The Pilgrims Society and Public Diplomacy, 1895–1945

Edinburgh Studies in Anglo-American Relations

Series Editors: Steve Marsh and Alan P. Dobson

Published and forthcoming titles

www.edinburghuniversitypress.com/series/esar

The Pilgrims Society and Public Diplomacy, 1895–1945

Stephen Bowman

EDINBURGH
University Press

Edinburgh University Press is one of the leading university presses in the UK. We publish academic books and journals in our selected subject areas across the humanities and social sciences, combining cutting-edge scholarship with high editorial and production values to produce academic works of lasting importance. For more information visit our website: edinburghuniversitypress.com

© Stephen Bowman, 2018

Edinburgh University Press Ltd
The Tun – Holyrood Road,
12(2f) Jackson's Entry,
Edinburgh EH8 8PJ

Typeset in 11/13 Adobe Sabon by
IDSUK (Dataconnection) Ltd

A CIP record for this book is available from the British Library

ISBN 978 1 4744 1781 5 (hardback)
ISBN 978 1 4744 1782 2 (webready PDF)
ISBN 978 1 4744 1783 9 (epub)
ISBN 978 1 4744 5215 1 (paperback)

The right of Stephen Bowman to be identified as the author of this work has been asserted in accordance with the Copyright, Designs and Patents Act 1988, and the Copyright and Related Rights Regulations 2003 (SI No. 2498).

Contents

Acknowledgements

I would firstly like to thank Professor Sylvia Ellis, Dr Michael Cullinane and Dr Tanja Buetlmann who, as the supervision team for the Northumbria University PhD upon which this book is based, were always constructive in their criticism and readily available during any crises in confidence. I also thank Northumbria University more generally for its financial support and thank the countless archival staff with whom I have come into contact. Thanks are also due to the Pilgrims Society for granting access to their publicly and privately held papers.

I would also like to thank my wider professional support network, which encompasses a variety of scholars across a range of universities. In particular, I thank Dr James Smyth at the University of Stirling for putting me on the path to academic study in the first place and for his continued guidance today. I also thank Dr Alastair Mann, also of the University of Stirling, for his always frank assessments of work and life. My colleagues at the University of the Highlands and Islands also deserve praise for the supportive and collegiate working environment at the Centre for History. I also thank the many friends I made whilst conducting the research for this book. They made my time at Northumbria University enjoyable.

On a more personal level I must thank my family, particularly my parents. They provided me with the opportunity and support to complete eight years of university education. My family also gave me a belief in the importance of education, formal or otherwise, which is so evidently important for navigating a world of post-fact and demagoguery. Finally, special thanks must go to my wife and life companion, Fiona. She has provided unstinting support and shown more patience during my academic pursuits than I have had the right to expect. For all of that and more I dedicate this book to her.

Introduction

This book is about the Pilgrims Society, an elite organisation known to most scholars of twentieth-century Anglo-American relations. References to the Pilgrims may be found in a variety of historical works; none, however, have given the Society more than passing mention. The present monograph, therefore, is the first detailed scholarly examination of this important transatlantic association and demonstrates the ways in which the Pilgrims Society has played a noteworthy role in both the history of Anglo-American relations and the history of public diplomacy. The Pilgrims was founded in 1902 as an elite dining club with the aim of improving cultural, diplomatic, and political relations between the United Kingdom and the United States of America. The Society had been formed during the period of Bradford Perkins' so-called 'great rapprochement' between Britain and the US, and was a part of the Anglo-Saxon impulse that helped bring the countries closer together at the turn of the nineteenth and twentieth centuries.[1] The Pilgrims Society still exists today and has branches in London and New York. It was founded principally as an exclusive dining club for British and American elites, in particular for those men it regarded as 'prominent in public or social life, science, art or literature'.[2] In both cities, it was entwined with the other brandy-fuelled upper-class clubs and societies that met amidst the cigar smoke of fashionable venues like Delmonico's, the Waldorf-Astoria, and Claridge's. The Pilgrims was originally supported by the likes of the famous British field marshal, Lord Frederick Roberts and the academic, Liberal politician, and British ambassador to the US from 1907 until 1913, James Bryce. Other notable British members included Lord Charles Beresford and the author Arthur Conan Doyle. Important members of the New York branch in its early years included Joseph Choate, who was the US ambassador to Britain between 1899 and 1905, bankers Jacob H. Schiff and J. P. Morgan, the industrialist Andrew Carnegie, and Adolph Ochs, owner of the *New York Times*.[3] In more recent years, prominent figures associated with the Society have included top British civil servant Gus O'Donnell and the former editor of *The Times*, Simon Jenkins. Other well-known guests have included people like the former British Secretary of State for Defence and Secretary General of NATO George Robertson, and the historian David Cannadine, while recent leading members have included Robert Worcester, founder of MORI, and Henry Luce III, one-time publisher of *Time* and *Fortune*.[4] Queen Elizabeth II described the Pilgrims as a 'special organisation' and, in a letter to the Society in 2002, said that it had made a 'unique contribution' to 'Anglo-American relations over the years'. Indeed, she recalled that her first public engagement following her marriage to Prince Philip was a Pilgrims event for Eleanor Roosevelt in 1948.[5]

The famous names listed above make it clear that the Pilgrims Society has occupied a privileged place in the Anglo-American relationship. It has operated with varying degrees of complicity with officialdom and has excluded people on the basis of wealth, status, and – at points in its history – gender and skin colour. As such, the Society exists in what Frank Costigliola has called 'the nexus between public and private'. Costigliola's referent was the importance of the personal relationships between Winston Churchill, Joseph Stalin, and Franklin D. Roosevelt to the Second World War's Grand Alliance, but this study of the Pilgrims Society similarly 'helps us see the messy way that history really happens'.[6] Proceeding from the central research aim of providing the first scholarly examination of the Pilgrims and establishing its precise role in Anglo-American relations in the first half of the twentieth century, this book has three broad objectives. Firstly, it will explore how the Pilgrims' status as an association helps explain its formation and activities. This will be done by tracing the Society's elite networks and by examining its inner workings and membership. Secondly, by scrutinising the overlap between official diplomacy and the Pilgrims' unofficial activities, this book will consider the extent to which the Pilgrims' activities can be regarded as a nascent form of public diplomacy. Thirdly, the book will examine the motives and values that underpinned the Society's activities. These values were initially coloured by notions of Anglo-Saxonism and English-speaking freedoms, which focused on Anglo-American ideas of liberal democracy, civilising imperialism, and the rule of law. Importantly, however, the desire for Anglo-American harmony was informed in large part by hopes for world peace in order to preserve international trade and commerce. In addition, this book will explore the key figures within the Society and will look at the connections its wider membership had to other political, business, journalistic, and state elites. The contention is that the Pilgrims Society contributed to Anglo-American relations during the first half of the twentieth century in a variety of ways, principally by public diplomacy activities.

Ultimately, this book considers the intersections that exist between associational culture and international relations, and between elite networking and public diplomacy. This approach offers new ways of looking at the history of the Anglo-American relationship, an area of scholarly and popular interest that has generated a large literature, not least because of its implications for understanding the much-discussed 'special relationship' that developed between the two countries after the Second World War.[7] This book covers the period up to the advent of that special relationship, but takes as its starting point a time when Anglo-American relations were only beginning to improve following the resolution of a number of nineteenth-century sources of friction. As originator of the term 'the great rapprochement', Perkins remains the standard introduction to this topic for new students of Anglo-American relations at the turn of the nineteenth and twentieth centuries, even if his work has largely been superseded by a more critical school of thought less inclined to use the adjective 'great'.[8] Nevertheless, that there was a rapprochement is generally accepted by most historians, many of whom agree that relations between Britain and the US were better at the end of the nineteenth century than they had been at the start.[9] There are a number of reasons why the Anglo-American relationship had been troublesome in the first place. As Perkins explains, the American Revolution meant that 'generation after generation' in the US had 'learned to look upon England as an enemy'.[10] This was at least partly due to American perceptions of British oppression, not only during the revolutionary period, but also during the 1812 war.[11] Likewise, some Americans had felt embittered by Britain's occasional interference in the American Civil War, with those on the Union side angry that Britain, although officially neutral, allowed the construction in Liverpool of the Confederate ship the *Alabama*. A diplomatic storm was also thrown up by the illegal seizure by Union forces in 1861 of the British ship the *Trent*, carrying two Confederate agents, with the British protesting in the strongest possible terms.[12] Some writers emphasise other reasons for the 'rather bitter, cold and frosty' Anglo-American relations in this period, as Iestyn Adams has described them.[13] Kathleen Burk, whose focus is often on the economic factors of international diplomacy, notes that Britain's insistence on the use of gold as the measure of currency angered a variety of people in the US, including the silver miners of the West and others who relied on the higher inflation characteristic of silver-based currencies.[14] Similarly, Crapol argues that Britain's status as 'national nemesis and chief economic rival' to America played a large part in perpetuating an anti-British feeling, with the US remaining a 'debtor nation' in the later nineteenth century.[15] This did not change until the First World War, over the course of which Britain became dependent on US credit. The issue of Britain's war debt to the US became a feature of Anglo-American relations into the 1920s.[16]

Alongside Britain's relative economic decline – which arguably predates the First World War and can be traced to the period 1870–1914 – the notion that Britain's ideal of 'splendid isolation' was becoming increasingly unworkable was another factor in the need for rapprochement.[17] This was partly due to the perceived danger of German naval expansion, with the Dual Alliance of France and Russia and the Triple Alliance of Germany, Austria-Hungary, and Italy leaving Britain 'awkwardly isolated'.[18] The British Admiralty, meanwhile, advised the government in 1903 that it would be unable to simultaneously fight a European war and control the seas around America. This made good relations with the US vital.[19] Improved relations with the US therefore allowed Britain to focus its military and naval strength away from the Western Hemisphere, while the 1902 Anglo-Japanese alliance protected its interests in the Pacific. Meanwhile, the Entente Cordiale with France in 1904 and the Anglo-Russian agreement in 1907 helped to end Britain's European isolation.[20] Crucially, the rapprochement between Britain and the US was solidified by British concessions and a policy of appeasement.[21]

Evidence of appeasement and of the rapprochement is generally seen in the handling of the Venezuela boundary dispute of 1895–6, in which the British eventually bowed to American pressure regarding the disputed border between Venezuela and British Guiana. Citing the Monroe Doctrine, President Grover Cleveland had told the US Congress that if Britain did not accept the findings of a US report into what the correct boundary was, then it was the

> duty of the United States to resist, by every means in its power, as a wilful aggression upon its rights and interests, the appropriation by Great Britain of any lands . . . which, after investigation, we have determined of right belongs to Venezuela.[22]

This was interpreted as a threat of war, and, along with the need to address other diplomatic issues – for example in South Africa, where the disastrous Jameson Raid had resulted in the German Kaiser expressing his support for the Transvaal republic's efforts to repel the British – ultimately resulted in the British submitting to American arbitration of the Venezuelan dispute.[23] Itself a bad-tempered affair, the Venezuelan boundary question, ahead of the Olney–Pauncefote arbitration treaty of 1897, was the main development that led to the great rapprochement.[24]

More evidence for rapprochement comes in Britain's response to the Spanish-American War and the concessions it granted to the US in relation to the isthmian canal. Britain had taken a less than neutral stance in favour of the US during the Spanish-American War of 1898, following which the US took possession of Spain's colonies in Cuba and the Philippines. This stood in contrast to the other European powers. Whereas elsewhere in Europe public sentiment was behind Spain, people in Britain generally supported the American position. This was demonstrated by the crowds waving American flags outside the US Embassy in London and by the British celebration that year of the Fourth of July. Britain had also allowed the US access to its port at Hong Kong, from which the US Navy launched its attack on Manila.[25] Meanwhile, the question of the isthmian canal – which centred on the US's desire to build, manage, and defend a canal linking the Atlantic and Pacific oceans, a development the British feared would provide the US with a significant naval advantage – was eventually settled in 1901 by the Hay–Pauncefote Treaty. It was a long-standing issue and had been the subject of the Clayton–Bulwer Treaty of 1850. This treaty had stipulated that any future canal should be a joint venture and that neither Britain nor the US could fortify it. It had become apparent to the US during its war with Spain, however, that not having control of a waterway across South America was a distinct military disadvantage. The 1901 treaty was the outcome of negotiations which had taken place in response to opposition in the US Senate to an earlier treaty of 1900 and represented a more favourable outcome for the US than the 1900 agreement. Whereas in 1900 the US was obliged not to fortify the canal, the 1901 treaty provided tacit consent for it to do just that. The treaty recognised the US's argument and essentially resulted in Britain ceding to the US its influence in the Western Hemisphere. Britain yielded to the US regarding the canal question in the interests of Anglo-American relations, not least because of its wider international isolation.[26] In any event, the US would have built the canal anyway: it was better for Britain to let the issue drop and therefore avoid unnecessary tensions.[27] Indeed, it seems likely that the settlement of the canal rights was a bigger issue for the US than it was for Britain. On the assumption that British and American interests in the Caribbean largely matched, Britain had freed up her navy from policing the Pacific; a role now undertaken by the US navy.[28]

Another marker of rapprochement, and the final significant obstacle to Anglo-American amity, was the resolution of the dispute over the precise location of the Canadian–US border in Alaska.[29] Like the isthmian canal, the Alaskan boundary dispute was a long-standing issue. It took on renewed urgency after the discovery of gold in the Yukon in the 1890s, with Canada claiming additional stretches of land than had been previously recognised by the admittedly unclear 1825 Anglo-Russian Treaty. The British government had initially attempted to have the Alaskan boundary dispute discussed at the same time as the isthmian canal question – with the Canadians hoping that if Britain accepted the US's position in relation to the canal, then the US would accept the Canadian position in Alaska – and had pushed for this during meetings of the Joint High Commission that had been set up in 1898 to address Canadian–US relations. The US did not agree, thus contributing to the ill-feeling that resulted in the Commission's adjournment the following year. Negotiations on the Alaska issue were, however, restarted in 1901 and ultimately led to the creation in 1903 of a British–Canadian–US commission to examine and settle the question of the boundary line. The commission eventually decided in favour of the US claims, with the British representative siding with the Americans rather than with the Canadians. While causing tension between Britain and its self-governing dominion, the settlement of the Alaskan boundary dispute in favour of the US was another example of British appeasement in an effort to solidify the Anglo-American rapprochement.[30]

The US was increasingly receptive to British efforts to improve relations between the two countries. One example of an American contribution to the rapprochement was during Britain's war with the Boers in South Africa between 1899 and 1902, when policy-making elites like John Hay (US ambassador to Britain, 1897–8, then Secretary of State, 1898–1905) and Theodore Roosevelt (Assistant Secretary of the Navy, 1897–8, Governor of New York 1899–1900, and US president, 1901–9), expressed their support for Britain's imperialist mission.[31] American imperialists saw a similarity between Britain's colonial war in South Africa and the US's engagement with insurgents in the newly acquired Philippines. In both cases, the imperial power aggressively suppressed native opposition.[32] Conceptions of Anglo-American imperialism speak to an important aspect of the rapprochement: namely, Anglo-Saxonism.[33] Anglo-Saxonism, as defined by Stuart Anderson, was a 'doctrine' prevalent in Britain and the US during the late nineteenth and early twentieth centuries that held that 'the civilization of the English-speaking nations was superior to that of any other group of people' and that the 'primacy of English and American civilization' was attributable to the 'innate racial superiority of the people who were descended from the ancient Anglo-Saxon invaders of Britain'.[34] Anglo-Saxonism was a concept closely related to the term 'English-speaking peoples', though Peter Clarke is perhaps overly optimistic in interpreting the latter as less racially charged than the former. Both concepts were also linked with the idea of 'Greater Britain', a term coined by Charles Dilke in the 1860s in a book written describing his travels across the 'English-speaking countries'.[35] These countries included Britain's dominions, like Canada and Australia, but Dilke also referred to the US. Such terms are evidence of the existence of perceptions of Britain and the US's shared cultural and racial heritage.[36]

Though not denying that diplomatic negotiation played an important part, Anderson argues that Anglo-Saxonism provided the 'primary abstract rationale' for the Anglo-American rapprochement. This he attributes partly to the central diplomatic and policy-making roles played by people like John Hay, British Cabinet minister and eventual Prime Minister Arthur Balfour, and Colonial Secretary Joseph Chamberlain, all of whom subscribed to the prevailing concept of Anglo-Saxonism. In this context, some people in Britain and the US perceived that they held a unique and shared talent for 'industry, intelligence, adventurousness', and 'self-government'. Similarly, some Anglo-Saxonists highlighted a combination of shared Protestantism, liberalism, democracy, and individualism.[37] This line of thinking posits that because elites in both countries considered themselves as sharing similar cultural and racial values, they were more likely to share a desire for similar policy outcomes. As this book will discuss, this notion has implications for understanding the Pilgrims Society's public and cultural diplomacy approach to Anglo-American relations. Anderson contends that Anglo-Saxonism was first evident as a force in diplomatic relations during the 1895 Venezuela boundary dispute. In this argument, a shared Anglo-Saxon identity played a large part in preventing a war between two countries that now saw themselves as blood brothers.[38] Anderson traces this line of thinking throughout the main reasons for the rapprochement, noting that British bias in favour of the US during the Spanish-American War was largely due to a belief that the US was fighting against Spain on behalf of the Anglo-Saxon race.[39] Anderson similarly argues that Anglo-Saxonism was crucial in ensuring that US policymakers were not more sympathetic to the Boers in 1899, though the American public felt less bound by race sentiment.[40] As Kramer has written, an important aspect of Anglo-American Anglo-Saxonism was a shared interest in imperialism, which anti-imperialists reacted against by challenging the idea that Anglo-Saxonism and Americanism were in any sense 'racial, historical, or political extensions of each other'.[41]

That Anglo-Saxonism played a part in improving Anglo-American relations is generally not disputed, though it is a question of degrees.[42] Some writers have emphasised the limited impact that Anglo-Saxonism had on diplomatic relations, with Burk arguing that it was unlikely to override national self-interest.[43] Bueltmann has argued that Anglo-American pan-Anglo-Saxonism was not more important to Britain than its connections with its empire, while Crapol suggests that the 1902 alliance between Britain and Japan indicates that racial views were not necessarily important in all diplomatic considerations.[44] Even Anderson argues that Anglo-Saxonism had lost its potency by 1905. Japan's defeat of Russia removed what had been termed the 'Slavic peril' and Progressive ideas, another point of transatlantic contact, began challenging racial theory.[45] Priscilla Roberts, however, argues that the pro-Allied feeling in the US during the First World War was in large part informed by Anglo-Saxonist sentiment and that the conflict 'was the decisive event in the creation of a cohesive and self-conscious group of American Atlanticists'.[46] This books shares this latter view and argues that Anglo-Saxonist ideas remained an important cultural milieu for the evolving Anglo-American relationship beyond the 1900s, including for many members of the Pilgrims Society.

Some of the intersections between Anglo-Saxonist concepts and the Pilgrims Society are best explained with reference to the work of Duncan Bell. Bell has written convincingly about the late nineteenth- and early twentieth-century developments in intellectual thought that resulted in Anglo-Saxonism and notions of race federation being regarded as possible facilitators of world peace. As such, Anglo-Saxonism was not simply a theoretical construction of perceived racial comity, but also reflected real-world considerations. As Cecilie Reid has written, the US in the 1890s was concerned with how to maintain economic growth at a time of increasing ethnic diversity and outside pressures.[47] These fears partly motivated those American peace advocates at the National Arbitration Conference in 1896 who believed that Britain and the US's racial comity meant that the two countries should work together to ward off the commercial and military challenge of inferior 'races' and countries, including Russia.

Anglo-Saxonist peace advocates believed that friendship between the two countries was important for the free flow of commerce and people.[48] For the British, meanwhile, Anglo-Saxon federation was also a way of containing the economic and military challenge of an increasingly powerful USA.[49] Some of these Anglo-Saxonist ideas – including those of legal theorist A. V. Dicey – called upon isopolitan ideas of common citizenship for Britons and Americans. Such ideas incorporated both realist security concerns and an element of utopianism, in particular the belief that, through cooperation and federation, the '"Anglo-Saxon" race would help to bring peace, order, and justice to the earth'.[50] Crucially, Anglo-Saxonism and concepts of Greater Britain motivated some members of the Pilgrims Society. Scottish industrialist and future Pilgrims Society member, Andrew Carnegie, was a proponent of these ideas, as were other future Pilgrims Charles Beresford and James Bryce. Beresford, a naval strategist and founding member of the Society, believed in an 'Anglo-Saxon patriotism' which was 'in addition to our domestic patriotism and our Imperial or American patriotism'.[51] Meanwhile, Bryce, an academic, Liberal politician, and future ambassador to the US, wrote in support of joint British–American citizenship. He was also famous for his 1888 book *The American Commonwealth*, which, according to Bell, 'presented his audience with a thoroughly anglicised account of American institutions', including the US constitution.[52] There were, however, diverse British and American usages of Anglo-Saxonism. While Bueltmann has noted that the British writer W. T. Stead expressed a desire for an 'English-speaking United States of the World' in his 1902 book *The Americanization of the World*, Kohn has argued that the 1900s witnessed a move away from North American Anglo-Saxonism towards 'Anglo-conformism'.[53] This was partly in response to the large numbers of immigrants arriving into the US, a development that 'forced Americans . . . to adapt their view of what it meant to be American' and resulted in an American identity focused 'less on race than on the ideas and cultural norms of the dominant "Yankee tradition"'.[54] A part of this process of Anglo-conformism was to highlight those cultural elements that the US was believed to share with Britain. As John Dumbrell has argued, fears about the 'de-Angloing' of America caused by immigration from Southern and Eastern Europe in the 1890s resulted in elites in both the US and Britain promoting 'ideas of the desired unity of English-speaking peoples and of "Anglo-America"'.[55] Similarly, in her article on the development of an East Coast 'Atlanticist' and Anglophile policy-making elite during and after the First World War, Roberts argues such elites felt that new immigrants 'failed to appreciate' that, to them, the 'United States embodied a constitutional, legal, political, and racial heritage which it shared with Great Britain'.[56] It was this heritage to which the Pilgrims Society appealed in its efforts towards Anglo-American friendship.

At this point, it is worth commenting on terminology, in particular the phrase 'Anglo-American relations'. As such, the Pilgrims Society's interpretation of the British–American past was Anglocentric. America was regarded as the recipient and custodian of ideas and values brought to the continent by seventeenth-century English settlers. While 'British–American relations' is the more correct (though by no means perfect) term for referring to state–state relations between the UK and the US, the elite cultural links were predominantly Anglo-American. In truth, it is unsurprising that British–American identity was Anglocentric given that British identity was similarly Anglocentric. This was true of British constitutional history, which, for example, 'subverted' Scotland's own constitutional and parliamentary past in pursuit of closer union after 1707. In this process, England's constitutional tradition came to dominate British identity. It was this tradition, including its 'individualist conception of the history of liberty', that contributed to the cultural tropes connected with the British–American rapprochement.[57] This analysis chimes with Robert Hendershot's notion of 'Anglo-American sentimentality', which he regards as the 'perception of cultural affinity' that was primarily evident 'amongst the Anglo-American foreign policy élite'.[58]

As this book will show, the perception of cultural affinity between the Anglo-American foreign policy-making elite is important to understanding the activities and approaches of the Pilgrims Society. With this in mind, the book interprets the Pilgrims' efforts to encourage Anglo-American friendship as a form of nascent public diplomacy and argues that the Society was a precursor to later, more official public and cultural diplomacy organisations. The book also calls upon themes of associational culture, and traces the connections between the Pilgrims and other elite urban clubs. As such, the Society acted as an elite, state–private network which facilitated contact between influential individuals. Precisely what is meant by public diplomacy, associational culture, and elite networking is outlined in Chapter 1. The book then goes on to consider the Society's cultural diplomacy activities in support of British–Canadian–US rapprochement in the early 1900s; some of its activities during and immediately after the First World War; the use of the Society in the 1920s as a venue for important policy announcements by US statesmen in London; and, finally, its contribution to Anglo-American relations in 1941, the final year of US neutrality during the Second World War.

Chapter 2 discusses in detail the founding of the Society in 1902 and examines the associational culture of London and New York from which it emerged. Chapter 2 also provides an examination of the precise aims of the Pilgrims and introduces some of the Society's principal figures. This serves to solidify the description of the Society as an elite network, something which is expanded upon in Chapter 3 in the course of a case study of an important banquet held by the Society in New York in 1906 for Earl Grey, the Governor General of Canada. This banquet also demonstrates some of the ways in which the Society attempted to facilitate better official Anglo-American relations, with particular reference to outstanding sources of diplomatic disagreement between the

US and Canada. Chapter 3 also provides a significant example of the Pilgrims' public diplomacy, including its appeals to Anglo-American cultural affinity and its use by a British statesman as a venue from which to publicly advocate diplomatic policy. This shows how important and influential the Society had become so soon after its founding.

Chapter 4, meanwhile, examines the activities undertaken by the Pilgrims and its members during the First World War, when the Society was involved in semi-official propaganda work and in instances of exchange diplomacy. US involvement in the war after April 1917 was regarded by the Pilgrims as an event of singular importance. After that date, and alongside supporting the work of the British domestic propaganda body the National War Aims Committee, the Pilgrims established the American Officers' Club in London in an effort to welcome American service personnel to Europe. In both these ventures the Society worked closely with officialdom. This meant that it was able to support the war effort whilst also promoting its agenda of Anglo-American friendship. This continued after the war, with the Society's involvement in the American celebration of wartime cooperation on what was termed 'Britain's Day' in December 1918. Ultimately, this chapter argues that the Society's activities during the conflict blurred the lines between official and unofficial action and between propaganda and public diplomacy.

Chapters 5 and 6 then examine the Pilgrims Society during the 1920s, a decade in which the Anglo-American relationship came under increasing strain. The Pilgrims Society also came under a great deal of suspicion from isolationist and anti-British figures in the US, many of whom tapped into a popular belief that the Society had been complicit in British propaganda efforts during the First World War, and that these efforts had continued in the years immediately following the conflict. This was a more difficult period for the New York branch than it was for the London branch, as the US Pilgrims also had to contend with a degree of internal division. At the same time, however, the 1920s witnessed the solidification of the Society's semi-official status, particularly with US ambassadors like George Harvey, Alanson Houghton, and Charles Dawes deliberately using their maiden speeches at Pilgrims functions in London to make important official policy announcements concerning matters such as US membership of the League of Nations, US financial support for Europe, and naval disarmament. In these ways the Pilgrims Society's activities in the 1920s provided a developmental stage between an earlier tradition of private involvement in international relations and later forms of state-sponsored public diplomacy. Chapter 6 also traces the Society's activities during the 1930s – a decade of particular interest to historians of public diplomacy, as the next chapter will show – and into the beginning of the Second World War, including by analysing Prime Minister Winston Churchill's speech at a Pilgrims event in March 1941.

This book will show how the Pilgrims Society participated in the Anglo-American relationship across the first half of the twentieth century. It eschews any simplistic notions of a special relationship, not least because the term has little currency for most of the time period covered here. Britain and the US in the 1900s – and indeed in the 1920s and 1930s too – were still coming to terms with how the former colony related to the mother country. The Pilgrims, constituted of Americans and Britons, had no one prescription for this other than seeking to ensure peace and understanding between the two countries. For most of the wealthy male Pilgrims this meant peace between white Anglo-Saxons. Accordingly, they articulated their appeals for Anglo-American friendship in these fairly circumscribed and elitist cultural terms. The Pilgrims Society never set the agenda for the official Anglo-American relationship, but it did play a leading role in the history of public diplomacy and, by extension, helped formulate how people have come to think about that relationship.

Notes

1. Bradford Perkins, *The Great Rapprochement: England and the United States, 1895–1914* (London, 1969).
2. 'The Pilgrims List of Members and Bye-Laws', 1909, Harry Brittain Papers, British Library of Political and Economic Science [BLPES], Box 5.
3. 'The Pilgrims List of Members and Bye-Laws', 1909, Brittain Papers, BLPES, Box 5; Minute Book 1, 6 December 1909, Pilgrims Society of the United States Mss, Pilgrims of the United States Head Office, New York City [NYC].
4. Christopher Robson 'The Pilgrims' Society of Great Britain', <http://www.pilgrimsociety.org/history.pdf> (last accessed 3 October 2011); Anne P. Baker, *The Pilgrims of Great Britain: A Centennial History*

(London, 2002), p. 69 and p. 204; Baker, *The Pilgrims of the United States: A Centennial History* (London, 2003), p. 51.

5. Elizabeth II to Lord Carrington, January 2002, Pilgrims Society of Great Britain Mss, London Metropolitan Archives [LMA], LMA/4632/A/05/001.

6. Frank Costigliola, *Roosevelt's Lost Alliances: How Personal Politics Helped Start the Cold War* (Princeton, 2012), p. 20.

7. For more on the 'special relationship' – including on the reasons authors so often place those words in inverted commas – see Alex Danchev, *On Specialness: Essays in Anglo-American Relations* (London, 1998); Henry Butterfield Ryan, *The Vision of Anglo-America: The US–UK Alliance and the Emerging Cold War, 1943–1946* (Cambridge, 1987); Howard Temperley, *Britain and America Since Independence* (Basingstoke, 2002); H. G. Nicholas, *The United States and Britain* (Chicago, 1975).

8. Perkins, *Great Rapprochement, passim*; Edward P. Crapol, 'From Anglophobia to Fragile Rapprochement: Anglo-American Relations in the Early Twentieth Century', in Hans-Jürgen Schroder (ed.), *Confrontation and Cooperation: Germany and the United States in the Era of World War 1, 1900–1924* (Providence, 1993), p. 23.

9. Kathleen Burk, 'Anglo-American Relations Before They Were "Special"', in Antoine Capet (ed.), *The Special Relationship: La 'relation spéciale' entre le Royaume-Uni et les États-Unis, 1945–1990* (Rouen, 2003), p. 12.

10. Perkins, *Great Rapprochement*, p. 4.

11. Lionel Gelber, *The Rise of Anglo-American Friendship: A Study in World Politics, 1898–1906* (London, 1938), p. 2.

12. Burk, *Old World, New World* (New York, 2007), p. 272.

13. Iestyn Adams, *Brothers Across the Ocean: British Foreign Policy and the Origins of the Anglo-American 'Special Relationship' 1900–1905* (London, 2005), p. 10.

14. Burk, *Old World, New World*, p. 384.

15. Crapol, 'Anglophobia to Rapprochement', p. 16.

16. Burk, 'Great Britain in the United States, 1917–1918: The Turning Point', *International History Review*, Vol. 1, No. 2 (April 1979), pp. 228–45; Burk, *Britain, America and the Sinews of War, 1914–1918* (London, 1985).

17. Max Beloff, 'The Special Relationship: An Anglo-American Myth', in Martin Gilbert (ed.), *A Century of Conflict: Essays in Honour of A. J. P. Taylor* (London, 1966), p. 152; Aaron L. Friedberg, *The Weary Titan: Britain and the Experience of Relative Decline, 1895–1905* (Princeton, 1988), p. 299; Keith Neilson, '"Greatly Exaggerated": The Myth of the Decline of Great Britain Before 1914', *International History Review*, Vol. 13, No. 4 (November 1991), pp. 695–725.

18. Crapol, 'Anglophobia to Rapprochement', p. 20; Adams, *Brothers Across the Ocean*, p. 14.
19. Donald C. Watt, *Personalities and Policies: Studies in the Formulation of British Foreign Policy in the Twentieth Century* (London, 1965), p. 28.
20. Crapol, 'Anglophobia to Rapprochement', pp. 15–16 and pp. 20–1; Charles S. Campbell, 'Anglo-American Relations, 1897–1901', in Paolo E. Coletta (ed.), *Threshold to American Internationalism: Essays on the Foreign Policies of William McKinley* (New York, 1970), p. 221; Adams, *Brothers Across the Ocean*, p. 79 and pp. 89–91.
21. Watt, *Personalities and Policies*, p. 23; Crapol, 'Anglophobia to Rapprochement', p. 23.
22. 'Venezuelan Boundary Controversy', 17 December 1895, Congressional Record – Senate, 54th Congress, 1st Session, Vol. 28, Part 1, p. 191; Burk, *Old World, New World*, p. 404; see also pp. 398–411; Perkins, *Great Rapprochement*, pp. 12–20.
23. Crapol, 'Anglophobia to Rapprochement', p. 18.
24. Ibid. p. 18.
25. Burk, *Old World, New World*, pp. 413–14; Crapol, 'Anglophobia to Rapprochement', p. 19; Perkins, *Great Rapprochement*, pp. 31–63.
26. Burk, *Old World, New World*, pp. 425–8; Crapol, 'Anglophobia to Rapprochement', p. 19; Adams, *Brothers Across the Ocean*, pp. 22–4; Campbell, 'Anglo-American Relations', pp. 243–8; Perkins, *Great Rapprochement*, pp. 173–85.
27. Campbell, 'Anglo-American Relations', p. 249.
28. Burk, *Sinews of War*, p. 3.
29. William N. Tilchin, *Theodore Roosevelt and the British Empire: A Study in Presidential Statecraft* (Basingstoke, 1997), p. 36.
30. Burk, *Old World, New World*, pp. 422–7; Perkins, *Great Rapprochement*, pp. 156–72; 'Decision of the Alaskan Boundary Tribunal under the treaty of January 24, 1903, between the United States and Great Britain', 20 October 1903, Foreign Relations of the United States [FRUS], University of Wisconsin Digital Collections, <http://uwdc.library.wisc.edu/collections/FRUS> (last accessed 12 May 2014).
31. Crapol, 'Anglophobia to Rapprochement', pp. 23–4; Burk, *Old World, New World*, pp. 421–2; Byron Farwell, 'Taking Sides in the Boer War', *American Heritage*, Vol. 27 (April 1976), pp. 21–5.
32. Paul A. Kramer, 'Empires, Exceptions and Anglo-Saxons: Race and Rule Between the British and United States Empires, 1880–1910', *Journal of American History*, Vol. 88, No. 4 (March 2002), p. 1335; for more on the links between British and US imperialism, see Stephen Tuffnell, 'Anglo-American Inter-Imperialism: US Expansion

and the British World, c. 1895–1914', *Britain and the World*, Vol. 7, Issue 2 (2014), pp. 174–95.

33. Kramer, 'Empires, Exceptions and Anglo-Saxons', pp. 1315–53.
34. Stuart Anderson, *Race and Rapprochement: Anglo-Saxonism and Anglo-American Relations, 1895–1904* (London, 1981), pp. 11–12.
35. Srdjan Vucetic, 'The Fulton Address as Racial Discourse', in Alan Dobson and Steve Marsh (eds), *Churchill and the Anglo-American Special Relationship* (London, 2017), pp. 96–115; Peter Clarke, 'The English-Speaking Peoples Before Churchill', *Britain and the World*, Vol. 4, No. 2 (2011), p. 224; Duncan Bell, *The Idea of Greater Britain: Empire and the Future of World Order, 1860–1900* (Princeton, 2007), *passim*; Joe Hardwick, 'An English Institution? The Colonial Church of England in the First Half of the Nineteenth Century', in Tanja Bueltmann, David Gleeson and Donald M. Mac-Raild (eds), *Locating the English Diaspora, 1500–2010* (Liverpool, 2012), p. 97; Charles Dilke, *Greater Britain: A Record of Travel in English-Speaking Countries During 1866–7* (London, 1869).
36. David Hackett Fischer, *Albion's Seed: Four British Folkways in America* (New York, 1992); James Belich, *Replenishing the Earth: The Settler Revolution and the Rise of the Anglo-World, 1783–1939* (Oxford, 2009).
37. Anderson, *Race and Rapprochement*, p. 12 and pp. 17–19.
38. Ibid. p. 13.
39. Ibid. pp. 118–19.
40. Ibid. p. 147.
41. Kramer, 'Empires, Exceptions and Anglo-Saxons', p. 1340.
42. Campbell, *From Revolution to Rapprochement: The United States and Great Britain, 1783–1900* (New York, 1974), pp. 201–4.
43. Burk, *Old World, New World*, p. 386.
44. Bueltmann, 'Anglo-Saxonism and the Racialization of the English Diaspora', in Bueltmann, Gleeson and MacRaild (eds) *Locating the English Diaspora*, p. 130; Crapol, 'Anglophobia to Rapprochement', pp. 20–1.
45. Anderson, *Race and Rapprochement*, pp. 174–5.
46. Priscilla Roberts, 'The First World War and the Emergence of American Atlanticism, 1914–1920', *Diplomacy and Statecraft*, Vol. 5, Issue 3 (1994), p. 570.
47. Cecilie Reid, 'American Internationalism: Peace Advocacy and International Relations, 1895–1916', unpublished PhD thesis (Boston College, 2005), p. 2.
48. Ibid. pp. 44–6.
49. Duncan Bell, 'The Project for a New Anglo Century: Race, Space, and Global Order', in Peter Katzenstein (ed.), *Anglo-America and*

Its Discontents: Civilizational Identities Beyond West and East (New York, 2012), p. 36.

50. Bell, 'The Project for a New Anglo Century', pp. 36–9 and p. 44; Bell, 'Dreaming the Future: Anglo-America as Utopia, 1880–1914', in Ella Dzelzainis and Ruth Livesey (eds), *The American Experiment and the Idea of Democracy in British Culture, 1776–1914* (Farnham, 2013), p. 207; as Bell has argued, 'the fanciful delusion of Anglo superiority never seems to die' and has characterised some perceptions of Anglo-American relations throughout the twentieth century and into the start of the twenty-first, for instance the work of the historian Andrew Roberts. See Bell, 'Beyond the Sovereign State: Isopolitan Citizenship, Race and Anglo-American Union', *Political Studies*, Vol. 62 (2014), p. 432; Bell, 'The Project for a New Anglo Century', p. 51; Andrew Roberts, 'Forging the Special Relationship', *The New Criterion*, Vol. 29, No. 10 (June 2011), p. 33; Srdjan Vucetic, *The Anglosphere: A Genealogy of Racialized Identity in International Relations* (Stanford, 2011).

51. Bell, 'The Project for a New Anglo Century', p. 40; Bell, 'Before the Democratic Peace: Racial Utopianism, Empire, and the Abolition of War', *European Journal of International Relations*, Vol. 20, Issue 3 (2014), p. 659.

52. Bell, 'Beyond the Sovereign State', p. 427; Frank Prochaska, *Eminent Victorians on American Democracy: The View from Albion* (Oxford, 2012), p. 102; James Bryce, *The American Commonwealth* (London, 1888).

53. Bueltmann, 'Anglo-Saxonism', p. 134; William T. Stead, *The Americanization of the World or The Trend of the Twentieth Century* (New York, 1902); Edward P. Kohn, *This Kindred People: Canadian–American Relations and the Anglo-Saxon Idea, 1895–1903* (Montreal, 2005), p. 202.

54. Kohn, *This Kindred People*, p. 201.

55. John Dumbrell, *A Special Relationship: Anglo-American Relations in the Cold War and After* (Basingstoke, 2001), p. 4.

56. Roberts, 'The Emergence of American Atlanticism', p. 594; Roberts has written a variety of pieces on US East Coast foreign policy-making elites. See also Roberts, 'Underpinning the Anglo-American Alliance: The Council on Foreign Relations and Britain Between the Wars', in Jonathan Hollowell (ed.), *Twentieth-Century Anglo-American Relations* (New York, 2001), pp. 25–43; Roberts, 'The Anglo-American Theme: American Visions of an Atlantic Alliance, 1914–1933', *Diplomatic History*, Vol. 21, No. 3 (1997), pp. 333–64; Roberts, 'The Transatlantic American Foreign Policy Elite: Its Evolution in Generational Perspective', *Journal of Transatlantic Studies*, Vol. 7 (2009), pp. 163–83.

57. Colin Kidd, *Subverting Scotland's Past: Scottish Whig Historians and the Creation of an Anglo-British Identity, c. 1689–1830* (Cambridge, 2003), p. 111.

58. Robert M. Hendershot, '"Affection Is the Cement which Binds Us": Understanding the Cultural Sinews of the Anglo-American Special Relationship', in Alan P. Dobson and Steve Marsh (eds), *Anglo-American Relations: Contemporary Perspectives* (London, 2013), p. 52 and pp. 55–6.

1 Public Diplomacy Conceptualised

There is a friendship of Governments and a friendship of peoples.
(James Bryce)

This book contends that concepts surrounding the role of elite
non-state actors are central to understanding the development of
the Pilgrims, just as they help explain the activities of other, bet-
ter-known, and more recent groups. Indeed, the argument here
is that the early activities of the Society were a form of nascent
public diplomacy. While members of the Society and others associated with the organisation did not use that term, the Society's
activities in the period up until the end of the 1920s not only
exhibited many of the characteristics of later forms of public
diplomacy but also contributed to their development in the 1930s
and 1940s. The Pilgrims Society was a semi-official public diplomacy actor in the realm of foreign relations, which means that
there is a line of descent from the Pilgrims to organisations like
the British Council and the Division of Cultural Relations in the
1930s, themselves precursors to Cold War organisations like the
United States Information Agency (USIA). This argument stands
in contrast to that of most writers on public diplomacy, many
of whom begin their examination of the subject with reference
to these later organisations. This chapter analyses the different
and changing ways in which public diplomacy has been understood across time and outlines why it can usefully be applied
to the early twentieth century. It also establishes how concepts
of public diplomacy, associational culture, and elite networking
intersect and demonstrates why this intersection is important to
the history of the Pilgrims Society. The chapter is divided into
four sections. The first section analyses the existing literature in
the field of public diplomacy and shows why the history of the

Pilgrims Society is an important addition to this canon. The second section establishes a working definition of the concept. The definition outlined in this section is used throughout the rest of the book. The third section presents some preliminary thoughts about how some of the antecedents to the Society helped shape its approach to international relations, while the final section argues that the Pilgrims' activities must be seen in the context of the history of other elite clubs and societies.

The history and historiography of public diplomacy

'Public diplomacy' has not been a fixed concept through time: it means different things to different people. For example, Nicholas Cull has defined public diplomacy as an 'international actor's attempt to conduct its foreign policy by engaging with foreign publics'.[1] According to Kenneth Osgood and Brian Etheridge, meanwhile, public diplomacy 'involves the cultivation of public opinion to achieve the desired geopolitical aims of the sponsor' by 'fostering a receptive climate for the sponsor's foreign policies'.[2] Such definitions, however, tend to relate primarily to later twentieth-century conceptions of public diplomacy. As Cull has explained in a short article that serves to demonstrate the relatively superficial attention given to pre-1930s forms of public diplomacy, in the nineteenth century 'public diplomacy' was typically used in relation to the idea of 'open diplomacy' as opposed to 'secret diplomacy'. It was not until after the Second World War that the term took on a new meaning, closer in conception to 'propaganda'. Edmund Gullion contributed to this change in its definition. 'Public diplomacy' was a euphemism for the more pejorative term 'propaganda', and was used to describe the activities of the USIA, the US government's official public diplomacy body formed in 1953.[3] In truth, it is difficult to disentangle 'public diplomacy' from 'propaganda', both in the present and in the past. Taylor has, however, argued that propaganda differs from 'publicity'. He argues that publicity 'imparts information which might not otherwise have been available' and provides an 'audience with opportunities to formulate opinions and to act accordingly', while propaganda goes a step further and 'tells its audience how to use those opportunities'. As such, propaganda is 'defined by reference to its aims', which Taylor regards as including the aim of eliciting a 'desired line of action' amongst an audience in order to 'serve the interest of the author'.[4] This, however, might equally serve as a definition for public diplomacy, especially as Osgood and Etheridge argue that public diplomacy can be regarded as 'propaganda in the service of a nation's foreign policy'.[5]

While the principal focus of Cull's research is the USIA, 1953 is not regarded by him or other historians as the beginning of US public diplomacy. For example, Justin Hart has published an important book covering the period 1936–53, which he describes as witnessing the 'first phase of US public diplomacy'.[6] Writers other than Hart have also discussed the adoption of public diplomacy policies by the British and US governments during the 1930s and 1940s, often focusing on ideas of 'cultural diplomacy'. For example, Frank Ninkovich has discussed the US State Department's cultural programmes of the mid-twentieth century in terms of the so-called 'diplomacy of ideas'. He traces the antecedents of such 'cultural policy' to the activities of philanthropic organisations like the Carnegie Endowment for International Peace. It was not until the 1930s, in response to the cultural diplomacy and propaganda of powers like Germany, the USSR, and Japan, that the State Department began to look more seriously at international cultural relations, for instance through the creation of the Division of Cultural Relations in 1938.[7]

For Hart, the US had additional motivations for wanting to project its image abroad during the 1930s and 1940s. He argues that state-sponsored cultural diplomacy grew from efforts to support Franklin Roosevelt's Good Neighbor policies in Latin America and that it developed in the context of 'four intersecting phenomena that came together to fundamentally reconfigure the global environment and the place of the United States therein'. The four intersecting phenomena identified by Hart are the 'arrival of the United States as the world's dominant power'; the threats posed by Germany, Japan, and Russia; 'the continuing proliferation of access to the technologies of mass communications'; and, finally, 'the disintegration of European empires', especially the British Empire.[8] Some of these developments, however, occurred in the earlier period covered by this book. Just as Hart argues that the geopolitical developments of the 1930s and 1940s necessitated a reappraisal of how the US presented itself to the world, the period of the Pilgrims' initial development from the 1890s to the 1920s was itself one of great flux in international affairs. As has been seen, this was the period of the 'great rapprochement' between Britain and the US, when the US's ever-growing economic and military strength and Britain's isolated position in Europe – and then its post-First World War relative decline – demanded a continuous reappraisal of the ways in which the two countries related to each other. The Pilgrims Society's public diplomacy had a role to play in helping elements in the two countries negotiate the terrain of this changing international environment. In other words, the relative decline of the British Empire necessitated public diplomacy on both sides of the Atlantic.

Similarly, while mass communications did expand in the 1930s and 1940s (and indeed the 1920s), there had been an earlier expansion that had helped facilitate the public diplomacy of the Pilgrims Society. Mass-circulation newspapers had come to prominence in Europe during the 1870s and 1880s, while the following decade witnessed the rise of the so-called 'yellow press' in the US, when the papers of William Randolph Hearst and Joseph Pulitzer contributed to pro-war feeling ahead of American intervention in Cuba against Spain in 1898. As a result of a larger reading public, and the concomitant belief that public opinion could impact upon official relations, it had become increasingly apparent to diplomats and other actors in international relations that it was necessary to engage with a wider constituency than just fellow statesmen.[9] This was demonstrated by the Pilgrims Society throughout the period covered by this book, when the organisation self-consciously courted press coverage in an effort to disseminate its core message of Anglo-American friendship. Indeed, it is worth noting that both the *New York Times* and the London *Times* had links with the Society and that both reported sympathetically on its activities. Adolph Ochs, the publisher of the *New York Times* since 1896 and then its owner from 1900, was an early member of the US Pilgrims, while Lord Northcliffe, the proprietor of the London *Times* from 1908, had various connections to important Pilgrims members, including to Harry Brittain, the first secretary of the British branch.[10] Similarly, Sir Campbell Stuart, the managing director of *The Times* from 1920 and the editor of the *Daily Mail* from 1921, was elected to the executive committee soon after his admission to the Society in 1918 and later became chairman of the London Pilgrims.[11]

The contention here is that there is a pre-history to official Anglo-American public diplomacy that extends earlier than even the propaganda efforts of the Creel Committee during the First World War, which Hart identifies as the principal precursor to the public diplomacy of the 1936 to 1953 period.[12] That this was the case is partly shown by Ninkovich's argument that the Carnegie Endowment was an antecedent to later versions of public diplomacy. Established in 1910, the Carnegie Endowment was indeed an early example of private involvement in international affairs. The Pilgrims Society, however, was founded in 1902, eight years before the Carnegie Endowment. As a result – and to borrow some of Ninkovich's words – 'cultural relations were institutionalized and tied, however tentatively, to foreign policy objectives' before the formation of the Carnegie Endowment.[13] If the Carnegie Endowment pre-empted the State Department's cultural programmes, then the Pilgrims Society pre-empted the Carnegie Endowment. In truth, the Pilgrims and the Carnegie Endowment were part of the same impulse that saw private bodies becoming involved in international affairs. For example, the Carnegie Endowment's first two presidents – Elihu Root and Nicholas Murray Butler – were both members of the Pilgrims Society, as, moreover, was Andrew Carnegie.[14]

Developments in public diplomacy were not confined to the US. This book also tackles the question as to whether the Pilgrims Society was also a precursor to organisations like the British Council, a body that Taylor believes 'injected a new dimension into the traditional conduct of British foreign policy – that of cultural diplomacy'.[15] Taylor notes that the establishment of the British Council in 1934 was indicative of a dawning realisation in the British Foreign Office that the state had a role to play in addressing the cultural aspect of international relations. As with the US State Department, this was partly in response to the propaganda activities of countries like Germany and Italy.[16] Taylor believes that the British authorities were hitherto aware that the Pilgrims – along with the Travel Association (formed in 1928 essentially as a body to promote tourism to Britain, but which also aimed to improve the country's image in an effort to promote international understanding) – provided a means of projecting British interests abroad. The Travel Association had received a grant from the British government and had the tacit support of the Foreign Office and the Department of Overseas

Trade. The Pilgrims' Harry Brittain was involved with the Association and it was led by Lord Derby, who became chairman of the London Pilgrims in 1930. According to Taylor, organisations like the Travel Association and the Pilgrims prevented the need for a fully official government agency responsible for overseas propaganda and public diplomacy.[17] Despite his mention of the Pilgrims Society, Taylor focuses almost entirely on the Travel Association. He spends very little time on the Pilgrims and does not use primary source material pertaining to the Society. This provides an opportunity for this book to examine whether there is a direct line of descent from the Pilgrims to the more official organs of public diplomacy in the 1930s and 1940s.

Importantly, the 1920s provide a middle ground between 1930s and nineteenth-century approaches to public diplomacy. As subsequent chapters will show, it was in the 1920s that the Pilgrims Society was used by ambassadors as a vehicle for making important policy-related speeches. This suggests an understanding in officialdom of both public diplomacy and of the Pilgrims' utility in ensuring messages were given appropriate legitimacy and publicity, even though it occurred before the full acceptance of state-sponsored public and cultural diplomacy. It also suggests that the activities of the Pilgrims in the first two decades of the century had indeed shaped opinions about public diplomacy ahead of the 1930s. Indeed, the question of the origins of public diplomacy primarily turns on which body is identified as the principal actor in any given activity. In Hart's period the initiative for public diplomacy had, for the first time to any great extent, come from governmental bodies.[18] Yet, this only occurred after a history of non-governmental bodies playing an active role in international relations. The history of the Pilgrims Society is one that witnesses a gradual shift from unofficial actors providing the main impetus in public diplomacy to official actors providing the main impetus.

Public diplomacy defined

So far the terms 'cultural diplomacy' and 'public diplomacy' have been used interchangeably. In truth, it is necessary to delineate the two. Cultural diplomacy is a concept very closely related to public diplomacy. For Nicholas Cull, cultural diplomacy is a form of public diplomacy.[19] Richard T. Arndt, a former cultural diplomat and USIA staff member, argues that such practices have been utilised throughout human history, for example when Ancient Rome 'reached outward with architecture as its compelling symbol'.[20] According to Jessica Gienow-Hecht, meanwhile, cultural diplomacy 'entails the effort to create a cultural liaison between or among people living in two or more different regions'.[21] Thus, the 'sponsor' involved in any of these diplomatic actions may or may not be a government, with Gienow-Hecht arguing that, in the nineteenth and early twentieth centuries, public and cultural diplomacy was largely undertaken by private non-state actors on behalf of their state.[22] Gienow-Hecht believes that this earlier model differs from American and Russian public diplomacy during the Cold War, which was undertaken with more cooperation and financial support from the respective government departments.[23] Cull argues, meanwhile, that public diplomacy can only be regarded as distinct from informal intercultural relations when it becomes part of an actor's 'policy'.[24] Neither the British nor US governments had such a policy in the period covered by this book. The Pilgrims, however, did.

With so many strands to public and cultural diplomacy, it is helpful to utilise Cull's five-point model describing what he regards as the principal methods and features of the USIA's public diplomacy in the Cold War period. This model is as follows: 'listening', for example through opinion polling; 'advocacy', for example through the 'creation and dissemination of information materials to build understanding of a policy'; 'cultural diplomacy', that is to say the 'dissemination of cultural practices as a mechanism to promote the interests of the actor'; 'exchange diplomacy', for example student exchange schemes; and 'international broadcasting', for example the 'transmission of balanced news over state-funded international radio'.[25] These definitions of the constituent parts of public diplomacy can usefully be applied to the Pilgrims Society: in particular, examples of cultural diplomacy, advocacy diplomacy, and exchange diplomacy as described here were among the early twentieth-century activities of the Society. By following this model, this book regards cultural diplomacy as a form of public diplomacy, though aspects of cultural diplomacy can also overlap with other forms of public diplomacy, including advocacy and exchange diplomacy. The important point is that many of these activities first occurred in an earlier time period than many authors have previously recognised.

Cull's definition of public diplomacy as an 'international actor's attempt to conduct its foreign policy by engaging with foreign publics' by means of the five methods described in his model – and which he regards as being 'traditionally government-to-people contact' – is also useful to this study. It can, however, be modified slightly to suit the purposes of this book.[26] Therefore, public diplomacy is here defined as an 'international actor's attempt to influence foreign and international relations by engaging with foreign publics'. This relies partly on Hart's conception of 'foreign relations', which he describes as the 'sum total of a nation's contacts with governments and peoples of other nations'. Hart differentiates this from 'diplomacy', which he regards as the 'high-level contacts between the official designated representatives of various nations', and from 'foreign policy', which he defines as 'all aspects of a government's approach to the external world'. According to Hart, this includes state–state diplomacy, but also, after the development of official public diplomacy initiatives in the 1940s, intercultural relations.[27] This book regards the Pilgrims Society as an 'international actor' and argues that its work represented one element of a 'nation's contacts with governments and peoples of other nations'.[28] This work was occasionally done in cooperation with official elements in the British or US governments and was, as such, semi-official. The 'foreign publics' with which the Pilgrims engaged, meanwhile, varied in size from the wider reading public who learned about the Society's events in the press, to the elite guests present at such events. Not all of these elites were official diplomats, though it was often hoped that they wielded some form of influence.

The Pilgrims' public diplomacy

The history of the Pilgrims Society challenges notions of what is and what is not 'traditional public diplomacy', a concept described by Nancy Snow as 'governments talking to global publics' and characterised by groups like the USIA. It is this version of public diplomacy that has been tarnished by its association with propaganda and which has led Snow to advocate a post-Cold War public diplomacy that 'involves the way in which both government and private individuals and groups influence directly and indirectly those public attitudes and opinions that bear directly on another government's foreign policy decisions'.[29] Snow's agenda was to challenge post-George W. Bush US governments to find new ways of improving the nation's international image, in which its 'soft power' is more important than its 'hard power'.[30] Central to this new version of 'public diplomacy' is the idea that international relations are discursive and not didactic, and include the 'active involvement of non-governmental actors such as the media, the business community, non-profit organizations, and individual Americans'.[31] This, however, is precisely what was already happening in the late nineteenth and early twentieth centuries and was what characterised the international tradition in which the Pilgrims Society had its origins.

The Pilgrims Society's form of public and cultural diplomacy emerged from a nineteenth-century tradition of internationalism. Frank Ninkovich has argued that the nineteenth century witnessed the formation of a 'global society', with many Americans – primarily liberals – taking an interest in ideas of progress and civilisation beyond the borders of what has traditionally been seen as an isolationist Gilded Age USA. Such internationalists believed that 'international relations were grounded in contacts between peoples and societies, not between states'.[32] This much was articulated by James Bryce during a Pilgrims dinner in London upon his return to Britain at the end of his term as ambassador in the US in 1913, when he said that '[t]here is a friendship of Governments and a friendship of peoples'. Whereas he regarded the former as an 'unstable thing, which may vary with the shifting of material interests, or with the formation of alliances with other Powers', the latter relied 'upon a more solid and enduring basis'. In the case of Britain and the US, this basis was characterised by a 'community of language, of literature, of institutions, of traditions, of ideals'.[33] Ideas such as these were especially important to the Pilgrims' cultural diplomacy.

Evidence for 'global society' is, meanwhile, found in the variety of international fairs and expositions held in the second half of the nineteenth century and at the start of the twentieth century. These fairs demonstrated an understanding of the potential

benefits to state–state relations accruing from the internationalism of private individuals and organisations.[34] Members of the
Pilgrims Society were involved in many of these fairs, including
the businessman and prominent Republican Chauncey Depew at
the 1901 exposition in Buffalo. As the US Secretary of State John
Hay said in relation to the Buffalo event, such expositions were
important because the 'benignant influences that shall emanate
from this great festival of peace shall not be bounded by oceans
nor by continents'.[35] The Pilgrims knew this to be true, which
is why its members were involved in the holding of an Anglo-
American Exposition in London in 1914 and why the Society
was deeply alarmed by the British government's decision in 1913
not to become officially involved in the 1915 Panama–Pacific
Exposition in San Francisco. The British government said that
it made this decision because of the costs associated with transporting exhibits, but it was widely interpreted as a protest over
tolls on the Panama Canal. Not attending was anathema to the
aims of the Pilgrims.[36] Members of the Pilgrims Society had also
been involved with New York's Hudson–Fulton celebrations in
1909, a large international festival and public fair held to jointly
mark the tercentenary of Henry Hudson's arrival from the Old
World on the river which eventually bore his name, and engineer
Robert Fulton's first steamship journey on the river in 1807. The
president of the Hudson–Fulton Celebration Commission was
Stewart L. Woodford, a former Pilgrims Society chairman, while
George T. Wilson, one of the New York Pilgrims' most active and
prominent members, was responsible for taking care of the British military officers visiting New York as part of the festivities.[37]
The Pilgrims Society's involvement with the Hudson–Fulton celebrations in 1909 and with the Anglo-American Exposition in
1914 locates its activities within a lineage of privately sponsored
public and cultural diplomacy, part of which had its roots in the
world's fairs and expositions of the previous century.[38]

If the Pilgrims Society developed from the period of 'global
society', then it also contributed to what Daniel Gorman had
described as the 'emergence of international society' in the
1920s. Though there were differences between liberal and conservative Anglo-American internationalists, particularly over
US membership of the League of Nations, Gorman believes that
'[c]onceptions of international society were advanced primarily by private interests during the 1920s, with official attitudes

ambivalent'.[39] The argument here is that private involvement in international relations was necessitated by difficult state–state relations, including between Britain and the US, and confirms the idea that elite transatlantic networks like the Pilgrims Society had a role to play in efforts to secure international amity. The features associated with the development of concepts like Gilded Age 'global society' and 1920s 'international society' show that the practice of public diplomacy predates both the Pilgrims Society and the formal recognition of the term by the British and US governments later in the twentieth century. It also means that present-day ideas – like those articulated by Nancy Snow – about the usefulness of less official channels of public diplomacy are not as new as they may at first appear. Importantly, however, the Pilgrims Society's activities helped ensure the existence of state-sponsored public diplomacy programmes in the first place.

Associational culture

The Pilgrims Society's ability to operate as a public diplomacy actor was underpinned by its status as an elite association. As a result, this book approaches the Pilgrims Society with reference to concepts of associational culture and builds upon the work done by other historians in the field. Such work is representative of a sub-discipline of history that regards the associational culture surrounding club and society membership as a prism through which to analyse wider historical issues, including migration, ethnicity, political activism, and social status. Associational culture is regarded here as referring to the ideas, habits, and activities that existed as a result of the coming together of individuals into collective organisations, such as clubs and societies. These organisations can often act as an 'identifiable carrier of ideals': in the case of the Pilgrims Society, the ideal of Anglo-American friendship.[40] Peter Clark's *British Clubs and Societies 1580–1800* – which traces the early modern 'origins of an associational world' – is the seminal text in the field of associational culture history. Operating in this earlier period, Clark suggests that it is necessary to approach the study of associations with the following questions in mind: 'what forms do [voluntary associations] take? Who joins them and for what reasons? Where are they located? What do they do? How stable and effective are they? And what is their impact?'[41] This book poses these questions of the Pilgrims Society. R. J. Morris has also conducted important research into the emergence of elite urban voluntary societies in Britain, and identifies the period between 1780 and 1850 as a time when, due to industrialisation and urbanisation, there was a notable growth in such associations.[42] American writers, meanwhile, have examined the development of associational culture in the US, particularly in New York. For example, Edward Pessen has studied the various clubs and societies that were founded in New York during the first half of the nineteenth century. Similarly, Eric Homberger has examined the social lives of the city's elites in the period up until the beginning of the twentieth century and has studied the ways in which networking, associations, power, and money helped create a New York 'aristocracy'.[43] Works such as these are important for this study because they relate to notions of an elite urban associational culture – of which the Pilgrims were undoubtedly a part – and because they have helped conceptualise the idea that associational culture provides a way in which to study wider social, political, and diplomatic issues. The Pilgrims Society was used as a vehicle, or a conduit, between, and for, official and unofficial agents and agency in international affairs, with the aim of promoting Anglo-American friendship. As a well-connected elite association, the Society enabled its prominent members, acting under its auspices and on its behalf, to participate in the field of international relations, including by coming into contact with official diplomats and statesmen. Conversely, the Society provided a means for these officials to engage with influential elites and with wider publics, for instance through networking at high-profile banquets.

The Pilgrims Society was able to act as a conduit between official and unofficial elements in Britain and the US in large part because it was an elite network which benefited from existing social, cultural, and associational links between its members and other influential individuals.[44] As is shown by the Pilgrims, clubs can provide a centre for international diplomatic networks. The idea that the study of clubs can inform an understanding of the ways in which social networks – regarded by this book as the personal and institutional links between and amongst individuals and organisations, broadly including state and non-state actors – can influence wider spheres relates to themes that have been explored in literature pertaining to associational culture. For example, writers like Kelly and Comerford have argued that '[o]ne way to explore social networks is to trace them through the structures of a developing associational culture, or in other words formal voluntary activity, such as participation in clubs'.[45] Such participation 'fostered participation in the public sphere by groups other than the traditional aristocratic and political elite of society'.[46] This also chimes with the notion that the Pilgrims Society provided a conduit for its (albeit elite) members to become involved in wider semi-official public diplomacy activity. While 'associations' is not a synonym for 'networks', associations can act as a looking-glass through which to study wider phenomena, including elite networking, public diplomacy, and international relations.

Conclusion

The Pilgrims Society channelled its public diplomacy activities via transnational associationalism. The Society plugged its high-status members into, and provided them with, a network of useful connections. What made the Society distinct from other associations is that its transatlantic network enabled its members to use the agency provided by the Society in order to participate in public diplomacy and, namely, to 'attempt to influence foreign and international relations by engaging with foreign publics'. The Pilgrims did this before the advent of more official public diplomacy programmes, but also emerged from an older tradition of elite-led internationalism partly characterised by the fostering of cultural and economic relations. The next chapter considers the precise ways in which the Society developed as a transatlantic association, while subsequent chapters provide case studies of its public diplomacy activities.

Notes

1. Nicholas J. Cull, *The Cold War and the United States Information Agency: American Propaganda and Public Diplomacy, 1945–1989* (Cambridge, 2008), p. xv.

2. Kenneth Osgood and Brian Etheridge, 'Introduction: The New International History Meets the New Cultural History: Public Diplomacy and US Foreign Relations', in Osgood and Etheridge (eds), *The United States and Public Diplomacy: New Directions in Cultural and International History* (Leiden and Boston, 2010), pp. 12–14.

3. Cull, 'Public Diplomacy Before Gullion: The Evolution of a Phrase', *USC Center on Public Diplomacy*, <http://uscpublicdiplomacy.org/blog/060418_public_diplomacy_before_gullion_the_evolution_of_a_phrase> (last accessed 7 April 2014); Cull, *American Propaganda and Public Diplomacy*, p. xv.

4. Philip M. Taylor, *The Projection of Britain: British Overseas Publicity and Propaganda, 1919–1939* (Cambridge, 1981), pp. 2–5.

5. Osgood and Etheridge, 'Introduction', pp. 12–13.

6. Justin Hart, *Empire of Ideas: The Origins of Public Diplomacy and the Transformation of US Foreign Policy* (Oxford, 2013), p. 2.

7. Frank Ninkovich, *The Diplomacy of Ideas: US Foreign Policy and Cultural Relations, 1938–1950* (Cambridge, 1981), pp. 8–34.

8. Hart, *Empire of Ideas*, p. 8.

9. Dominik Geppert, 'The Public Challenge to Diplomacy: German and British Ways of Dealing with the Press, 1890–1914', in Markus Mösslang and Torsten Riotte (eds), *The Diplomats' World: A Cultural History of Diplomacy, 1815–1914* (Oxford, 2008), pp. 133–8; George C. Herring, *From Colony to Superpower: US Foreign Relations Since 1776* (New York, 2008), p. 311; Cull, *American Propaganda and Public Diplomacy*, p. 5.

10. *New York Times*, 9 April 1935; Baker, *Pilgrims of Britain*, p. 184; the connection between Brittain and Northcliffe was solidified during the course of the organisation of the 1909 Imperial Press Conference. See Harry Brittain to Lord Northcliffe, 26 June 1909, and the undated account of the conference by Harry Brittain, Lord Northcliffe Papers, British Library [BL], Add MSS 62166; D. George Boyce, 'Harmsworth, Alfred Charles William, Viscount Northcliffe (1865–1922)', *Oxford Dictionary of National Biography* (Oxford University Press, 2004), <http://www.oxforddnb.com/view/article/33717> (last accessed 24 July 2014).

11. 'Speeches at a dinner of the Executive Committee of the Pilgrims in honour of Sir Campbell Stuart', 23 October 1958, Brittain Papers, BLPES, Box 4; W. Haley, 'Stuart, Sir Campbell Arthur (1885–1972)', *Oxford Dictionary of National Biography* (Oxford University Press, 2004), <http://www.oxforddnb.com/view/article/31732> (last accessed 2 April 2012); Sir Campbell Stuart to Sir Roderick Jones, 25 March 1918, Records of the Foreign Office, The National Archives, Kew, [TNA], FO/395/223.

12. Hart, *Empire of Ideas*, pp. 6–7.

13. Ninkovich, *Diplomacy of Ideas*, pp. 8–34; for more on the Carnegie Endowment, and also the Rockefeller Foundation, see Katharina Rietzler, 'Beyond the Cultural Cold Wars: American Philanthropy and Cultural Diplomacy in the Inter-War Years', *Historical Research*, Vol. 84, No. 223 (February 2011), pp. 148–64. See also Volker R. Berghan, *America and the Intellectual Cold Wars in Europe* (Princeton, 2001).

14. Ninkovich, *Diplomacy of Ideas*, pp. 8–34.

15. Taylor, *British Propaganda in the Twentieth Century: Selling Democracy* (Edinburgh, 1999), p. 76.

16. Ibid. pp. 76–7.

17. Taylor, *Projection of Britain*, pp. 93–125; Minutes, 24 October 1929, Pilgrims Mss, LMA/4632/A/01/001.

18. Hart argues that the Creel Committee was something of a wartime anomaly, with those involved believing that such an organisation was not appropriate in peacetime. See Hart, *Empire of Ideas*, p. 7. Even so, this book will show that developments during the First World War were part of the pre-1930s lineage of public diplomacy.

19. Cull, *American Propaganda and Public Diplomacy*, p. xv.

20. Richard T. Arndt, *The First Resort of Kings: American Cultural Diplomacy in the Twentieth Century* (Washington DC, 2005), p. 5.

21. Jessica Gienow-Hecht, 'The Anomaly of the Cold War: Cultural Diplomacy and Civil Society Since 1850', in Osgood and Etheridge (eds), *The United States and Public Diplomacy*, p. 32.

22. Ibid. pp. 29–30.

23. Ibid. p. 30.

24. Cull, *American Propaganda and Public Diplomacy*, p. xvi.

25. Ibid. p. xv.

26. Ibid. p. xv.

27. Hart, *Empire of Ideas*, p. 12.

28. Accordingly, this book agrees with the University of Southern California's Center on Public Diplomacy that public diplomacy 'involves a multitude of actors and networks', some of them non-state. See USC Center on Public Diplomacy, 'What Is PD?', <http://uscpublicdiplomacy.org/page/what-pd> (last accessed 13 September 2014).

29. Nancy Snow, 'Rethinking Public Diplomacy', in Nancy Snow and Philip Taylor (eds), *The Routledge Handbook to Public Diplomacy* (New York, 2009), p. 6.

30. Snow's use of the term 'soft power' connects theories of public and cultural diplomacy with the work of Joseph Nye. Nye describes 'soft power' as an 'attraction to shared values' which can include an attraction to a country's institutions and culture, including films and music. The soft power thesis helps conceptualise the ways in

which the Pilgrims Society appealed to shared Anglo-American values in their pursuit of international friendship. As the term 'power' implies the 'ability to get the outcomes one wants', Nye's concept also speaks to the notion that the people involved with the Pilgrims Society were a power elite. As such, this book is located within the soft power concept, especially as Osgood and Etheridge have suggested that public diplomacy is 'one component of a nation's soft power'. See Joseph S. Nye, *Soft Power: The Means to Success in World Politics* (New York, 2004), pp. 1–7 and pp. 99–125; Osgood and Etheridge, 'Introduction', p. 13; Charles Wright Mills, *The Power Elite* (New York, 1959), p. 62.

31. Keith Reinhard, 'American Business and Its Role in Public Diplomacy', in Snow and Taylor (eds), *Public Diplomacy*, p. 195.

32. Ninkovich, *Global Dawn: The Cultural Foundation of American Internationalism, 1865–1890* (Cambridge, MA, 2009), pp. 3–4.

33. 'Dinner in Honour of The Right Honourable James Bryce Given by The Pilgrims at the Savoy Hotel', 6 November 1913, Brittain Papers, BLPES, Box 5.

34. Ninkovich, *Global Dawn*, p. 37.

35. Robert W. Rydell, *All the World's a Fair: Visions of Empire at American International Expositions, 1876–1916* (Chicago, 1984), pp. 127–53.

36. *The Times*, 15 October 1913; *New York Times*, 31 July 1913; George T. Wilson to Harry Brittain, 11 June 1914, Pilgrims Mss, LMA/4632/A/05/002/01.

37. Kathleen Eagen Johnson, *The Hudson–Fulton Celebration: New York's River Festival of 1909 and the Making of a Metropolis* (New York, 2009), *passim*; Minute Book 1, 2 September 1902, Pilgrims Mss, NYC; Wilson to Brittain, 18 April (no year), Pilgrims Mss, LMA/4632/A/05/002/01; Sir Edward Hobart Seymour, the Admiral of the British fleet, was the official representative of the British government at the Hudson–Fulton celebrations, and was a guest of the Pilgrims at a banquet in New York on 4 October. See *New York Times*, 5 October 1909.

38. Michael Sanders and Philip M. Taylor, *British Propaganda During the First World War, 1914–1918* (London, 1982), pp. 194–5.

39. Daniel Gorman, *The Emergence of International Society in the 1920s* (Cambridge, 2012), p. 3, p. 183 and p. 211; on his definition of 'international society', Gorman writes: 'Political scientist Hedley Bull defined "international society" as the shared norms and values of states and non-state actors and the means by which they regulate and shape international relations. I argue that the concept emerged to underwrite the international peace and

functional cooperation projects of the 1920s, re-conceptualizing pre-1914 liberal internationalism as a more robust vision of international relations at the nexus of supra-state, state, and sub-state politics'. See ibid. p. 16.

40. Bueltmann, Andrew Hinson and Graeme Morton, 'Introduction: Diaspora, Associations and Scottish Identity', in Bueltmann, Hinson and Morton (eds), *Ties of Bluid, Kin and Countrie: Scottish Associational Culture in the Diaspora* (Ontario, 2009), p. 7.

41. Peter Clark, *British Clubs and Societies 1580–1800: The Origins of an Associational World* (Oxford, 2000), p. viii.

42. R. J. Morris, 'Introduction: Civil Society, Associations and Urban Places: Class, Nation and Culture in Nineteenth-Century Europe', in Morton, Boudien de Vries and Morris (eds), *Civil Society, Associations and Urban Places: Class, Nation and Culture in Nineteenth-Century Europe* (Aldershot, 2006); Morris, 'Clubs, Societies and Associations', in F. M. L. Thompson (ed.), *The Cambridge Social History of Britain 1750–1950, Volume 3: Social Agencies and Institutions* (Cambridge, 1990), pp. 395–443; Morris, 'Voluntary Societies and British Urban Elites', *The Historical Journal*, Vol. 26, No. 1 (1983), pp. 95–118. Morris argues that nineteenth-century voluntary societies, in contrast to their twentieth-century counterparts (which tended to 'act as pressure groups upon government'), did not need to operate with reference to what was then a weaker state.

43. Eric Homberger, *Mrs. Astor's New York: Money and Social Power in a Gilded Age* (New Haven, 2002); Edward Pessen, 'Philip Hone's Set: The Social World of the New York City Elite in the "Age of Egalitarianism"', *New-York Historical Society Quarterly*, Vol. 56 (1972), pp. 285–308. See also Bueltmann, *Scottish Ethnicity and the Making of New Zealand Society, 1850–1930* (Edinburgh, 2011), p. 15; Amy Milne-Smith, 'Club Talk: Gossip, Masculinity and Oral Communities in Late Nineteenth-Century London', *Gender and History*, Vol. 21, No. 1 (April 2009), pp. 86–106; Antonia Taddei, 'London Clubs in the Late Nineteenth Century', *University of Oxford Discussion Papers in Economic and Social History*, Number 28 (April 1999); Jose C. Moya, 'Immigrants and Associations: A Global and Historical Perspective', *Journal of Ethnic and Migration Studies*, Vol. 31, No. 5 (September 2005), pp. 833–64. See also Jennifer Kelly and R. V. Comerford (eds), *Associational Culture in Ireland and Abroad* (Dublin, 2010); P. H. J. H. Gosden, *Self-Help: Voluntary Associations in Nineteenth-Century Britain* (London, 1974); Donald M. MacRaild, Sylvia Ellis and Stephen Bowman, 'Interdependence Day and Magna Charta: James Hamilton's Public

Diplomacy in the Anglo-World, 1907–1940s', *Journal of Transatlantic Studies*, Vol. 12, Issue 2 (2014), pp. 140–62.
44. Mills, *Power Elite*, p. 62.
45. Kelly and Comerford, 'Introduction', in Kelly and Comerford (eds), *Associational Culture in Ireland and Abroad*, p. 1.
46. Ibid. p. 1.

2 The Founding of the Society

Men <u>ask</u> to be permitted to join and if they are up to the standard, we graciously permit 'em.
(George T. Wilson)

The Pilgrims Society's functions were extravagant and colourful affairs stereotypical of the excesses of upper-class Edwardian Britain and Gilded Age America. The *New York Times* in 1907 reported from one such Society dinner, describing the grand ball room of New York's prestigious Waldorf-Astoria Hotel, where the event was being held, as 'lavishly decorated with American and British flags'.[1] Then, following an event in 1909, the walls of the same venue were described as bedecked by 'two clasped hands outlined in electric lights, and over them an arrangement of electric bulbs spelled "Hands Across the Sea"'. The 'gold epaulets and gold lace' which adorned the military uniforms of some of the 500 guests 'glittered in the glare of lights at almost all of the fifty tables'.[2] Sometimes the decorations chosen for Society events had a symbolic significance, for example on one occasion when tables were embellished by 'sprays of trailing arbutus', chosen because they were the species of plant that had purportedly been the first flower encountered by the Pilgrim Fathers when they landed at Plymouth Rock in the seventeenth century. While official histories of the Pilgrims Society claim that the club did not take its name from the Pilgrim Fathers, the Society was evidently prepared to evoke the spirit of America's early modern English and European settlers. It is noteworthy, for example, that the London branch utilised what was called the 'Mayflower Room' in the Hotel Victoria, a room named after both the Pilgrim Fathers' ship and the trailing arbutus (the trailing arbutus is also called the mayflower, due to this connection with the seventeenth-century Pilgrims).

Such sentiments concerning the Pilgrim Fathers were consistent with what Joseph Conforti has termed a 'new, politicized meaning' to the word 'Pilgrim', which emerged in the early nineteenth century. Largely distinct from religious connotations, 'Pilgrim', and the Pilgrim Fathers, 'connoted the pioneering status of New England's founders; the old comers were now imagined as the pioneers of civil and religious liberty in America'.[3] This is what James Sheffield – the US ambassador to Mexico – meant when he, at the Pilgrims Society's twenty-fifth anniversary dinner in 1928, spoke of the 'fundamental principles of government' which the Pilgrim Fathers had brought to America from England. He said that he believed that the 'spirit' of that pilgrimage 'rests with [the Society]'.[4]

This chapter examines the founding of the Pilgrims Society and the development of its early aims and activities, which were formulated amidst those bright lights of elite London and New York. It does so across five sections. The first section traces the origins of the Society and establishes precisely who was responsible for its foundation. It also considers why people were motivated to become involved with the Society in the first place. The second section examines how the Society's membership was constituted and what processes were involved in joining. The third section places the Society in the context of the elite associational cultures of London and New York. It does so with reference to a variety of other clubs, including some with similar aims to those of the Pilgrims. The fourth section looks in greater detail at some internal debates had by the Society in relation to how best to achieve its aims. Meanwhile, the final section examines the ways in which the Pilgrims engendered links with diplomatic officials and why this meant that the Society was more successful, more quickly, than many of its contemporaries.

The development of the Pilgrims

The improvement in Anglo-American relations at the turn of the nineteenth and twentieth centuries was noted in 1903 by the London *Times* in its coverage of one of the first meetings of the Pilgrims Society in New York, an occasion which the paper regarded as a 'sign of the change which has taken place, and a pleasant means of extending its scope and of promoting its continuance'. While the rapprochement was often articulated in the rhetoric of Anglo-Saxonism, the work of the Pilgrims, according to *The Times*, was also about bringing Britain and the US together as the two 'great manufacturers and traders of the world, and therefore the great advocates of international peace'.[5] It had been amidst this milieu of English-speaking rapprochement and international friendship that the Pilgrims Society was first established in London the year before, in 1902. The Society was founded with an explicit aim 'to increase and perpetuate the present friendly relations between the peoples of the two countries'.[6] It was established across the summer of 1902, following meetings held at the city's Carlton Hotel. The Society's first function was a banquet to Lord Roberts at the Carlton Hotel on 8 August, the day before the coronation of King Edward VII. Harry Brittain later recalled that the coronation had 'kept very many distinguished people in London', which was helpful for securing the attendance of such people for the Society's first function. Roberts welcomed the Pilgrims' American guests 'as brothers of the same stock who share all the proud traditions of the Anglo-Saxon race'.[7] The New York branch was founded in January 1903 and held its first recorded meeting on 9 February.[8] Speaking at the Society's first public function in New York a few days previously, which was, in fact, done under the auspices of the existing London branch, founding member and senior British naval commander Charles Beresford highlighted what he believed were the benefits of Anglo-American friendship: namely, that it would 'help to maintain the peace of the world, which, if assured, will give a trading and commercial century'.[9] Beresford was a proponent of the 'Open Door' policy regarding trade with China, and – following a visit to both China and the US in 1899 – partly influenced US Secretary of State John Hay's formulation of his Open Door Notes.[10] This underlines that the motivation behind some Pilgrims' support for improved Anglo-American relations had a commercial aspect.[11]

The creation of an American branch was a natural development for an organisation with the aim of promoting transatlantic links. With New York such an important point of arrival for many travellers, the choice of the city as a locus for a Pilgrims branch was partly motivated by the belief that the Society's role was to facilitate 'pilgrimages' or, as in Brittain's words, the 'peregrinating' of elite individuals, between the two countries. As such, it was hoped that international amity would be served by the personal experience of travel and social intercourse.[12] Each branch of the Pilgrims had its own executive committee, which usually met once a month under the leadership of a chairman. The British Pilgrims' first chairman was William Sinclair, the Archdeacon of London, while the first chairman of the American Pilgrims was a lawyer named Lindsay Russell. Russell was originally from North Carolina, but was associated with legal firms in both New York and London. He later said that he had been inspired to work towards Anglo-American friendship partly because he had lived in Detroit, Michigan, in the 1890s, close to the Canadian–US border, and had witnessed 'English and American mingling daily in friendly intercourse, with no forts or ships to guard either side of the international line'.[13] He had a wide-ranging interest in international relations that stretched beyond Anglo-American rapprochement. For example, he served as a director of the New York Peace Society and in 1907 founded the city's Japan Society with the aim of promoting better relations between Japan and the US.[14] After the First World War, Russell was also chairman of the Council on Foreign Relations, a group founded in 1918 to promote international peace and commerce and which merged in 1921 with the American Institute of International Affairs to create the present-day Council on Foreign Relations.[15]

In addition to the chairman, the Pilgrims Society's branches also each had a president. This was largely a ceremonial and honorary position. The first president of the British Pilgrims was Field Marshal Lord Frederick Roberts, while Henry Codman Potter, the Bishop of New York, was the first in the US. With Lord Roberts acting as the figurehead of the British Pilgrims, the Society was immediately associated with a man of considerable imperial and military prestige. Roberts was commander-in-chief of the British army and was famous for his participation and leadership in a number of nineteenth-century British military engagements, including in India, Afghanistan, and South Africa. He was well connected and was friends both with Lord Lansdowne, the British Foreign Secretary between 1900 and 1905, and with the London *Times* journalist C. F. Moberly Bell, who was also a member of the Pilgrims.[16] The Pilgrims' military connections were enhanced by the involvement of the American General Joseph Wheeler, a Confederate veteran of the Civil War who was based in Lindsay Russell's London office at the time of the founding of the Pilgrims in 1902. It was then that Russell had suggested – somewhat presumptuously, but in line with wider notions of the importance of Anglo-American relations for international order and peace – that Wheeler and Roberts 'should devote the remainder of their lives to the promotion of peace and good will, and brought about a meeting of the two military leaders to discuss plans for organising The Pilgrims Society'.[17] While Roberts served as president until his death in 1914, Wheeler did not hold an official role in the Society. Other positions on the executive committee included the honorary secretary and the honorary treasurer, neither of which were in practice 'honorary' but were instead labour-intensive and influential roles. This was particularly the case for the honorary secretary, as was well demonstrated by the energetic Harry Brittain. Brittain very much made the role of secretary of the London branch his own. He subsequently served as chairman until 1919.[18]

The Society, meanwhile, worked to establish links with the heads of state in both Britain and the US. These links were sometimes personal but were on other occasions largely symbolic. The Duke of Connaught, for example, served as president of the London branch from 1917 until 1942.[19] Queen Elizabeth II has, meanwhile, been the Society's patron, though previous monarchs do not appear to have served this function. The British Pilgrims in 1995 decided against going through what was regarded as an expensive and time-consuming process of applying for a royal charter as it already had the patronage of the monarch. The US president acted as honorary president of the New York branch only since Dwight Eisenhower in the 1950s until Ronald Reagan in the 1980s. Toasts at Society functions, meanwhile, were typically given to the British monarch and to the US president.[20]

There was some controversy in later years about precisely who was the principal founder of the Pilgrims, with Harry Brittain eventually receiving (and claiming) most of the credit in Britain. Similarly in New York, George T. Wilson – who was a director and vice-president of the Equitable Life Assurance Society – enjoyed most of the plaudits for the success of the American Pilgrims.[21] Yet, in the case of both Brittain and Wilson (both strong characters who worked closely together during their years in office and who were something of a Pilgrims double act), their undeniably important work in building up the Society in subsequent years has obscured the crucial roles initially played by others, including the lawyer Lindsay Russell. Russell was working in London in the early 1900s and was described by J. Arthur Barratt, a Pilgrim and legal adviser to the US Embassy in London, as the Society's 'real "founder"'.[22] It was largely Russell – in a role that he described as 'Chairman of the Committee on Organization', which appears to have been a temporary organisational body – who brought together the various interested parties, both in London and in New York.[23] A number of letters addressed to Russell in response to invitations to join the Pilgrims, sent immediately prior to its first meeting in London, further demonstrate that Russell was indeed the focal point for the Society's establishment in Britain. Likewise, a letter sent in January 1903 to Russell from Whitelaw Reid – the proprietor of the *New-York Tribune* and later the American ambassador to Britain – regarding the founding of the New York branch, shows that he was also behind the Society's expansion into the US.[24] For some Pilgrims, however, the processes that led to the founding of the Society were obscured by the passage of time. This was demonstrated in the late 1940s by correspondence between then president of Columbia University, and president of the New York Pilgrims between 1928 and 1946, Nicholas Murray Butler, and Sir Evelyn Wrench, the founder of the English-Speaking Union (ESU). Wrench was writing a book about 'American landmarks and associations with London' and asked Butler for information regarding the founding of the Pilgrims Society, which he erroneously thought was first established in New York. In reply, Butler explained that he had 'recollection of an informal conference at the Athenaeum in London some time in 1902 or 1903' with Lindsay Russell and Joseph Wheeler, at which was discussed the 'advisability of organising an association to bring the people and the public sentiment of Great Britain and the United States in closer contact with each other', though he admitted that he did 'not know that the word Pilgrims was used'. While this informal discussion may well have happened in 1902, it is unclear how important Butler was to the eventual creation of the Society. Even though Butler told Wrench that '[a]lmost immediately the movement to found the Pilgrims began, and I have done what I could to carry it forward from that day to this', Butler did not in fact join the Society until 1909.[25]

The lack of clarity about the precise origins of the Pilgrims is caused not only by the haziness of some people's memories, but is also partly due to tensions that existed between the principal members and is manifest in the contradictory nature of the primary source material. In the 1930s, Barratt wrote to a number of the original members seeking confirmation of who had been responsible for the Society's founding. He was motivated by a desire to produce what he regarded as the correct history of the Society, in contrast to the version of events then being written for publication by Harry Brittain. William Goode, one of the founding members, told Barratt that the

> idea of the Pilgrims originated from a conversation in the Carlton Hotel smoking room between George Wilson, then a vice-President of the New York Life [Insurance Company], Lindsay Russell, who had recently opened an office in London for the Maryland Trust Company, and myself.[26]

According to Goode, Russell had originally suggested that he should become the honorary secretary, but Goode's employer – Walter Neef, the European Superintendent of the Associated Press – thought that he had too many outside interests. Instead, 'Russell then said he had a nice young chap named Brittain who had recently come down from Oxford, working in his office with practically nothing to do and he would bring him along and get him to act as Secretary'.[27] Slightly contradicting Goode's statement regarding the role played by George Wilson, Russell wrote to Barratt making clear that Wilson had 'nothing to do with the preliminary organization'.[28] Russell did, however, corroborate Goode's statement that Brittain was working in his office as a clerk in January 1902, explaining that Brittain served under him at the firm of Alexander and Colby and also that 'whatever he did during the first two years of The Pilgrims was under my direction'.[29] Russell accepted that Brittain had managed the Pilgrims as a '"going concern" very skilfully', but also noted that Brittain 'had not the training or connections' to have founded the Society.[30] Having received information from Lindsay Russell and William Goode, Barratt pointedly wrote Brittain that

> you will do well and avoid possible adverse criticism by giving due credit, as no doubt you will, to those who helped to organise the club. For you did not do, and, of course, could not have done it alone, as a comparatively unknown young man in London and New York at that time.[31]

In response, Brittain insisted that he had no problem giving Russell 'full credit for the suggestion of the Pilgrims, and all praise for the work he did during our early stages'. He took exception, however, to the suggestion that he had merely been Russell's clerk, arguing instead that Russell had 'asked me whether I would like to be associated with him, with the idea of advising on the English side of things' for Alexander and Colby. Brittain told Barratt that 'I was then no particular stripling for I reached the age of 29 in 1902, having taken my degree at Oxford and been Called to the Bar several years previously'.[32] While Brittain had indeed attended the University of Oxford (from where he graduated with a third-class degree in law), he omitted to mention that he had given up his legal career one week after arriving in London in 1897, initially receiving financial support from an allowance from his father, before eventually finding work as the private secretary to William Ingram, the managing director of the *Illustrated London News*. He also spent a period of introspection swimming and playing sport at the Bath Club, where he met Arthur Pearson, founder of the *Daily Express* and owner of *The Standard* and the *Evening Standard*, for whom he also became secretary.[33]

The discussion in the 1930s about the origins of the Pilgrims occurred outside of the Society itself, with Barratt, Brittain, and Russell corresponding privately with one another. Barratt did, however, write to the then secretary of the British Pilgrims, John Wilson Taylor, explaining that he had 'written Brittain my account of the origin of the Pilgrims . . . so that he can be under no misapprehension as to the origins of the Club'.[34] In reply, Taylor wrote that it was 'obvious that the origin of The Pilgrims was decided upon before Brittain came on the scene', but 'also that he did good service for the cause in its early years and until after the war'. Taylor promised to 'carefully preserve the letters you have sent me among the archives of the Society', acknowledging that he did 'not know what Brittain will say in his book but I know that he considers The Pilgrims as the particular product of his industry and enterprize'.[35] Taylor was subsequently 'glad' that Barratt had written to Brittain, as he believed that there was 'no excuse now for any wrong publication of the facts of the origins of The Pilgrims'.[36] The contrasts between the accounts provided by Brittain and those provided by Lindsay Russell and his friends – which ring more truthfully – were doubtless provoked by the success of the Pilgrims over the first thirty years of its existence, with a number of people clearly keen to highlight the role that they played in helping to establish the Society. This was also true of Nicholas Murray Butler's statement made in the 1940s that he was involved in discussions at the Athenaeum in London in the early 1900s.[37] There was, meanwhile, an additional personal element to the dispute between Lindsay Russell and Harry Brittain, as Russell had had an unsuccessful engagement to one of Brittain's sisters, with Brittain feeling that Russell had 'let my sister down rather badly'.[38] Whatever the underlying reasons – and judging by the tone of the 1930s correspondence – the passage of over thirty years had done little to soften the strength of feeling over who was primarily responsible for the founding of the society.

The Barratt correspondence in the 1930s was not the first occasion when differences between Brittain and Russell had come to the fore. Russell had left the Society some time before 1909 but had been re-elected to the New York Pilgrims in 1913, much to the displeasure of George Wilson who wrote to Brittain that he regarded Russell as 'a mischief maker, and in view of his history and certain things known to me, I am free to say that he is not the kind of a man I wish to be associated with myself, in any intimate capacity'.[39] Then in 1918, Lindsay Russell wrote a letter to the *New York Times* explaining that – contrary to popular belief, and rehearsing the arguments made in the Barratt correspondence in the 1930s – Harry Brittain had not founded the Society.[40] This was a notably open airing of the Society's internal tensions and suggests that Russell was motivated to clarify a perception amongst the reading public that Brittain had founded the Pilgrims. Newspaper reports did usually describe Brittain as the 'co-founder', or as 'one of the founders' of the Society, for example when in 1917 the *Atlanta Constitution* said that Brittain had 'in association with . . . the late Lord Roberts and the late General "Joe" Wheeler, founded the Pilgrims' club'.[41] It also demonstrates that the Pilgrims, within the first twenty years of its existence, had developed a significantly large public profile for the newspaper and its readers to take an interest in the story of the Society's founding.

Regardless of the later fallout between Russell, Brittain, and Wilson, the weight of evidence does indeed indicate that Russell was the principal figure in the founding of the Pilgrims Society. Russell also outlined the Society's initial motivations and influences. By his account, one of the original motivations for forming the Society was to address the need for London-based American journalists to network with important men in the British capital.[42] Indeed, early support for the Society came from people like the aforementioned Neef, European manager of the Associated Press, and Isaac N. Ford, the London correspondent for the *New-York Tribune*.[43] Russell's description of the Society's aims immediately associates the Pilgrims with the press, demonstrating that it believed that improved dissemination of information between Britain and the US could contribute to the rapprochement between the two countries. The relationship between the Pilgrims and the press took two forms. Firstly, it welcomed into its membership senior staff like Neef and Ford, but also newspaper proprietors like the *New York Times*' Adolph Ochs. Other senior newspaper men like the *Observer*'s James Garvin and the *Spectator*'s John St. Loe Strachey joined the Society later.[44] Secondly, the Society engaged on a more practical level with journalists in an effort to ensure publicity for its functions. This was evidenced by the practice of providing a table for press reporters at Society events and locating it directly in front of the speakers' table.[45] Russell's presentation of the Society as working to connect journalists with politicians and diplomats chimes with its later activities. As such, the Pilgrims' activities were informed by a desire to provide a conduit between British and American elites, including between official and unofficial actors, in an effort to promote international peace to ensure, in Charles Beresford's words, the advent of 'a trading and commercial century'.[46] That this was the case is shown by an interview given by Harry Brittain in 1912 for the *Pall Mall Gazette*, in which he said that Pilgrims events had ensured 'innumerable friendships have been made between men "who count", which have, I know, in many cases, been of real practical service to the two countries'.[47] This underlines that the role of the Society was to facilitate better international relations by encouraging personal contact between elites from the two centres of London and New York.

There is some indication, meanwhile, that wider European geopolitics motivated some of those involved with the formation of the Pilgrims Society. Russell recalled in the 1930s that 'Lord Roberts, in approving the plans for the organisation of the society, said that he saw the need for closer relations between England and the United States to counteract the war tendencies of the Imperial German government.'[48] This was precisely the period in which Britain was feeling increasingly isolated in Europe, part of neither the Triple Alliance between Germany, Austria-Hungary, and Italy, nor the Dual Alliance between France and Russia. Whereas 'splendid isolation' had hitherto been the accepted British foreign policy, by 1907 Britain had entered the Triple Entente with France and Russia, itself preceded by the Entente Cordiale with France in 1904. While agreements between Britain and France were principally designed to address sources of imperial friction in North Africa, Britain was also increasingly cognisant of the potential threat posed by Germany, in particular on account of the extension of its naval power.[49] The US also regarded Germany with increasing suspicion, especially following the 1903 Venezuelan crisis. Though this crisis had involved both Germany and Britain taking naval action against Venezuela in an effort to collect debts from the South American country in breach of the Monroe Doctrine, Britain had quickly bowed to US pressure for arbitration, while Germany proved more recalcitrant.[50] Lord Roberts' wish for the Society to play a role in bringing Britain and the US closer together in an effort to counteract Germany matched the British policy of acceding to American naval supremacy in the Western Hemisphere. Public sentiment in Britain was also hardening against Germany, with a number of fictional books presenting stories of a German invasion proving popular. Such books included one published in 1906 by William Le Queux, whom Lord Roberts had personally backed.[51] Roberts was also president of the National Service League (NSL), an organisation which – partly in response to inadequacies exposed by the Boer War – campaigned for compulsory military conscription. Harry Brittain also volunteered to help with the NSL, with Roberts telling him that '[w]hat you can do is to try and get money for us, and if you can persuade any of your rich friends to help in that, we shall be greatly obliged'. Other Pilgrims involved in the NSL included Charles Beresford and C. F. Moberly Bell.[52] This shows that for these individuals an interest in the Pilgrims' aim of Anglo-American friendship was informed by a wider concern for the defence of Britain's position as a world power and was connected to such concerns partly through their involvement in other organisations, like the NSL.

The Pilgrims' membership

Membership of the Society was restricted to 'Englishmen and Americans, and those prominent in public or social life, science, art or literature'.[53] Its membership was not illustrative of wider

British–American society, but was representative of the elite from both countries with an interest in Anglo-American friendship. Indeed, some Pilgrims were not resident in Britain or the US, meaning that the membership was a global body of elites with shared interests. This section looks at precisely how the Society's membership was constituted and also at the methods by which individuals were permitted entry into the organisation.

Women were not permitted to join the Pilgrims until 1977, when the New York branch was obliged to change its attitude to gender in response to the US Secretary of State Cyrus Vance and the US President Jimmy Carter refusing to accept honorary memberships of a society that had no female members. As membership in one branch provided membership in the other, this meant that the London Pilgrims also had to admit women.[54] In its exclusion of women the early twentieth-century Pilgrims Society was similar to many other elite urban clubs whose associational culture had long been a male-dominated sphere, partly on account of male chauvinism and the inferior legal status of women.[55] The role of women in the Pilgrims was, however, debated from a relatively early point in the Society's existence. In the aftermath of the First World War, during which many women had taken on traditionally male jobs as replacements for the men who had become soldiers, there was an expectation that women would enjoy greater employment opportunities and social equality. The granting of the franchise to (some) British women in June 1918 was another element to this.[56] Such hopes were entertained by Mrs Welsh-Lee, the London Pilgrims' business secretary – a position distinct from the position of honorary secretary on the executive committee, and consistently filled by a woman – who wrote in July 1919 to the Society's committee of 'the coming political and professional equality of men and women', and of her belief that women should be permitted to join the Pilgrims 'in the not too distant future'. Failing that, she suggested that the 'attendance of wives and women friends of members at certain gatherings and lectures would prove of educational value and stimulate interest'.[57] Yet Welsh-Lee and those other women who had anticipated greater equality after the First World War were disappointed. Not only were returning soldiers given back their old jobs at the expense of female employees, but the Pilgrims Society showed no sign of changing its policy towards women members. Indeed, some in the Society had been critical of women's rights in the past, including the author Arthur

Conan Doyle.[58] Conan Doyle, and those Pilgrims members with similar views, would clearly have been unsympathetic to Welsh-Lee's prediction of 'the coming political and professional equality of men and women'. Then in 1921, in response to a correspondent who wrote to say that 'it has always seemed to me a mistake for the Pilgrims not to admit [women]', especially as this was 'a course adopted by the English-Speaking Union at their functions', Wilson Taylor said that 'it is not proposed that ladies shall be invited to dine', as the Society's large membership meant that this would result in an impracticably large increase in attendance at functions.[59] Rather than heralding a new era of equality for women in wider society and for those women involved with the Pilgrims Society, the period immediately after the First World War remained one of gender-based segregation. For example, from the early 1920s until after the Second World War, the Pilgrims' female secretaries sat behind a screen and wore evening dress and a hat when working at Society events.[60] A step forward was made in 1930 during Nicholas Murray Butler's tenure as president of the New York branch, when the Society began providing separate dinner functions for women if the guests of honour brought their wives.[61] This physical separation of males and females represented an uneasy compromise between inclusion and exclusion but, like the screen hiding the secretary, was a long-standing aspect of male-dominated associational culture. It was ostensibly the manifestation of a desire to shield women from any male behaviour which could be regarded as inappropriate or un-gentlemanly.[62]

There were financial as well as gender barriers to membership of the Pilgrims. Any member who became bankrupted had to leave the Society, but could be reinstated if the committee felt 'he has done nothing to injure his reputation as a gentleman'. There was no entrance fee, though there was an annual subscription of £2 2s in 1909, compared with a maximum of £2 in 1902.[63] These were sizeable sums of money and were considerably greater than the shilling per year in 1898 for membership to the more inclusive Anglo-American League, and stood in contrast to the £1 1s annual subscription demanded by the Atlantic Union (though the Union also required a £1 1s entrance fee). It also was over double the cost of the highest level of membership to the Royal Society of St. George (RSStG), an organisation whose leadership included some individuals of a similar social status to many of the Pilgrims. Gilbert Parker MP, for example, was a vice-president of the RSStG and a member of the executive committee of the London Pilgrims. Harry Brittain was also involved with the RSStG, while the London Pilgrims' president from 1917, the Duke of Connaught, was one of the RSStG's vice-patrons.[64]

The Pilgrims also invested money and had £500 worth of bonds with the Japanese imperial government and $3,000 with the Pennsylvania Railroad.[65] Society functions were supposed to be paid for by the money raised from the sale of tickets, though there were occasions when expenditure on events was greater than the income, for example the New York branch's dinner in 1906 for Earl Grey. The executive committee believed that they would have been in credit had the tickets been sold for $15 instead of $10, but nevertheless felt that the deficit was 'fully justified by the importance of the occasion'.[66] In truth, auditors' reports undertaken for the London Pilgrims indicate that the cost of dinners was frequently greater than the income from tickets. Even so, this cost was absorbed by the Society's admittedly healthy finances.[67]

In 1906, the Pilgrims decided that members who did not live in the UK or the US did not need to pay a subscription, as there was little chance of such people having the opportunity to attend functions. This was directed particularly at members from across the British Empire, such as the Bishop of Perth, Australia, who had tendered his resignation from the Society, but was persuaded to stay by the offer of free membership. The London executive committee explained that it was 'desirous of retaining the interest of all prominent colonists in the organization'.[68] The Anglican Bishop of Perth was a man named Charles Owen Leaver Riley, who was originally from Birmingham and who went to Australia in 1895. He was a staunch imperialist and was, for example, Perth's official representative at the coronation of King George V in 1911 before going on to serve as Anglican chaplain general for the Australian forces during the First World War. He was also an Anglo-Saxonist, as shown by his sermon on Empire Day in 1913, when he 'prayed that the day might come when the Anglo-Saxon race might be firmly knitted together into one solid force, so powerful, so strong, that it might be able to ensure the peace of the word'.[69] Riley's membership of the Pilgrims – though long-distance and necessarily inactive – provided the Bishop with a link both to his homeland and to the Anglo-Saxonist and imperialist ethos that was clearly important to him. People like Riley also provided another element to the activities of the Pilgrims Society, beyond Anglo-American relations. Indeed,

Harry Brittain felt able to describe the Pilgrims as a 'British Empire–American institution', due to the number of members who were, in his words, 'prominent Colonials'. This was also demonstrated by the Pilgrims dinners held in 1907 and 1911, at the request of the British government, for the prime ministers of the British dominions who were in London for those years' imperial conferences.[70] As such, the Pilgrims' membership had a global reach.

Membership to the Pilgrims was by election, overseen by a sub-committee of the executive committee of each branch. George Wilson encapsulated the exclusive spirit of the Pilgrims' attitude to membership when he wrote to Harry Brittain to say that the Society was 'not making a general canvass for members. Men <u>ask</u> to be permitted to join and if they are up to the standard, we graciously permit 'em.'[71] Potential members required a proposer and a seconder to support their application, in addition to written statements from 'at least two other members' confirming the 'eligibility of the candidate'.[72] Even when these requirements were ostensibly fulfilled, the committee could decide 'not to recommend' the candidate for membership, for instance because one of the candidate's supporters had not paid their most recent subscription.[73] This also implies that the candidate was not deemed 'up to the standard'. Then in 1914, the New York Pilgrims decided that 'every candidate for membership must be known to at least one member of the Committee on Admissions or to at least one member of the Executive Committee present at the meeting at which the candidate's name is presented'. The London Pilgrims enacted this rule in 1930.[74] Despite George Wilson's statement to the contrary, potential members were sometimes approached by prominent figures from within the Pilgrims. This was the case when the Society was first established, with founding members calling upon personal contacts to encourage fellow elites to join. A good example of this was Richard Watson Gilder, the editor of the *Century* magazine and a poet. Gilder was elected onto the Pilgrims' executive committee in New York, having been invited to its founding meeting in February 1903 by Lindsay Russell at the request of the Society's first president, Bishop Potter.[75] Potter and Gilder were close acquaintances who kept up a long correspondence over many years and were themselves notable New York figures, both with a keen interest in the social affairs of the city.[76] Both Potter and Gilder came to the Pilgrims with a degree of reservation, with Gilder having written Potter, on receipt of Lindsay Russell's invitation, to say that he was 'very anxious about this matter' and that he did 'not care to be connected with a foolish or inept movement'.[77] As will become apparent, Gilder was concerned about some of the people involved with the Pilgrims. It is also likely that Gilder was unsure whether the Pilgrims would add anything new in the field of Anglo-American relations. He was a long-standing supporter of Anglo-American fellowship and told Potter that he had previously supported a venture in London similar to the Pilgrims; presumably the Anglo-American League, of which Gilder was a member.[78] Likewise, amidst the Venezuelan boundary dispute in 1895–6 the *Century* had editorialised its concern about the 'two great English-speaking nations giving up their position side by side in the vanguard of civilization'.[79] In relation to the Pilgrims, however, Gilder questioned whether a 'permanent organization on this side would not do more harm than good'.[80] Potter sympathised, writing that it would be 'easy enough for an international society to go astray', but he harnessed his friend's concern, urging him to join on the basis that 'it would be worthwhile for you and me to try and keep it in the right track'.[81] Potter had done enough to induce Gilder to join, but his concerns were not assuaged permanently and he resigned from the Pilgrims two years later. This was precipitated by an incident that occurred between Gilder and George Wilson at a Pilgrims dinner chaired by Wilson in June 1905. The next day Gilder wrote frantically to Potter, complaining that he had never been to 'a public dinner in New York of such low tone. It was one hip, hip, hurrah! and roaring, aggressive commonness, from beginning to end.'[82] Quite what happened between Gilder and Wilson is unclear, though it seems likely that Gilder's polite sensibilities had been shocked by a man who apparently was not averse to throwing bread rolls across the Pilgrims' top table towards distinguished guests.[83] Yet, and though Gilder later admitted that Wilson's main fault was his 'exuberance and boyishness' and insisted that his desire to resign from the Pilgrims was due to health reasons, Gilder's outburst against one of the club's leading figures surely had deeper motives.[84] In his original letter to Bishop Potter, which was mistakenly forwarded to the Pilgrims' chairman William Butler Duncan, Gilder wrote that as 'nearly as I can tell, no one insurance company is running the Pilgrims, but there seems to be a group who, for reasons of their own, are active'. He also seems to have had his early fears about the Pilgrims confirmed and, reminding Potter that it was he who had gotten him involved in the Society in the first place, revealed that in 1903 'certain prominent men told me that they feared that the active men in it [the Pilgrims] were, some of them, not what should be in such an organization, but I felt with you that there was, possibly, a patriotic duty to be done'.[85] Gilder was demonstrating the reforming liberal's concern about the corrupting influence of big business, in this case the New York insurance companies of which Wilson was a representative; a concern that would have been doubly excited in 1905 by that year's investigation into the workings of such companies. The investigation centred on Wilson's Equitable Life Assurance Society and an internal dispute over control of the company between its president, James W. Alexander, and its vice-president, James H. Hyde. The investigation was partly motivated by a public distaste for some of the indulgences of these wealthy entrepreneurs, but it also exposed some significant conflicting interests at the heart of New York commerce.[86] For instance, Jacob Schiff as both president of Kuhn, Loeb and a director of Equitable, was accused of impropriety over the sale of securities to Equitable by Kuhn, Loeb.[87] Hyde's testimony to the investigation, meanwhile, revealed that the Equitable had been solicited for a $25,000 donation to the Republican Party, in exchange for which the former US Secretary of the Interior Cornelius Bliss, Chauncey Depew, and Jacob Schiff attempted (unsuccessfully) to have Hyde appointed US ambassador to France.[88] Chauncey Depew, at the time still a US senator and another director of Equitable, was further criticised for receiving a $20,000 annual retainer from the company for his services as 'special counsel'.[89] With all of these men members of the Pilgrims, Gilder's concerns about some of the people he was associating with as part of the Society were not unfounded.

Potter was disappointed when Gilder finally made the decision to leave the Society, though he also confided to Gilder that the Pilgrims had 'too narrow a scope' and that they should 'offer an equal welcome to all travellers, Russian, Chinese, Austrian, or Italian, as well as those who are merely British. Enlarged in that way, it might serve a very benign and useful purpose.'[90] It is striking that a founding member and the incumbent president of the US Pilgrims should write about the club in such terms. Potter's and Gilder's remarks appear incongruous alongside the chauvinistic Anglo-Saxon and unapologetically capitalistic rhetoric that was a more readily identifiable feature of the Pilgrims. Their comments are suggestive of another side to the Society, an arguably more progressive and (relatively) less elitist side that was potentially crowded out by the ascendancy to positions of influence of people like George T. Wilson, Harry Brittain, and Chauncey Depew.

The Pilgrims' associational matrix

The founding of the Pilgrims Society occurred in the context of the founding of a variety of other elite-led associations whose aim it also was to promote Anglo-American friendship, for example the Anglo-American League and the Atlantic Union, formed in London in 1898 and 1900 respectively.[91] The Atlantic Union aimed to facilitate improved contact between British and American elites by means of its members acting essentially as tour guides for American visitors visiting Britain. Specifically, the Union wanted to attract 'those who help to form public opinion in the Colonies and the States'. A document outlining the Union's aims and objectives made it clear that it was 'essential that the English members shall themselves belong to the class of those who make and lead public opinion in this country'. Thus, like the Pilgrims, membership was only for 'professional men', including statesmen, journalists, educators, and 'leaders in the world of finance and commerce'.[92] With the hope of improving international sentiment through sympathetic exposure to foreign cultures, this was an early form of cultural exchange; a term which, in more recent years, has become associated with initiatives such as study abroad programmes for university students.[93] The Anglo-American League was, however, more significant than the Atlantic Union. Established in London in 1898, the League was supported and led by a number of prominent individuals, some of whom went on to become involved with the Pilgrims Society. Such individuals included Earl Grey, James Bryce, Horace Plunkett MP, and Charles Beresford. The author Sir Walter Besant was, meanwhile, involved with both the Atlantic Union and the Anglo-American League.[94] For its part, the Anglo-American League believed that the 'peoples of the British Empire and of the United States of America are closely allied in blood, inherit the same literature and laws' and that they shared 'common interests in many parts of the world'.[95] The League aimed to promote the 'most cordial and constant co-operation between the two nations' and hoped to do so by the creation of branches throughout the country. Though it was an elite-led organisation, membership of the League was open to anyone who could afford to pay the relatively modest entrance fee.[96]

Nobody at the inaugural meeting of the Anglo-American League explicitly mentioned the still ongoing Spanish-American War, with one newspaper noting that 'not a single word was dropped by any speaker calculated to wound the feelings of the most sensitive Spaniard . . . In fact, there was no direct reference, scarcely an allusion, to the war now fortunately coming to a speedy termination.'[97] Nevertheless, that the newspaper felt the need to mention it only serves to underline that Britain's support for the US in the conflict provided the immediate context for the founding of the Anglo-American League. For example, one of the League's honorary secretaries, Sir Frederick Pollock (a prominent jurist who also later became a Pilgrims member, and who had a well-known friendship with the famous American judge Oliver Wendell Holmes), wrote in a pamphlet for the League that Britain's stance during the Spanish-American War was an example of the 'spontaneous cooperation of England with the United States' and was caused not only by an 'affinity of race', but also by the

> common stock of traditions and institutions, the ideal of political and intellectual freedom which was framed by England by centuries of toil and conflict, and has gone round the world with the law happily called by a name neither distinctively English or American – our Common Law.[98]

The extent of the Anglo-American rapprochement in the late 1890s and the development of a related associational culture was encapsulated in the make-up of the organising committee of the New York branch of the Anglo-American League. As the *Pall Mall Gazette* noted, the committee included 'three members of that Cleveland Cabinet which got pretty near to involving the United States and England in war over the Venezuelan difficulty'. These three men were John G. Carlisle (Secretary of the Treasury), Daniel S. Lamont (Secretary of War), and William C. Whitney (Secretary of the Navy).[99] The rapprochement was by no means complete in 1898, but this shows the changes that had been wrought in just a few years. Whereas in 1895 these men were members of a US government whose relationship with its British counterpart was decidedly uneasy, in 1898 they were members of an association founded to promote the idea of the underlying comity of Britain and the US.

Like the Anglo-American League and the Atlantic Union, the Pilgrims Society was a product of this improvement in Anglo-American relations. Also like these other organisations, the Pilgrims Society was linked to elite urban associational culture. While there was indeed a global element to the Society's membership, it is nevertheless clear that the Pilgrims Society was primarily part of the exclusive social scenes of London and New York. As such, both cities allowed the Pilgrims Society to tap in to existing networks of exclusive associations. Indeed, New York had the largest number of gentlemen's clubs of any American city.[100] Some of the London clubs, meanwhile, had their origins in the coffee-houses of the seventeenth and eighteenth centuries, with associations like White's Chocolate House, Boodle's, and the Cocoa Tree all transforming from coffee-houses into elite clubs partly in response to their popularity amongst social elites.[101] With greater industrialisation and urbanisation – and with the undermining of traditional status symbols like craft guild membership caused by the rise of a middle class with a disposable income – clubs and associations provided a way of safeguarding social position and networks.[102] By the nineteenth century – particularly after the Napoleonic wars – the London clubs witnessed a considerable growth in membership. Many of these associations not only acted not only as social clubs for the wealthy and powerful elites, but also catered for a variety of interests, including political, artistic, military, and academic. Some examples of such clubs were the Reform, the Carlton, the St. James's (which was frequented by diplomats and foreign officials), the Athenaeum, and the Marlborough. The majority of these associations provided luxurious clubhouses and other amenities, many of which were located in the city's West End and financial district.[103]

Though the Pilgrims did not have a clubhouse, the Society did share certain other characteristics with the London clubs, including their use of waiting lists, elections, and subscriptions for entry. Like the pre-existing clubs, the Pilgrims also provided an elite 'homosocial' space in which status was simultaneously symbolised, granted, and safeguarded by membership. This was the closed domain of the Victorian and Edwardian 'gentleman', guaranteeing what one writer has termed a 'commonality of interest' among its members.[104] Even though the Pilgrims did not have rooms and so perhaps did not fulfil quite the same social function as some of the other associations, London's 'clubland' was nevertheless the environment from which the Pilgrims originated and with which they were irrevocably linked. For example, Harry Brittain – who was a also member of the Tory Carlton Club – later contextualised the founding of the Pilgrims with reference to London's associational culture, writing in 1962 that it was always a 'simple matter to find a few genial companions with whom to discuss the events of the day' in one of the city's clubs, while J. Arthur Barratt recalled that he had based the Pilgrims' rules 'on those of some of the best Clubs in town'.[105] Similarly, correspondence between members of the London Pilgrims' membership sub-committee show that the Society was sure to note which other club memberships were held by those men applying to join. Lists of candidates for the Pilgrims from 1906 include men who were members of associations like the National Liberal Club, the Athenaeum, the Constitutional, and the St. James's.[106] For example, Donald Macmaster, a Scots-Canadian lawyer who arrived in London in 1905, and who later became a Member of Parliament, joined the Pilgrims having already been a member of the Constitutional Club and the 1900 Club.[107] Macmaster is a good example of the business and political elite that constituted the Pilgrims' membership. He also demonstrates that some individuals in the Pilgrims were 'joiners'; in other words, they were individuals who habitually joined a variety of clubs and societies without taking on particularly active roles.

Like the London branch, the New York Pilgrims was located firmly in its elite social setting. Most of the American Pilgrims were also 'joiners' of a variety of other famous New York clubs such as the Knickerbocker, the Metropolitan, and the Union. For example, Edward J. Berwind, chairman of a coal mining company, was a member of each.[108] Exclusive clubs such as these were modelled on the London clubs. They were a product of New York's development in the eighteenth and nineteenth centuries and a feature of its ever-increasing prosperity in the twentieth. This had seen the rise of an urban aristocracy which flaunted its prodigious wealth at ostentatious balls and whose social status was symbolised and reinforced by membership of elite associations. Access into this upper class was not simply predicated on money – especially if that money was 'new' – and it was equally important to make and sustain the right connections, ideally with the Astors or the Vanderbilts.[109] Entry into elite clubs was, of course, limited, with the Union Club and the Union League Club both admitting a maximum of 1,000 members. The Democratic Party's Manhattan Club – co-founded by the chairman of the New York Pilgrims, William Butler Duncan – was more exclusive still and restricted membership to 600.[110] Duncan, who had been chairman of the Ohio Railroad Company and head of the Butler Exchange Company in Providence, Rhode Island, was one of the original members of a select group of fifty society figures, called the Patriarchs, which was formed in the 1870s by the socialite Ward McAllister.[111] For its part, the Pilgrims originally restricted membership to 500 in each city, though by 1918 this limit had been increased to 1,000 on both sides.[112]

The New York Pilgrims particularly had links to the Lawyers' Club and the Bankers' Club, whose clubrooms they used for their monthly committee meetings.[113] The Lawyers' Club – the membership of which was not restricted to lawyers, and which had rooms in the Equitable Life Assurance Society Building at 120 Broadway – was described in 1896 as the 'handsomest and most luxurious dining club in the world'. Later Pilgrims Chauncey Depew, George T. Wilson, John J. McCook, and William Allen Butler all served on the Lawyers' Club executive committee, while other future Pilgrims R. A. C. Smith, Alton B. Parker, Frederic Coudert, William C. Demorest, and Samuel W. Fairchild were prominent members.[114] The Equitable Building was destroyed by a massive fire in January 1912 – in which George Wilson lost many of his private papers, including his 'Pilgrims memorabilia', which he regarded as a 'sentimental tragedy' – and so the Pilgrims were required to find another regular meeting place. They initially met at some of the other New York clubs, but settled in the Lawyers' Club's new rooms at 115 Broadway when they opened in October 1912.[115] The Pilgrims moved back into 120 Broadway when the new Equitable Building opened in 1915, this time using rooms belonging to the Bankers' Club.[116] This new club, the 'keynote' of which was 'bigness', was not just for bankers and its members were said to 'represent bigness in a business way'. The clubrooms were described by the *New York Times* as the largest in the world in terms of floor space, occupying, as they did, the top three floors of this skyscraper. The view from the club's dining room, meanwhile, provided guests with a 'panorama including the North and East Rivers, the bay and the greater city, without leaving their tables'. George T. Wilson was one of the club's vice-presidents, while his fellow Pilgrim and the chairman of Chase

National Bank, A. Barton Hepburn, was its president.[117] In contrast to the American Pilgrims, the British Pilgrims generally did not use other clubs' rooms for meetings. Instead, they kept an office in one of London's leading hotels. The significant overlap of senior members between the New York Pilgrims and, in particular, the Lawyers' Club, and the resultant ease of access to the latter's rooms, suggests one reason for this difference. The London Pilgrims Society was not, however, entirely without regular accommodation. Though it had been founded following meetings at the Carlton Hotel, the branch later had offices at the famous Savoy Hotel, and then at the Hotel Victoria on Northumberland Avenue.[118] In addition to Claridge's, these were the venues principally used by the Society to host their banquets and functions. Then, during the First World War, the Society occasionally met at 9 Chesterfield Gardens, the luxurious home of Lord Leconfield, which was then being used by the Pilgrims to host the American Officers' Club (a club established by the Society during the war to cater for visiting American military officers, and which is discussed in greater detail later).[119] The executive committee also met in rooms at the House of Commons in July 1919, having already been invited to dine there in June by Harry Brittain, who had by then become the Member of Parliament for the London constituency of Acton. On these occasions, members of the Pilgrims Society were quite literally rubbing shoulders with political elites.[120]

The Pilgrims' activities and attempted expansion

While the Pilgrims excluded people on the basis of class, gender, status, and wealth, the criteria that members should be English or American was altogether more flexible. The Society was not an ethnic organisation in the strictest sense. It is true that some Pilgrims subscribed to an English national identity. Some, including Edward K. Beddall, Frederick Cunliffe-Owen, and Henry Clews, were members of New York's St. George's Society. Harry Brittain, meanwhile, was associated with the Royal Society of St. George.[121] In addition, some American candidates for membership believed that an English lineage strengthened their application. For example, J. C. Curtiss, of the United Publishers Corporation in New York, wrote that he was 'duly qualified to become a member . . . being a descendant of an illustrious family, who emigrated from England in 1630 on the ship "Lyon", and settled at Situate, Mass'.[122] Yet, with members of Scots and Irish descent, like James Bryce, Charles Beresford, and the Clydeside shipbuilder William Beardmore – as well as William Butler Duncan and A. Barton Hepburn, both of whom served as president of the Saint Andrews Society of New York – it is clear that the Pilgrims Society itself usually took 'English' to mean 'British'.[123]

Nevertheless, the founding members of the Society in 1902 were aware of the non-English aspect of their work, for example the Irish dimension to British politics and Anglo-American relations. According to Lindsay Russell, the Pilgrims ensured that 'care was taken to include Irishmen or Members of Parliament who were friendly to Ireland, such as Lord Roberts, Admiral Lord Charles Beresford, Hon. Burke Roche MP, and Sir Thomas Lipton'. Even Harry Brittain was part of this effort, with some in the Society believing that 'even an Irish-American would respond to his ready wit'.[124] Such concerns about the racialist assumptions of the Society's aims were not confined to their implications for Celtic members. As has already been shown, the New York Pilgrims' first president, Henry Potter, believed that the Society focused too narrowly on Anglo-Saxon ideas and that it should instead explicitly include members from across the world. His statement that this would result in the Society serving a 'very benign and useful purpose' demonstrates his belief that the inclusion, not exclusion, of all nationalities was more conducive to international goodwill.[125] In truth, and even though the Scottish entertainer Harry Lauder, in response to a misstatement made by an earlier speaker, reminded the New York Pilgrims in 1918 that 'there is no such thing as an English Navy', such debates about the logic of the overarching Englishness of the Pilgrims' approach to Anglo-American relations rarely seeped into the content of speeches made at Society events.[126]

The Pilgrims Society not only debated how best to frame its activities, but also debated what those activities should be. For example, Harry Brittain telegraphed his American colleagues in 1918 to inform them that the London Pilgrims 'unanimously recommended' the creation of branches not only in American cities like Boston, Chicago, and San Francisco, but also in Montreal and Melbourne. Brittain believed that such branches would serve the 'purpose of supporting the senior foundations in London and New

York', and said that a network of branches through the US and the British Empire was part of the 'original scheme' for the Pilgrims. Indeed, at the New York Pilgrims' first function in February 1903, George Wilson had envisioned the Society 'extending its branches into all English-speaking countries – the United States, Canada, India, and Australia'.[127] The North American 'local committees' were not to become 'branches' in their own right but would have been accountable to the executive committee in New York, who jealously guarded the title of 'The Pilgrims of the United States'.[128] This was well demonstrated in 1909 by the New York Pilgrims' opposition to an unrelated group in California, which called itself the Pilgrims of the Pacific and which had similar designs on Anglo-American friendship. Though the original Pilgrims explained that they were 'most sympathetic with the object', they also made clear to the San Franciscans that the New York club was 'The Pilgrims of the United States, which embraced membership all over the United States', and that they 'would prefer not to have them use the same name'.[129] In the end, the Pilgrims of the Pacific disappeared from history, while no local committees of the Pilgrims of the United States were formed. The American Pilgrims were irrevocably linked to the New York social scene. As Nicholas Murray Butler told George Wilson in January 1919, the 'prestige and dignity of the Pilgrims would be ended if we were to have chapters or branches in different parts of the United States'.[130] As the US's financial centre, and with its heritage of elite social clubs – not to mention the symbolic significance of its role as a major port into the New World – New York provided the organisation with greater prestige and social capital than could most other American cities.

In contrast to the New York Pilgrims' desire to safeguard its position as the only American branch of the Society, Harry Brittain oversaw the Pilgrims' only practical attempt at a branch outside of London or New York. Between 1918 and 1920, efforts were made to establish a Pilgrims committee in Liverpool, 'the function of which would be to welcome and look after any well-known American visitors arriving in this country, or leaving for America'.[131] With the two main transatlantic shipping lines – Cunard and White Star – based in Liverpool, a Pilgrims branch in what was a major point of embarkation to and from the US was a logical development. Moreover, the general manager of Cunard, Andrew D. Mearns, was a Pilgrim, and the company offered members of the Society reduced fares on passage between Britain and America.[132] The idea of a Liverpool branch received the full backing of the executive committee in London, with John Sandeman Allen – a prominent figure in marine insurance and later a Conservative Member of Parliament in Liverpool – taking responsibility for the new venture.[133] Sandeman Allen organised a lunch in January 1919 in Liverpool's Exchange Club to inaugurate the city's new Pilgrims committee. Harry Brittain attended as the guest of honour and was joined at the event by around twenty others, including Liverpool's Lord Mayor, Lt. Col. John Ritchie.[134] Despite the support for the venture from the London Pilgrims, and in spite of his own self-proclaimed wish for organisational expansion, New York's George Wilson expressed his doubts. In a somewhat meandering and exuberant (and probably drunken) letter to Harry Brittain, he acknowledged the creation of the Liverpool branch, but dismissed Brittain's hope that it would act as a 'connecting link' between London and New York: 'Ha ha! "Connecting" nothing! New York–London – a straight route and you and I are the "connecting" – not "missing" – links. Cheers!'[135]

Wilson's flippant remark about the prospects of the Liverpool Pilgrims ultimately proved more foresightful than he probably intended it. In October, Sandeman Allen had told Wilson Taylor that the Liverpool branch was 'a little bit in the air at the moment. Its affiliation, or status, with the "Pilgrims" has not yet been clearly defined. I rather understood that the Liverpool Committee would be represented on the General Committee.'[136] By July 1920, it was decided by the London Pilgrims that they were 'not in favour of extending the operations of the Society beyond its original conception as a dining club in London'. They felt that 'with Mr Allen on the Committee they will be able always to secure the help they need from Liverpool without the embarrassment of a separate branch with its attendant drawbacks'.[137] The final mention of Pilgrims activity in Liverpool was in July 1922, when a 'deputation of the Liverpool Pilgrims' bid farewell to William H. Taft, the former US president, prior to his return to America at the conclusion of a trip made to Britain in his capacity as Chief Justice of the Supreme Court. The Pilgrims had also held a dinner in Taft's honour at the Hotel Victoria in London in June.[138]

Even though the committee had supported the idea when it was first suggested, the impetus for the Liverpool branch had been lost when Harry Brittain resigned as chairman of the British Pilgrims in the summer of 1919 due to his other commitments, including his parliamentary duties, to be replaced by Lord Desborough.[139] This resulted in the dropping of other planned developments by the Society's new leadership, including the building of permanent clubrooms. Following the wartime experience of the American Officers' Club – which had successfully accommodated American military officers in temporary clubrooms in Lord Leconfield's Mayfair townhouse – a circular in the name of Harry Brittain, dated June 1918, was sent to the membership arguing that the time was right to

> create in the heart of London a first-rate Anglo-American centre, with the best Club-house available, a complete Anglo-American Library, Information Bureau, Rooms for Meetings, etc., together with any other items which would be of interest and utility to our visitors from overseas, as well as to resident Pilgrims.[140]

George Wilson had held a similar ambition for the US branch. He envisioned a clubhouse in New York 'where distinguished and the right sort of Britons could stop in preference to an hotel – and which would be the headquarters and clearing house of Anglo-American friendship and co-operation'. Wilson understood, however, that these plans were ambitious and that the New York branch was unsure about extending the Society's activities much further. He admitted that he did 'not see the realization of this vision at once but I think the future holds it'.[141]

In addition to the Liverpool branch, Harry Brittain and the British Pilgrims went further in exploring new options for the Society than did George Wilson and the US Pilgrims. Neither branch would, however, ultimately expand its role to any great degree. In July 1919, immediately before Brittain resigned, the executive committee of the London branch decided that any expansion of the Society's scope was 'much too ambitious' and that the Pilgrims was a 'dining club and having been very successful in the past' there should be 'no alteration in its policy'. Brittain agreed that any subsequent developments were the responsibility of his successor.[142] This discussion had taken place in response to a memorandum sent by the Society's secretary (and so not an official member), Mrs Welsh-Lee, outlining ideas for new Pilgrims activities, but which Brittain said he had not seen before it was issued. It is interesting that the Society's secretary should take it upon herself to do this, and unusual (and unlikely) that Brittain was not aware of her doing so.[143] Welsh-Lee's July 1919 memorandum was indeed very ambitious and outlined plans for a significant expansion in the role of the Society. It was motivated by her belief that the Pilgrims had to radically change its approach to its work lest 'someone or other of the various Anglo-American societies will cut the ground from under the Pilgrims' feet, and the only alternative will be union with that body or an emasculated existence'.[144] For example, she wanted the Pilgrims to establish a 'Propaganda Sub-Committee' and to ensure that as many newspaper editors and university chancellors as possible would become members of the Society. This demonstrated her desire for the Pilgrims to take more direct steps in influencing public opinion than it had done before. It also demonstrates the cross-over between notions of propaganda and public diplomacy. Welsh-Lee was suggesting that the Society produce and distribute written material in support of its aim of Anglo-American friendship. Though she used the term 'propaganda' – and did so immediately after the First World War, when the term was beginning to take on a pejorative meaning – Welsh-Lee was suggesting the use of 'advocacy' public diplomacy. Like Brittain, she also suggested the creation of a 'British-American Library' – an example both of advocacy diplomacy and cultural diplomacy – and the establishment of permanent clubrooms. According to Welsh-Lee, clubrooms would provide 'an admirable headquarters both in a business and a social sense'. Demonstrating her understanding that an elite club could indeed sustain important networks and foster shared interests, Welsh-Lee said that a permanent clubroom – something the more traditional London clubs tended to have, and something that the newly founded American Club had in Piccadilly – would 'give prominence to the Pilgrims' name, increase its influence', and 'would enable the society to have more frequent gatherings'.[145]

Despite rightly acknowledging that the New York branch was 'still hesitating to extend its activities' across the US, and despite the concurrent difficulties with the Liverpool branch, Welsh-Lee outlined another plan for establishing Pilgrims branches elsewhere in the world. In addition to a branch in Canada – which would help reconcile the 'differences of outlook and feeling between the Mother Country and the younger British Nations'– Welsh-Lee wanted branches in 'Paris, Rome or Milan, Geneva, Buenos Ayres, anywhere, in fact, where there are large British and American colonies'. She hoped that such branches would gather together 'Britishers and Americans in residence or in business in foreign countries who would at the same time keep British and American Pilgrims advised as to the state of feeling in these countries, and endeavour to represent British and American ideas and spread knowledge on all sorts of subjects.' She also wanted to create sub-committees in Scotland and Wales, and was particularly keen on having a Pilgrims presence in Ireland. She felt that an Irish sub-committee would assist in the gathering of 'information on the Irish question other than that obtainable in England' and enable the sending 'to America literature and possibly speakers in co-operation with headquarters to make plainer the much misunderstood Irish question in that country – a question which is endangering friendly relations between the United States and Great Britain'.[146] Welsh-Lee was referring to what was the beginning of the Irish war of independence, the opening shots of which were fired in 1919. In January, the new Sinn Féin Members of Parliament had declined to sit at Westminster in favour of meeting in Dublin, and had declared Irish independence. During the following two years of conflict, which were marked by the brutality of the infamous 'Black and Tans', support amongst many in America for Irish independence was a source of Anglo-American ill-feeling. The arrival in the US in June of Éamon de Valera, the president of the new Irish republic, on a fundraising trip – during which he stayed in New York's Waldorf-Astoria hotel, somewhere the Pilgrims frequently used for their functions – provided the immediate context for Welsh-Lee's July memorandum.[147] Welsh-Lee would have wanted to influence the opinions towards Ireland held by some American Pilgrims: Chauncey Depew had expressed his support for Irish home rule in the 1880s, while George Harvey, the US ambassador to Britain from 1921 until 1923, and a Pilgrims member of the Society since at least 1909, was also sympathetic to the Irish cause.[148]

Welsh-Lee's plans represented a significant enlargement of the scope of the Society: in short, she envisaged 'the Pilgrims becoming an international force'.[149] Arguably the Society already was an 'international force', and the following chapters of this book will discuss some of the ways in which this was the case. Yet, the Society's influence was of a much more discreet, and less explicit, type than that advocated by Welsh-Lee. As a result, it was decided at the annual general meeting in October 1919 that 'the aim of the Pilgrims in the future will be to maintain the policy that has answered so well in the past', namely that the Society was 'the premier Anglo-American dining Club, and our propaganda is to work unostentatiously and [in] intimate channels by bringing Eminent American citizens into friendly fellowship with their British Brethren'.[150] This re-emphasises the point that it is correct to regard the Society's activities in terms of public diplomacy. As such, this statement shows that the Society self-consciously acted as an elite transatlantic network in an effort to promote Anglo-American friendship by means of 'advocacy' and 'exchange' public diplomacy. It did this even while stopping short of Welsh-Lee's proposals. The Society considered itself, meanwhile, as having 'fathered' the other British–American associations, and felt that the 'overlapping work already so well done by kindred organizations like the English-Speaking Union' meant that there was no need for the Pilgrims to 'enter upon hazardous schemes of development, involving perhaps heavy financial liability'.[151]

Diplomatic connections

As had happened in relation to the possibility of branches in other British and American cities, the Pilgrims Society ultimately decided against the expansion of its role in its existing London location. The Society remained an exclusive dining club whose importance and prestige was at least partly linked to its proximity to the seat of British imperial government and to its presence in America's principal metropolis. It was its exclusivity and its location that contributed to the Society's notably rapid success. From early on in its existence, it was able to attract some of Britain and America's biggest names, both as members and as guests. Indeed, in 1903 the London branch entertained Joseph Choate, the US ambassador to Britain, at a banquet at the Hyde Park Hotel, while the US Pilgrims held a dinner for the British ambassador, Sir Michael Herbert, in New York that same year. Then in 1905, the Pilgrims hosted Whitelaw Reid, Choate's replacement, upon his arrival in Britain.[152] This was the beginning of the practice of newly appointed British–American ambassadors making their first public appearances in the respective countries at a Pilgrims dinner in either London or New York. This continued when James Bryce arrived in the US as British ambassador in 1907, when George Wilson admitted to his colleagues that he was 'anxious that this Dinner should be his first public function' as 'there seems to be some rumour that the Union League Club, the Lotos Club or the St. George's Club are expecting the first privilege'.[153] The Pilgrims felt that it was 'quite natural and appropriate' that Bryce should visit them first, with Louis Hay – an American member of the British Pilgrims who had moved to London in 1897 as part of his work as a lumber merchant, and who returned to New York in 1907 to join the stock exchange and become secretary of the Pilgrims there – urging Isaac N. Ford – a Pilgrim and the London correspondent for the *New-York Tribune* – to 'present the matter to Mr Bryce so that he would allow the New York Pilgrims to have the first Dinner'.[154] By the 1920s, a number of US ambassadors to Britain benefited from this tradition by using their maiden speeches to make important official policy announcements. As will be discussed later, the heritage attached to an ambassador's first Pilgrims speech gave their statements added impact. That ambassadors throughout the period agreed to make their first speeches at Pilgrims events demonstrates that embassies regarded the Society as a legitimate organisation, whose connections and status were of use to newly arrived diplomats.

The Pilgrims Society's ability to offer hospitality to visiting statesmen was assisted by its connections with officialdom. George Wilson, for example, received a letter from the British Embassy in Washington in 1919 informing him of the arrival into the US of some prominent British figures, including the new Naval Attaché in Washington, Captain Tottenham, whom Wilson wanted to welcome upon his arrival in New York on board the *Olympic*.[155] The Society also had links with the British Government Hospitality Fund, a body formed in 1908, and answerable to Parliament, 'in order to provide the Government with the necessary means for offering hospitality to distinguished visitors from abroad'.[156] The relationship between the Fund and the Pilgrims was demonstrated in 1921, when the Fund contacted John Wilson Taylor ahead of a Pilgrims event on behalf of the Japanese Embassy confirming the attendance of the Japanese ambassador and seeking confirmation of the arrangements for the function. Then, the following year, the secretary of the Fund, E. E. Beare, was amongst the guests at a Pilgrims banquet in London.[157]

There were, meanwhile, debates within the Pilgrims Society about how best to relate to the embassies. British ambassadors in the US and US ambassadors in Britain were honorary members of the Society, but there was some discussion about how to involve other ambassadorial and consular staff.[158] For example, ahead of a Pilgrims event in London in 1903 there was discussion amongst some in the Society over whether representatives from the US Embassy – in addition to Ambassador Choate – should receive invitations. Demonstrating the desired extent of the Pilgrims' unofficial networking, Louis Hay felt that other staff at the Embassy – including Choate's secretary Henry White – did not need specific invitations. Instead, he hoped that 'all of them will become Members' on their own account and that 'this question will not have to be agitated every time'.[159] Even so, this represented something of a laissez-faire approach to the recruitment of members from amongst Embassy staff. Indicating that this approach had not proven successful, Welsh-Lee's July 1919 memorandum suggested that, in the future, 'certain Embassy officials should always be made Honorary Members of the Pilgrims during their tenure of office'. This practice was eventually adopted by the London Pilgrims in 1925. Further showing that links between the Society and the embassies were not as solid as they might have been, the memorandum emphasised that the 'importance of obtaining the active and brotherly support of the American Embassy in London, and of the British Embassy in Washington is undeniable, and an effort should be made to establish this on a firm basis of mutual understanding and sympathy'.[160] By contrast, the New York branch confirmed in the late 1920s that it wished to 'continue the policy of the Society heretofore in inviting members of the British Embassy as guests of the Society rather than making them Honorary Members'.[161] In all of these cases, however, the Society was acting to ensure a meaningful connection with the embassies. Hay hoped in 1903 that ambassadorial staff would become fully-fledged and active members, while the New York branch in 1927 evidently felt that a personal invitation was a more significant gesture than Welsh-Lee's idea of honorary membership. In addition to J. Arthur Barratt, examples of diplomatic staff with links to the Society included Sir Percy Sanderson, the British Consul-General in New York between 1894 and 1907, who was an active member during his time in the US. Subsequent Consul-Generals also had close relationships with the New York branch, for example when Sir Courtney Walter Bennett and Richard L. Nosworthy, the Vice-Consul, attended a meeting of the executive committee in 1914 as 'invited guests'.[162] Henry White eventually joined the London Pilgrims, though not until 1922, while Philip B. Kennedy and James K. Lynch of the US Embassy in London were made members in 1918.[163] Meanwhile, the British Consul-General in Boston, Gloster Armstrong, saw the benefits of being associated with the Pilgrims Society and wrote in 1919 of his desire to see a branch established in the Massachusetts city. Though this was never achieved, this demonstrates that the Society was considered by some in official-dom as a useful aid to Anglo-American friendship.[164] Interactions such as these between the Pilgrims and diplomatic staff ensured that the Society was regarded as an important and friendly organ-isation, and meant that it was easier to secure the attendance of ambassadors and other diplomats at functions.

Conclusion

Established in 1902, the Pilgrims built upon existing Anglo-American sentiment and transatlantic connections. The Society emerged around the same time as a number of other associations, like the Anglo-American League, which were influenced by the Anglo-Saxon sentiment that was informing the developing Anglo-American rapprochement. There was, however, a realist aspect to the Pilgrims Society's desire for Anglo-American friendship, par-ticularly in light of the US's growing strength and Britain's isola-tion in Europe. In addition, rapprochement was also about the need for international peace and stability in order to ensure the advent of a 'trading and commercial century'.[165]

The Pilgrims Society was rooted in the elite associational cul-ture of London and New York. Not only was there a crossover in membership between the Pilgrims and other elite clubs, but the Society also took steps to safeguard its exclusivity by not establish-ing branches in other towns and cities and by discouraging the use of its name by an unrelated group in San Francisco. Its exclusivity – and its loci in the imperial centre of Britain and the financial and journalistic centre of the US – meant that this network remained grounded in shared elite experience. This partly explains why it was so successful so quickly, as shown by its ability to rapidly establish itself as the forum at which British–American ambassa-dors made their first public appearances in each other's countries. Maintaining a consistently high level of prestige meant that the

Pilgrims was unique amongst the various British–American associations formed in this period.

The precise aims and activities of the Society were, meanwhile, open to discussion during the first twenty years of the organisation's existence. These centred on efforts to make the Pilgrims into more than simply a dining club and demonstrate why it is correct to consider the aims and activities of the Society in terms of public diplomacy. It is true that efforts to extend the Society's activities, like Welsh-Lee's ambitious plans in 1919, met with opposition from members who felt that the Pilgrims enjoyed a unique position as the most exclusive and prestigious of all the existing British–American associations. It is also true that the Pilgrims Society never officially extended its activities beyond hosting banquets and functions for visiting statesmen and other prominent figures. Yet the rejection of Welsh-Lee's plans in 1919 does not tell the full story. As the rest of this book will show, the Pilgrims – even if it was not recognised officially in the Society's constitution – carried out activities that did indeed go beyond its remit as a dining club. In fact, some of these activities took place before Welsh-Lee wrote her memorandum, as Chapter 4's examination of the Society during the First World War will show. Not that the Pilgrims would have been without influence had it restricted itself to the role of a banqueting club. With reference to a banquet held by the Society in 1906 in an attempt to contribute to the Anglo-American diplomatic rapprochement, and which provides a practical example of the Society's public diplomacy, the next chapter demonstrates some of the reasons why.

Notes

1. *New York Times*, 24 March 1907.
2. *New York Times*, 5 October 1909.
3. *Boston Daily Globe*, 1 April 1906; Harry Brittain wrote that the name of the Society was chosen 'to express the idea of members of the English-speaking world peregrinating from one country to another'. See Brittain, *Pilgrim Partners* (London, 1942), p. 12; there are contradictory statements about who chose the name of the society. Lindsay Russell said that the name was chosen by the Irish MP James Boothby Burke Roche, while Elihu Church – a later secretary of the New York Pilgrims – suggested that it had been

chosen by Lord Frederick Roberts, the British Pilgrims' first president. See Lindsay Russell to J. Arthur Barratt, 25 January 1939, and a 'Brief History of the Meeting Between Two Englishmen and Two Americans Which Brought About the Formation of The Pilgrims', undated, both documents LMA4632/C/05/001. Given that Lindsay Russell was the principal founder, his account is most likely correct; Minutes, 19 July 1922, Pilgrims Mss, LMA/4632/A/01/001; *The Times*, 18 October 1921; see Joseph A. Conforti, *Imagining New England: Explorations of Regional Identity from the Pilgrims to the Mid-Twentieth Century* (Chapel Hill, 2000), p. 180.

4. 'Speeches at the Dinner to celebrate the Twenty-Fifth Anniversary of the Founding of the Pilgrims of the United States', 9 February 1928, Pilgrims Mss, NYC.

5. *The Times*, 28 May 1903.

6. Report of the Committee on Organization, 11 July 1902, quoted in Baker, *Pilgrims of the US*, p. 5.

7. *Washington Post*, 9 August 1902; Brittain, *Pilgrim Partners*, pp. 15–16; Baker, *Pilgrims of Britain*, p. 14.

8. Baker, *Pilgrims of the US*, pp. 5–6; Minute Book 1, 9 February 1903, Pilgrims Mss, NYC; the London branch is properly referred to as the Pilgrims of Great Britain, while the New York branch is the Pilgrims of the United States.

9. *New York Times*, 5 February 1903.

10. H. C. Allen, *Great Britain and the United States: A History of Anglo-American Relations (1783–1952)* (London, 1954), pp. 586–9; *New York Times*, 14 May 1899; Thomas McCormick, 'Insular Imperialism and the Open Door: The China Market and the Spanish-American War', *Pacific Historical Review*, Vol. 32, No. 2 (May 1963), pp. 155–69.

11. This chimes with Tuffnell's argument that the 'social webs that connected Americans and Britons in London', including through associations like the Atlantic Union, the American Club, and the Anglo-American League, facilitated inter-imperial 'privileged access to networks of expertise and finance'. Tuffnell, 'Anglo-American Inter-Imperialism', pp. 188–90.

12. Kramer, 'Empires, Exceptions and Anglo-Saxons', p. 1334; Baker, *Pilgrims of Britain*, pp. 13–14; Brittain, *Pilgrim Partners*, p. 12.

13. Lindsay Russell to J. Arthur Barratt, 25 January 1939, Pilgrims Mss, LMA/4632/C/05/001; Baker, *Pilgrims of Britain*, p. 178; Baker, *Pilgrims of the US*, p. 152.

14. *Boston Daily Globe*, 20 May 1907; for obituaries of Russell, see *New York Times* and *Washington Post*, 9 October 1949; David S. Patterson, 'Japanese–American Relations: The 1906 California Crisis, the Gentlemen's Agreement, and the World Cruise', in Serge

Ricard (ed.), *A Companion to Theodore Roosevelt* (Chichester, 2011), pp. 391–416.

15. The Institute of International Affairs grew out of British–American contact at the Paris Peace Conference, and had its British counterpart in the Royal Institute of International Affairs, an organisation also known as Chatham House and which also still exists today. See Chatham House, The Royal Institute of International Affairs, <http://www.chathamhouse.org/about> (last accessed 24 August 2014); *New York Times*, 31 October 1920; Roberts, 'Underpinning the Anglo-American Alliance', pp. 25–43; Roberts, 'The Transatlantic American Foreign Policy Elite', pp. 163–83; Peter Grose, *Continuing the Inquiry: The Council on Foreign Relations from 1921 to 1996* (New York, 1996), pp. 7–8.

16. Baker, *Pilgrims of Britain*, p. 178 and p. 181; Baker, *Pilgrims of the US*, p. 152; Brian Robson, 'Frederick Sleigh Roberts, first Earl Roberts (1832–1914)', *Oxford Dictionary of National Biography* (Oxford University Press, 2004), <http://www.oxforddnb.com/view/article/35768> (last accessed 18 November 2013); *Pall Mall Gazette*, 26 September 1898.

17. Russell to Barratt, 25 January 1939, Pilgrims Mss, NYC; Wheeler also commanded the brigade under which Theodore Roosevelt's 'Rough Riders' fought during the Spanish-American War; Edward G. Longacre, *A Soldier to the Last: Maj. Gen. Joseph Wheeler in Blue and Gray* (Washington DC, 2007), pp. xii–xiii; John P. Dyer, *From Shiloh to San Juan: The Life of 'Fightin' Joe' Wheeler* (Baton Rouge, 1961), p. 259.

18. Baker, *Pilgrims of Britain*, p. 178.

19. Ibid. p. 178.

20. Elizabeth R to Lord Astor of Hever, 25 January 1972, and Robert Worcester to Sir Ronald Grierson, 12 October 1995, Pilgrims Mss, LMA/4632/A/05/001; Baker, *Pilgrims of the US*, p. 143; Baker, *Pilgrims of Britain*, p. 14.

21. For Wilson's obituary, see *New York Times*, 30 September 1933.

22. J. Arthur Barratt to Lindsay Russell, 26 February 1939, Pilgrims Mss, NYC; for details about Barratt, see *Chicago Daily Tribune*, 19 October 1913, and Brittain, *Pilgrim Partners*, p. 12.

23. *New York Times*, 14 July 1918.

24. Whitelaw Reid to Russell, 27 January 1903, Pilgrims Mss, NYC.

25. Sir Evelyn Wrench to Nicholas Murray Butler, 5 February 1947, and Butler to Wrench, 7 March 1947, Nicholas Murray Butler Papers, Columbia University Butler Library [CUBL], Box 469; Minute Book 1, 28 December 1909, Pilgrims Mss, NYC; Butler is not on the original list of members. See Baker, *Pilgrims of the US*, p. 152; Baker, *Pilgrims of Britain*, p. 181. He did, however, attend some Pilgrims functions,

for example a dinner at Delmonico's in 1905. See *Washington Post*, 10 June 1905.

26. William Goode to Barratt, 25 July 1938, Pilgrims Mss, LMA/4632/C/05/001.

27. Ibid.

28. Russell to Barratt, 25 January 1939, Pilgrims Mss, NYC.

29. Ibid.

30. 'Notes on the Founding of the Pilgrims Society (Addenda for Hon. J. Arthur Barratt, London and New York), by Lindsay Russell', 7 May 1939, Pilgrims Mss, LMA/4632/C/05/001.

31. Barratt to Brittain, 30 July 1938, Pilgrims Mss, LMA/4632/C/05/001.

32. Brittain to Barratt, 31 August 1938, Pilgrims Mss, LMA/4632/C/05/001.

33. Baker, *Pilgrims of Britain*, p. 15 and p. 105; Baker, 'Brittain, Sir Henry Ernest [Harry] (1873–1974)', *Oxford Dictionary of National Biography* (Oxford University Press, 2004), <http://www.oxforddnb.com/view/article/30852> (last accessed 20 February 2012); Alida Harvie, *Those Glittering Years* (London, 1980), pp. 13–14.

34. Barratt to John Wilson Taylor, 31 July 1938, Pilgrims Mss, NYC.

35. Wilson Taylor to Barratt, 28 July 1938, Pilgrims Mss, NYC.

36. Wilson Taylor to Barratt, 3 August 1938, Pilgrims Mss, NYC.

37. Wrench to Butler, 7 March 1947, Butler Papers, CUBL, Box 469.

38. Brittain to Barratt, 31 August 1938, Pilgrims Mss, LMA/4632/C/05/001.

39. Wilson to Brittain, 25 June 1913, Pilgrims Mss, LMA LMA/4632/A/05/002/01; Russell is not on the 1909 list of members. See 'The Pilgrims List of Members and Bye-Laws', 1909, Brittain Papers, BLPES, Box 5.

40. *New York Times*, 14 July 1918.

41. *Atlanta Constitution*, 14 January 1917; *New York Times*, 25 April 1915; this perception was never really successfully challenged. Brittain's obituary in the *Washington Post* described him as 'the founder', while *The Times* said that he was the 'co-founder'. See *Washington Post*, 12 July 1974, and *The Times*, 10 July 1974.

42. Lindsay Russell's letter to the editor, *New York Times*, 14 July 1918.

43. Brittain, *Pilgrim Partners*, p. 22; for information on Neef, see *New York Times*, 16 May 1905; for information on Ford, see *The Times*, 9 August 1912.

44. 'The Pilgrims List of Members and Bye-Laws', 1909, Brittain Papers, BLPES, Box 5; Minutes, 7 May 1917, Pilgrims Mss, LMA/4632/A/01/001.

45. Plan of tables for dinner for Arthur Balfour, 20 February 1922, Pilgrims Mss, LMA/4632/D/01/027.

46. *New York Times*, 5 February 1903.

47. Clipping from a 1912 (no further date information) edition of the *Pall Mall Gazette*, Brittain Papers, BLPES, Box 3.

48. 'Notes on the Founding of the Pilgrims Society (Addenda for Hon. J. Arthur Barratt, London and New York), by Lindsay Russell', 7 May 1939, Pilgrims Mss, LMA/4632/C/05/001.

49. Eric Hobsbawm, *The Age of Empire, 1875–1914* (London, 1987), pp. 318–20; Burk, *Old World, New World*, pp. 428–32.

50. Alan P. Dobson, *Anglo-American Relations in the Twentieth Century: Of Friendship, Conflict and the Rise and Decline of Superpowers* (London, 1995), pp. 26–7; the point is not that the Pilgrims Society was overwhelmingly influenced by a wish for Anglo-American friendship in opposition to Germany, only that this wider context did inform the views of some of its members, including Lord Roberts.

51. Burk, *Old World, New World*, pp. 429–30.

52. Lord Roberts to Brittain, 4 May 1913, Brittain Papers, BLPES, Correspondence Box R; Bernard Semmel, *Imperialism and Social Reform: English Social-Imperial Thought, 1895–1914* (London, 1960), pp. 248–51; R. T. Stearn, 'National Service League (*act.* 1902–1914)', *Oxford Dictionary of National Biography* (Oxford University Press, 2004), <http://www.oxforddnb.com/view/theme/95555> (last accessed 1 May 2012).

53. 'The Pilgrims List of Members and Bye-Laws', 1909, Brittain Papers, BLPES, Box 5.

54. Baker, *Pilgrims of the US*, pp. 28–9 and p. 143; Baker, *Pilgrims of Britain*, p. 44; Carter and Vance were also allegedly displeased that the Pilgrims had no black or Jewish members, though, like women, the Society had no explicit rule preventing their membership. The exclusion of women, however, was an unwritten assumption which the British Pilgrims discussed in 1955 and agreed to maintain.

55. Clark, *British Clubs and Societies*, pp. 202–4; even so, it is worth noting that the Pilgrims' eventual decision to admit women occurred significantly later than the period in which Clark operates. As such, it took a long time for the Society to admit women, which goes some way to demonstrating its conservatism.

56. Charles Loch Mowat, *Britain Between the Wars, 1918–1940* (London, 1955), p. 6 and p. 23; in the US, the Nineteenth Amendment to the Constitution, which granted female suffrage, was ratified in time for the 1920 presidential election. See David Morgan, 'Woman Suffrage in Britain and America in the Early Twentieth Century', in H. C. Allen and R. Thompson (eds), *Contrast and Connection: Bicentennial Essays in Anglo-American History* (London, 1976), pp. 272–95.

57. 'Suggestions for the immediate re-organisation and for the future of the Pilgrims' Society', July 1919, Pilgrims Mss, LMA/4632/A/05/004; Welsh-Lee also suggested that a man could become the Pilgrims' business secretary. Amidst the process of demobilisation following the end of the war, Welsh-Lee's ideal candidate was a 'demobilised officer between the ages of thirty and forty. He should be well educated, well read, travelled, he should be progressive in his ideas and have ideas.'

58. In December 1895, shortly after Grover Cleveland's message to the US Congress regarding the Venezuelan border crisis, Conan Doyle had written a letter to the London *Times* in which he said he wanted to see an 'Anglo-American Society started in London, with branches all over the Empire, for the purpose of promoting good feeling, smoothing over friction, laying literature before the public which will show them how strong are the arguments in favour of an Anglo-American alliance'. See *The Times*, 7 January 1896 (written 30 December 1895); 'Venezuelan Boundary Controversy', 17 December 1895, Congressional Record – Senate, 54th Congress, 1st Session, Vol. 28, Part 1, p. 191; in addition to joining the Pilgrims Society, Conan Doyle was a member both of the Anglo-American League and the Atlantic Union. See list of names of the general committee of the Anglo-American League, undated, Grey Papers, Durham University Special Collections [DU], File 176/10; 'Atlantic Union: objects, methods, membership, entrance fee and subscription', undated, Pilgrims Mss, LMA/4632/C/05/001; his desire for Anglo-American friendship was also sometimes manifest in his fiction writing, for example in the Sherlock Holmes story 'The Adventure of the Noble Bachelor', when Holmes admits that he 'was one of those who believe that the folly of a monarch and the blundering of a Minister in forgone years will not prevent our children from being someday citizens of the same world-wide country under a flag which shall be a quartering of the Union Jack with the Stars and Stripes'. Published in 1892, the story involves a marriage between an American woman and a British lord. This speaks to the trend of elite transatlantic marriages in this period, while the Holmes quote is demonstrative of the desires for some sort of Anglo-Saxon union that were held by people like William Stead and Cecil Rhodes. See Arthur Conan Doyle, 'The Adventure of the Noble Bachelor', in *The Adventures of Sherlock Holmes* (London, 2007), p. 295; Doyle, *The Adventures of Sherlock Homes* (New York, 1902), copyrighted 1892; Anderson, *Race and Rapprochement*, pp. 49–50; another of his books, *The White Heather*, dealt with similar themes. See Bell, 'The Project for a New Anglo Century', p. 43; *The Sun* (New York), 29 May 1914; Russell Miller, *The*

Adventures of Arthur Conan Doyle (London, 2008), p. 314; Dana Cooper, *Informal Ambassadors: American Women, Transatlantic Marriages, and Anglo-American Relations, 1865–1945* (Ashland, OH, 2014); Maureen E. Montgomery, *'Gilded Prostitution': Status, Money, and Transatlantic Marriages, 1870–1914* (London, 1989).

59. Correspondence between Wilson Taylor and an unnamed individual, 2 November 1921, Pilgrims Mss, LMA4632/D/01/026.
60. 'To be a Pilgrim', by Ada Doyle, undated, Pilgrims Mss, NYC.
61. Baker, *Pilgrims of the US*, p. 15.
62. Clark, *British Clubs and Societies*, p. 203.
63. 'The Pilgrims List of Members and Bye-Laws', 1909, Brittain Papers, BLPES, Box 5; Baker, *Pilgrims of Britain*, p. 16 and p. 44; *The Times*, 25 May 1928.
64. *The Times*, 28 July 1898; 'Atlantic Union: objects, methods, membership, entrance fee and subscription', undated, Pilgrims Mss, LMA/4632/C/05/001; *The English Race*, September 1913; *The English Race*, February 1908; 'The Pilgrims List of Members and Bye-Laws', 1909, Brittain Papers, BLPES, Box 5; *The English Race*, September 1923, p. 33; *The English Race*, August 1910.
65. Investments, undated, Pilgrims Mss, LMA/4632/A/01/001.
66. Minute Book 1, 6 April 1906, Pilgrims Mss, NYC.
67. Auditors' Reports, 1906–1916, Pilgrims Mss, LMA/4632/B/01/001/01–14.
68. Stephen W. Gambrill to the Bishop of Perth, 16 March 1906, and the Bishop of Perth to Gambrill, 23 April 1906, Pilgrims Mss, LMA/4632/C/05/002/02.
69. Peter Boyce, 'Riley, Charles Owen Leaver (1854–1929)', *Australian Dictionary of Biography* (National Centre of Biography, Australian National University, 1988), <http://adb.anu.edu.au/biography/riley-charles-owen-leaver-8213/text14371> (last accessed 10 June 2014); *The Western Australian*, 26 May 1913.
70. *Pall Mall Gazette*, June 1912; Brittain, *Pilgrim Partners*, p. 75; Baker, *Pilgrims of Britain*, p. 17.
71. Wilson to Brittain, 18 April (no year), Pilgrims Mss, LMA/4632/A/05/002/01. The emphasis on the word 'ask' is Wilson's own.
72. 'The Pilgrims List of Members and Bye-Laws', 1909, Brittain Papers, BLPES, Box 5.
73. Louis C. Hay to H. D. Hutchinson, 18 June 1906, Pilgrims Mss, LMA/4632/C/05/002/02.
74. Minute Book 2, 7 January 1914, Pilgrims Mss, NYC; Minutes, 28 February 1930, Pilgrims Mss, LMA/4632/A/01/001.
75. Minute Book 1, 9 February 1903, Pilgrims Mss, NYC; Russell to Richard Watson Gilder, 7 January 1903, Richard Watson Gilder Papers, New York Public Library [NYPL], Box 13.

76. Leaflet on behalf of Charles S. Fairchild, 29 November 1893, Gilder Papers, NYPL, Box 13.
77. Gilder to Henry C. Potter, 8 January 1903, Gilder Papers, NYPL, Box 21.
78. *Pall Mall Gazette*, 26 September 1898; there were, however, a variety of other British–American societies with liberal roots formed in the second half of the nineteenth century. Thomas Hughes attempted to start an 'Anglo-American Committee' in the late 1860s, while an 'Anglo-American Association' was formed in 1871 in London. An 'Anglo-American Union', meanwhile, was formed in 1896 to campaign for arbitration of the Venezuelan dispute and was largely made up of Liberals. See Leslie Butler, *Critical Americans: Victorian Intellectuals and Transatlantic Liberal Reform* (Chapel Hill, 2007), p. 94, and T. Boyle, 'The Venezuela Crisis and the Liberal Opposition, 1895–1896', *Journal of Modern History*, Vol. 50, No. 3 (1979), p. 1187 and p. 1204. See also *The Times*, 4 February 1871.
79. 'The Anachronism of War', *Century*, March 1896, p. 790; Butler, *Critical Americans*, p. 242.
80. Gilder to Potter, 8 January 1903, Gilder Papers, NYPL, Box 21.
81. Potter to Gilder, 12 January 1903, Gilder Papers, NYPL, Box 13.
82. Gilder to Potter, 10 June 1905, Gilder Papers, NYPL, Box 21.
83. Barratt to Russell, 26 February 1939, Pilgrims Mss, NYC. Barratt recalled 'Those Wilson dinners' with some fondness.
84. Gilder to William Butler Duncan, 12 July 1905, Gilder Papers, NYPL, Box 21.
85. Gilder to Potter, 10 June 1905, Gilder Papers, NYPL, Box 21.
86. *New York Times*, 27 July 1959.
87. Naomi W. Cohen, *Jacob H. Schiff: A Study in American Jewish Leadership* (Hanover, 1999), pp. 25–8.
88. *Washington Post*, 15 November 1905.
89. *Chicago Daily Tribune*, 30 June 1905; *Boston Daily Globe*, 7 December 1905; Ron Chernow, *The House of Morgan: An American Banking Dynasty and the Rise of Modern Finance* (New York, 1990), p. 110.
90. Potter to Gilder, 1 July 1905, Gilder Papers, NYPL, Box 13. There is no suggestion from Potter that these non-British 'travellers' would have been anything other than elite. He only explicitly mentioned opening up the Society's membership in terms of nationality, not social status. Potter also wrote that James Bryce seemed to be in the process of establishing a new society, which he hoped would be along such lines. It is not clear which society this was.
91. *The Times*, 22 February 1900 and 18 March 1901.

92. 'Atlantic Union: objects, methods, membership, entrance fee and subscription', undated, Pilgrims Mss, LMA/4632/C/05/001.

93. Cull, *American Propaganda and Public Diplomacy*, p. xv.

94. *The Times*, 14 July 1898; Walter Besant, *Autobiography of Sir Walter Besant: With a Prefatory Note by S. Squire Sprigge* (London, 1902), p. 266–73.

95. *The Times*, 14 July 1898; Kramer, 'Empires, Exceptions and Anglo-Saxons', p. 1334.

96. *The Times*, 14 July 1898 and 28 July 1898; the Duke of Sutherland presided over the first meeting and later became the League's treasurer. James Bryce became chairman.

97. *Belfast News-Letter*, 14 July 1898.

98. 'Anglo-American League of Great Britain; The Monroe Doctrine by Sir Frederick Pollock; List of General and Executive Committees of the Anglo-American League', undated pamphlet, Grey Papers, DU, File 176/10; 'The Pilgrims List of Members and Bye-Laws', 1909, Brittain Papers, BLPES, Box 5; Mark DeWolfe Howe (ed.), *Holmes–Pollock Letters: The Correspondence of Mr Justice Holmes and Sir Frederick Pollock, 1874–1932* (Cambridge, MA, 1961); during the Spanish-American War, Holmes wrote that 'England has behaved nobly to us it seems to me and I hope we may draw closer together.' See Oliver Wendell Homes to Lady Pollock, 13 May 1898, in DeWolfe Howe, *Holmes–Pollock Letters*, p. 86.

99. *Pall Mall Gazette*, 26 September 1898.

100. Homberger, *Mrs. Astor's New York*, p. 10; Pessen, 'Philip Hone's Set', pp. 294–6.

101. Taddei, 'London Clubs', p. 4.

102. Clark, *British Clubs and Societies*, p. 158.

103. Taddei, 'London Clubs', pp. 1–26; Milne-Smith, 'Club Talk', p. 89.

104. Milne-Smith, 'Club Talk', pp. 86–106.

105. Biographical notes, undated, Brittain Papers, BLPES, Box 3. Brittain avoided a nine-year waiting list for the Carlton, having been invited to join at the invitation of its chairman, Lord Claude Hamilton, in 1914; 'How We Launched the Pilgrims, by Sir Harry Brittain', 1962, Pilgrims Mss, NYC; Barratt to Wilson Taylor, 27 July 1938, Pilgrims Mss, NYC.

106. Hay to Hutchinson, 18 June and 23 June 1906, Pilgrims Mss, LMA/4632/C/05/002/02.

107. Hay to Hutchinson, 18 June 1906, Pilgrims Mss, LMA/4632/C/05/002/02; for Macmaster's obituary, see *The Times*, 4 March 1922.

108. 'The Pilgrims List of Members and Bye-Laws', 1909, Brittain Papers, BLPES, Box 5; for Berwind's obituary, see *New York Times*, 19 August 1936.

109. Homberger, *Mrs. Astor's New York*, pp. 8–10; Pessen, 'Philip Hone's Set', pp. 294–6; the St. George's Society of New York, for example, was founded in 1770. See Anon., *A History of the St. George's Society of New York from 1770–1913* (New York, 1913), p. 21.

110. Homberger, *Mrs. Astor's New York*, pp. 1–10 and p. 191.

111. Ibid. p. 10, p. 185 and pp. 191–2; J. P. Morgan joined the Patriarchs in the 1880s; for Duncan's obituary, see *New York Times*, 21 June 1912. Duncan was born in Edinburgh and was a president of the Saint Andrew's Society of New York. See Harlan D. Whatley, *Two Hundred Fifty Years: The History of Saint Andrew's Society of the State of New York* (New York, 2008), p. 108.

112. 'The Pilgrims List of Members and Bye-Laws', 1909, Brittain Papers, BLPES, Box 5; Minute Book 2, 27 December 1918, Pilgrims Mss, NYC; Minutes, 22 March 1918, Pilgrims Mss, LMA/4632/A/01/001.

113. Minute Book 1, 5 April 1904, Pilgrims Mss, NYC.

114. *New York Times*, 26 January 1896 and 28 January 1912; for information on McCook, who was a lawyer and a member of the Pilgrims' executive committee, see *New York Times*, 1 September 1911; Alton B. Parker was a judge and had been Democratic presidential nominee in the 1904 election, standing against Theodore Roosevelt; Frederic Coudert was a lawyer, and had also been a member of the Anglo-American League. See *Pall Mall Gazette*, 26 September 1898; Demorest was a property dealer and another Pilgrims treasurer. See *New York Times*, 7 November 1933, and Minute Book 1, 27 January 1908, Pilgrims Mss, NYC; Fairchild founded a manufacturing chemist. See *New York Times*, 14 November 1927.

115. *New York Times*, 10 January 1912 and 25 October 1912; Minute Book 2, 25 October 1912, Pilgrims Mss, NYC; Wilson to Brittain, 30 January 1912, Pilgrims Mss, LMA/4632/A/05/002/01.

116. Minute Book 2, 22 September 1915, Pilgrims Mss, NYC.

117. *New York Times*, 26 February 1915.

118. Circular from Harry Brittain to the Pilgrims Membership, 28 May 1919, Pilgrims Mss, LMA/4632/A/05/002/01; Baker, *Pilgrims of Britain*, p. 79.

119. Minutes, 20 June 1918, Pilgrims Mss, LMA/4632/A/01/001; Baker, *Pilgrims of Britain*, p. 102.

120. Minutes, 29 May and 17 July 1919, Pilgrims Mss, LMA/4632/A/01/001.

121. Anon., *History of the St. George's Society of New York*, pp. 242–3; *The English Race*, February 1908 and August 1910.

122. J. C. Curtiss to Brittain, 11 September 1917, Pilgrims Mss, LMA/4632/C/05/003.
123. Minutes, 19 November 1917, Pilgrims Mss, LMA/4632/A/01/001; Whatley, *Two Hundred Fifty Years*, p. 108 and p. 111.
124. 'Notes on the Founding of the Pilgrims Society (Addenda for Hon. J. Arthur Barratt, London and New York), by Lindsay Russell', 7 May 1939, Pilgrims Mss, LMA/4632/C/05/001; Thomas Lipton was brought up in the Gorbals area of Glasgow to Irish parents.
125. Potter to Gilder, 1 July 1905, Gilder Papers, NYPL, Box 13.
126. 'Addresses delivered at a Luncheon given by the Pilgrims of the United States in honour of the British Army and Navy on "British Day"', 7 December 1917, Pilgrims Mss, NYC.
127. Minute Book 2, 11 September 1918, Pilgrims Mss, NYC; Circular from Harry Brittain to the Pilgrims Members, June 1918, Pilgrims Mss, LMA/4632/A/01/001; *New York Times*, 5 February 1903.
128. Minute Book 1, 20 November 1903, and Minute Book 2, 27 December 1918, Pilgrims Mss, NYC.
129. Minute Book 1, 8 April 1909, Pilgrims Mss, NYC.
130. Butler to Wilson, 10 January 1919, Pilgrims Mss, NYC.
131. Minutes, 29 October 1918, Pilgrims Mss, LMA/4632/A/01/001.
132. General Manager's Office, Cunard, Water Street, Liverpool to Harry Brittain, 22 September 1908, Pilgrims Mss, LMA/4632/C/05/002/02; 'The Pilgrims List of Members and Bye-Laws', 1909, Brittain Papers, BLPES, Box 5; Cunard, Cockspur Street, London to Brittain, 26 May 1908, Pilgrims Mss, LMA/4632/C/05/002, Folder 1; in 1908, the concession did not apply for some of the summer months.
133. Minutes, 29 October 1918, Pilgrims Mss, LMA/4632/A/01/001; see Allen's obituary in *The Times*, 4 June 1935. He had also served as a marine insurance adviser at the Paris Peace Conference after the First World War. Allen was knighted in 1928, and his son – also John Sandeman – was an MP in Birkenhead.
134. 'Complimentary luncheon given by the Liverpool Committee of "The Pilgrims" to Sir Harry Brittain, MP at the Liverpool Exchange Club, on Friday, the Seventeenth Day of January, MDCCCCXIX, upon the occasion of the inauguration of the Liverpool committee of "The Pilgrims"' and loose piece of paper, Pilgrims Mss, LMA/4632/A/05/004; on 11 January 1919, Sandeman Allen said that Liverpool had 'some eighteen or so leading men here elected members'. See Sandeman Allen to A. H. Heal, 11 January 1919, Pilgrims Mss, LMA/4632/A/05/004.
135. Wilson to Brittain, 18 April 1919, Pilgrims Mss, LMA/4632/A/05/002/01.

136. Sandeman Allen to Wilson Taylor, 23 October 1919, Pilgrims Mss, LMA/4632/A/05/004.
137. Minutes, 18 July 1920, Pilgrims Mss, LMA/4632/A/01/001.
138. Minutes, 19 July 1922, Pilgrims Mss, LMA/4632/A/01/001; *The Times*, 20 June 1922.
139. Minutes, 5 June 1919, Pilgrims Mss, LMA/4632/A/01/001; Baker, *Pilgrims of Britain*, p. 67; Brittain became one of the vice-presidents of the Society; Minutes, 27 October 1919, Pilgrims Mss, LMA/4632/A/01/001.
140. Circular from Harry Brittain to the Pilgrims Members, June 1918, Pilgrims Mss, LMA/4632/A/01/001; Brittain, *Pilgrim Partners*, pp. 116–25.
141. Wilson to Brittain, 18 April 1919, Pilgrims Mss, LMA/4632/A/05/002/01.
142. Minutes, 17 July 1919, Pilgrims Mss, LMA/4632/A/01/001.
143. Ibid.; 'Suggestions for the immediate re-organisation and for the future of the Pilgrims' Society', July 1919, Pilgrims Mss, LMA/4632/A/05/004; Circular from Harry Brittain to the Pilgrims Members, June 1918, Pilgrims Mss, LMA/4632/A/01/001.
144. 'Suggestions for the immediate re-organisation and for the future of the Pilgrims' Society', July 1919, Pilgrims Mss, LMA/4632/A/05/004.
145. Ibid.; Taylor, *Projection of Britain*, pp. 1–4; *The Times*, 15 July 1919; Baker, *Pilgrims of Britain*, p. 20.
146. 'Suggestions for the immediate re-organisation and for the future of the Pilgrims' Society', July 1919, Pilgrims Mss, LMA/4632/A/05/004.
147. F. S. L. Lyons, 'The War of Independence, 1919–21', in W. E. Vaughan (ed.), *A New History of Ireland VI: Ireland Under the Union, 1870–1921* (Oxford, 1989), pp. 240–59; John E. Moser, *Twisting the Lion's Tail: Anglophobia in the United States, 1921–48* (London, 1999), p. 21; *New York Times*, 27 June 1919.
148. Robert D. Parmet, 'The Presidential Fever of Chauncey Depew', *New-York Historical Society Quarterly*, Vol. 54 (1970), p. 281; 'The Pilgrims List of Members and Bye-Laws', 1909, Brittain Papers, BLPES, Box 5; *Boston Daily Globe*, 20 March 1921. Indeed, Harvey's son-in-law, Marcellus H. Thompson, was indicted in 1922 for attempting to ship weapons from the US to Ireland for use by the IRA. See *New York Times*, 20 June 1922.
149. 'Suggestions for the immediate re-organisation and for the future of the Pilgrims' Society', July 1919, Pilgrims Mss, LMA/4632/A/05/004.
150. 'Report of the Executive Committee of the Pilgrims on the work of the year 1918–1919', 27 October 1919, Pilgrims Mss, LMA/4632/A/01/001.

151. Ibid.
152. *The Times*, 4 March 1903; *New York Times*, 26 May 1903 and 24 June 1905.
153. Louis Hay to I. N. Ford, 11 February 1907, Pilgrims Mss, LMA/4632/C/05/034.
154. Hay to Ford, 11 February 1907, Pilgrims Mss, LMA/4632/C/05/034; that this was indeed Bryce's first public appearance in America as ambassador is confirmed in a letter from Hay to Whitelaw Reid. See Hay to Reid, 19 March 1907, Pilgrims Mss, LMA/4632/C/05/034; for Hay's obituary, see *New York Times*, 16 July 1938. See also Ford's obituary, *New York Times*, 9 August 1912.
155. Charles Bridge to Wilson, 4 October 1922, and Wilson to Brittain, 14 October 1922, Pilgrims Mss, LMA/4632/A/05/002/01; *The Times*, 26 September 1922.
156. *The Times*, 28 November 1910.
157. Conway Davies to Wilson Taylor, 28 October 1921, Pilgrims Mss, LMA4632/D/01/026; *The Times*, 21 February 1922.
158. 'The Pilgrims List of Members and Bye-Laws', 1909, Brittain Papers, BLPES, Box 5.
159. Hay to Ford, 11 September 1903, Pilgrims Mss, LMA/4632/C/05/034.
160. 'Suggestions for the immediate re-organisation and for the future of the Pilgrims' Society', July 1919, Pilgrims Mss, LMA/4632/A/05/004; Baker, *Pilgrims of Britain*, p. 120.
161. Minute Book 3, 6 April 1927, Pilgrims Mss, NYC.
162. Baker, *Pilgrims of Britain*, p. 184; for Sanderson's obituary, see *The Times*, 15 July 1919; Minute Book 2, 7 January 1914, Pilgrims Mss, NYC.
163. Minute Book 3, 25 January 1922, Pilgrims Mss, NYC; Philip B. Kennedy to Brittain, 1 July 1918, and James K. Lynch to Brittain, 2 July 1918, Brittain Papers, BLPES, Box 7.
164. Gloster Armstrong to W. H. Harrison, 29 September and 17 September 1919, Pilgrims Mss, LMA/4632/A/05/004.
165. *New York Times*, 5 February 1903.

3 Earl Grey's Public Diplomacy

... a demonstration organized by the pro-British toadies and sycophants of New York to boom the Anglo-American alliance.
(*Gaelic American*)

In the months and years immediately following its establishment,
the Pilgrims Society was involved with some of the most pressing
questions of contemporary Anglo-American diplomacy. While the
British and German naval blockades of Venezuela in 1902 caused
a short spell of acrimony, it was the relationship between the US
and the British dominions of Canada and Newfoundland that
came to dominate much of the diplomacy of the 1900s. With the
North American aspect of the official Anglo-American relationship
proving so important in these years – in particular Canadian–US
relations – the Pilgrims Society focused much of its unofficial and
semi-official activities on attempts to foster greater understanding
between Britain, Canada, and the US. This speaks to the development of what John Bartlet Brebner termed the 'North Atlantic
Triangle', namely the concept that Canadian international relations have been framed by the country's links with Britain and the
US. Brebner traces the beginnings of such a triangle to the 1871
Treaty of Washington – when Britain and the US came to an agreement following disputes relating to the American Civil War, for
example the *Alabama* affair, and discussed other issues, including
the US–Canadian border and the North Atlantic fisheries – and
argues that the outcome of the Alaskan boundary dispute of 1903
led to a further differentiation of Canada as a third party in Anglo-
American relations. Canada faced the challenge of ensuring that it
had Britain's support against its powerful neighbour to the south,
while simultaneously trying to avoid Britain sacrificing its interests
on the altar of Anglo-American friendship.[1]

With matters such as the Alaskan boundary dispute and the North Atlantic fisheries ensuring that the strategically important rapprochement between Britain and the US remained incomplete, the Pilgrims worked to ensure that relations between all of the actors were as cordial as possible and that they were rooted in themes of Anglo-American harmony and similarity. The Society sought to do this both within its remit as a banqueting club and by cultivating links with those in officialdom. This is best shown by an event held on Saturday 31 March 1906 by the Pilgrims of the United States for the 4th Earl Grey, the Governor General of Canada, in New York's Waldorf-Astoria Hotel. At this function, both Grey and Elihu Root, the US Secretary of State, made significant and widely publicised speeches regarding the ongoing North Atlantic fisheries dispute. While it might today seem an obscure and esoteric chapter in the history of the Anglo-American relationship, the dispute over fishing rights in fact provided an opportunity for the Pilgrims Society to make its first noteworthy public diplomacy intervention. This simultaneously contributed to the Pilgrims' growing prestige and demonstrated a belief on the part of Root and Grey that the Society could lend legitimacy to their official utterances. These speeches should be regarded as examples of advocacy diplomacy. Of additional interest is Earl Grey's conspicuous attempt at what would now be termed cultural diplomacy, when he used the Pilgrims dinner to announce that he was gifting to the US a portrait of Benjamin Franklin which had been removed by the British during the American Revolution. The 1906 event illustrates the wider purposes of the Pilgrims Society and provides the clearest proof of the Society's nascent public diplomacy in this early period. This chapter is divided into four sections. The first section outlines the diplomatic context of the 1906 dinner, while the second and third sections analyse the significance of the event firstly in terms of elite networking and then with reference to the history of public diplomacy. The chapter's final section considers the specific cultural characteristics of the Pilgrims Society's cultural diplomacy.

The background to the 1906 dinner

In 1906, the British ambassador to the US, Sir Mortimer Durand, informed the Foreign Office that 'there are no questions pending' between Britain and the US 'which ought to create serious friction', 'with the possible exception of the Newfoundland Fishery dispute'.[2] The issue of US and French fishing rights in the seas off Newfoundland was a long-standing one and had been the subject of a number of treaties in the eighteenth and nineteenth centuries. Both countries possessed rights to fish there, even though this had an adverse effect on the local fishing industry. Negotiations had taken place to establish a reciprocity agreement between Newfoundland and the US in 1890, but the Canadian government voiced its opposition, which resulted in the British government blocking the deal. The 1898 Joint High Commission also failed to fully address the matter. Then, by the start of the 1900s, some in Newfoundland expressed their unhappiness with an agreement that had allowed American boats to use Newfoundland ports to buy bait. In light of this, Lord Lansdowne, the British Foreign Secretary, permitted Sir Robert Bond, the Newfoundland prime minister, to independently negotiate with the US. Sir Wilfrid Laurier, the Canadian prime minister, objected to this as he was afraid that a settlement favourable to Newfoundland – which he wanted to become part of Canada – would undermine the interests of Canada, which also had an agreement with the US regarding fishing in the North Atlantic.[3] The British government's sympathetic attitude to Newfoundland was a cause of further disillusionment for some Canadians, many of whom were already unhappy that the Alaskan boundary dispute had been settled in favour of the American claim. By 1905, a draft treaty had been drawn up between Bond and the US Secretary of State, John Hay. This was ratified by the US Senate in February 1905, but with significant concessions to senators representing New England fishing interests, so much so as to make the treaty unacceptable to Newfoundland. As a result, the Newfoundland government ended the agreement that had allowed American fishermen to buy bait and supplies and it was this development that sparked a period of acrimony between the US and Newfoundland. With Elihu Root – Hay's successor as Secretary of State from July 1905 – suggesting that a US battleship be sent to Newfoundland to safeguard the rights of the American fishermen, and rumours having emerged that Newfoundlanders were physically obstructing American fishing boats, the potential significance of the dispute became apparent to the Foreign Office. Root urged Britain to rein in Newfoundland, while the US ambassador in Britain, Whitelaw Reid, made similarly strong representations to the British government. Lansdowne was unhappy that Bond's actions had threatened to undermine the Anglo-American rapprochement, and a settlement was eventually reached in September 1906, with Sir Edward Grey, the new Foreign Secretary, reversing the punitive measures that had been taken by Newfoundland in 1905.[4] The Canadian and Newfoundland fishery disputes did not end fully until 1910, when a court of arbitration in The Hague – to which the cases had been referred in August 1907 – largely upheld the claims of the British dominions. Nevertheless, during the diplomatic wrangling of the previous decade, it was apparent that Britain had been willing to sacrifice the interests of Newfoundland and Canada in pursuit of Anglo-American accord.[5]

The Canadian aspect of the entangling North Atlantic fishery disputes was of primary importance to the Pilgrims dinner for Earl Grey in March 1906. Grey had been appointed Governor General of Canada in December 1904 and nearly from the start had sought to address the issues standing in the way of better Canadian–American relations. His efforts, combined with those of Elihu Root, resulted in a set of draft proposals in early May 1906. These proposals addressed the issues that had been raised at the Joint High Commission of 1898–9, including the seal and fishing disputes. As will become clear, it is significant that these proposals came so soon after the Pilgrims dinner. The discussions arising from the proposals, however, had broken down by the end of 1906, partly on account of Prime Minister Laurier's objections. Negotiations were rejuvenated by the replacement of the unpopular Mortimer Durand with James Bryce as Britain's ambassador in Washington in 1907. As the author of *The American Commonwealth*, Bryce was well respected, well known, and well connected in the US. Perhaps more so than Durand – with whom Theodore Roosevelt had had a difficult relationship – Bryce was thoroughly committed to the cause of Anglo-American friendship. He had been involved with the founding of the Anglo-American League in 1898 and would go on to become president of the British Pilgrims in 1915. Bryce regarded good Canadian–American relations as a way to solidify the Anglo-American rapprochement and worked with Grey, Root, and Laurier to progress talks to the extent that Laurier agreed to place the fishery dispute under arbitration in 1907.[6] Along with Earl Grey, Bryce worked to address Canada's dissatisfaction with the British Empire's diplomatic structures and attempted to represent Canada's interests too. It was Bryce, for example, who facilitated the creation in 1909 of the Canadian Department of External Affairs, providing for a further degree of Canadian autonomy.[7]

The extent to which the North Atlantic fishery disputes or the other outstanding issues concerning Canada and the US, including the entire boundary between the two countries, would impact on Anglo-American relations was unclear when the Pilgrims welcomed Earl Grey to New York. Sir Mortimer Durand was still concerned in August 1906 that the 'attitude of the Massachusetts fishermen is not reassuring, nor, I think, is that of the United States' Government, and in view of the coming elections it is impossible not to feel some uneasiness'. The ambassador – whose despatches one writer has likened to pulp fiction in their lurid and occasionally paranoid interpretation of American affairs – felt that the 'temptation to wave the Stars and Stripes in the face of Great Britain will be considerable'.[8] Nevertheless, Earl Grey's visit was part of a stage-managed attempt to markedly improve Canadian–American relations and, by extension, remove the principal sources of friction between Britain and the US. The Pilgrims dinner was a central component of this attempt. Indeed, Grey had always been alive to the importance of social functions as a means to facilitate such an improvement and had often entertained prominent Americans at his Ottawa residence. It was following one such occasion, at the start of February 1906, that Joseph Choate suggested to Grey that he visit New York as a guest of the Pilgrims Society.[9] Choate's invitation to Grey was made before Root had approached Sir Mortimer Durand on 27 February, when the Secretary of State initially made it known to the British that he desired to 'take advantage of the present opportunity, when there are no vexed questions between the United States and Canada, to examine and settle if possible a number of questions, such as the lake fisheries, which may hereafter give rise to friction'.[10] This presents the possibility that Root had privately asked Choate and the Pilgrims Society to make this unofficial approach to Earl Grey, in the hope that the gesture would complement his own official diplomacy. Alternatively, Grey believed that Root's communication was 'the result of Mr Choate's visit to me here last month', when Grey had 'had more than one conversation with Mr Choate on the desirability of using the opportunity which the present friendly relations between Canada and the United States offered for the purpose of settling all outstanding questions between the two countries'.[11] Choate had only the year before retired as US ambassador to Britain, in which capacity he had been associated with the London Pilgrims. He also went on to become a vice-president of the New York branch, and was then elected its president in 1912.[12]

For his own part, especially in light of his proactive approach to diplomacy, Grey would have been keen to accept Choate's invitation. Nevertheless, as per diplomatic protocol, he sought the advice of the British government before doing so. Perhaps indicating that the Pilgrims Society remained something of an unknown quantity in the corridors of Whitehall, Grey felt the need to explain that the 'Pilgrim's Club aims at promoting good feeling between the United States of America and Great Britain'. Grey also explained that the prime minister had already expressed the belief that it would be 'desirable I should accept'.[13] In response, the Colonial Office said that it had 'no objection from our point of view, quite the contrary'.[14] It is not clear whether Grey was referring to the British or Canadian prime minister, but it is likely that he meant the latter. When Elihu Root had approached Ambassador Durand in February 1906 to raise the possibility of addressing Canadian–American differences, Laurier – in contrast to the uncertain and indecisive response from the British – wished to seize the opportunity.[15] This provides a more nuanced understanding to interpretations of the Canadian prime minister's resentment over Alaska in 1903 as having 'poisoned' Canadian–American relations.[16] Laurier's wish for Grey to attend the Pilgrims dinner instead points to a subtle gesture towards rapprochement on the part of the Canadian prime minister.[17]

Thus wider geopolitical events were converging in Manhattan when the Pilgrims' reception gathered at 8 p.m. on 31 March 1906 in the Waldorf-Astoria's salubrious Astor Gallery. The Waldorf-Astoria was one of New York's most famous and exclusive hotels, and was frequently used for high-society functions. It was located on Fifth Avenue, which had long been associated with New York's social elites, many of whom lived on the street in large mansions. The Waldorf-Astoria was, in fact, two separate buildings, the Waldorf and the Astoria, joined by a connecting corridor. The Hotel Waldorf had been built in 1893 by William Waldorf Astor, while the Astoria was built four years later by William's cousin, John Jacob Astor IV.[18] The Astor family was one of the foremost families in elite New York society, and John Jacob IV – who would die in 1912 on the *Titanic* – was a member of the Pilgrims Society. The Pilgrims

Society would often use the Waldorf-Astoria as a venue for its functions, something that serves to highlight that the Society truly was a part of New York's elite associational culture. Indeed, the Pilgrims was one of a variety of New York clubs and societies that gathered together for a final banquet at the hotel in 1929, before it was closed and demolished to clear the site for the construction of the Empire State Building. Nicholas Murray Butler chaired the organising committee for the 1929 event, while George Wilson acted as toastmaster, in which capacity he read out a cablegram from Harry Brittain describing the hotel as 'a hall of golden memories'.[19] Exclusive hotels were a crucial component of elite urban networking. Paul Groth, in a study of the US's 'palace hotels' – large, expensive hotels of which the Waldorf-Astoria was one example – has noted that such hotels were naturally more sociable than private residencies and thus 'enveloped residents in an international network of architectural distinction'. The public spaces of a prestigious hotel – for example its lobby, ballroom, and restaurant – were 'known to virtually everyone in the city' and 'were generally accessible only to the truly elite'.[20] Upmarket hotels were in these ways integral to the essence of the exclusivity of the Pilgrims and New York elite society. As it did for whatever event was held there, the Waldorf-Astoria raised the prestige, status, and importance of the Pilgrims dinner for Earl Grey in 1906.

The significance of the dinner, I: elite networking

The Pilgrims had originally hoped that Theodore Roosevelt would attend the event, with William Butler Duncan, the Society's chairman, having visited Washington DC in an effort to establish whether this was possible. This was another example of the Society self-consciously attempting to cultivate its elite network, in this case by a personal visit to the centre of US government. Joseph Choate – having discussed the date of the dinner with Duncan – also spoke with the president in an effort to secure his attendance. The former ambassador was, however, left with the impression that Roosevelt would not come due to 'his present public duties and engagements'.[21] Duncan, meanwhile, had been told that Roosevelt's involvement 'was not considered practicable, because of precedents'. This was perhaps because it was regarded as inappropriate for the president to attend a function and not be the guest of honour. It was, for instance, explained to the assembled guests during the banquet that Roosevelt would have attended 'if it were possible for the President to play second fiddle to even the governor general of Canada, or share his honors with any one'. Instead, Duncan had been assured that it was very likely that the Secretary of State would attend instead. Indeed, the date of the Pilgrims dinner was chosen partly because it was deemed most convenient for guests from the US capital, including politicians and officials.[22] Guests included Robert Bacon, the Assistant Secretary of State (later Root's successor), and Robert Adams, the acting chairman of the Committee on Foreign Relations in the House of Representatives, who had overseen the passage through the House of the declaration of war against Spain in 1898, and who in 1906 – before he committed suicide in June – was working on legislation aimed at reforming the US consular service.[23]

Newspaper reports the day after the dinner described Root as having 'pushed through the crowd, and grasped the earl's hand' in friendship, before proceeding into a banquet room decorated by British, Canadian, and American flags, Florida palm trees, branches of Canadian pine, and ice sculptures of 'Uncle Sam, John Bull, and other figures emblematic of the two countries'. After the toasts to the king and the president, the 'band started up with "The Star Spangled Banner", played a few bars, and switched rapidly into "God Save the King", repeating each national air time after time'.[24] To be sure, Newfoundland was not represented at what was clearly a British–Canadian–US affair. This was likely because of a perception amongst the British and the Canadians that Newfoundland was of lesser importance. It may also have been a response to Newfoundland's more assertive approach to relations with the US, of which Earl Grey was critical. Still, the Newfoundland dispute was bound up both with British–American and Canadian–American relations, and the settlement of fishing rights was of as much importance to Canada as it was to Newfoundland and the US.[25] Thus the fishery dispute, along with the recent memory of the Alaskan boundary dispute and, indeed, the matter of the entire Canadian–US border – which was not finally settled until 1908 – provided the context for the Pilgrims dinner. It was for all of these reasons that, according to Elihu Root in his speech to the Pilgrims, some newspapers had reported that, at the event, 'an announcement would be made that all existing questions between Canada and the United States had been settled'.[26] The *Evening Statesman* in Washington State, for example, had written that disputes such as the 'protection of the fisheries in international waters, including the Great Lakes and the St Lawrence River, the fur seal fisheries dispute, the protection of the Niagara Falls and regulation of water to be taken for power, the Newfoundland fisheries and several minor boundary disputes' had been resolved.[27] In a room literally draped in the symbols of Anglo-American friendship, the Secretary of State mournfully admitted: 'I wish it were so'.[28]

The British government received printed copies of Root's speech, on which passages and sentences of particular interest had been underlined in pencil by the diplomatic staff. Highlighted sections included Root's contention that the US's traditional policy of avoiding *de jure* alliances did not matter when there was *de facto* cooperation. Using the metaphor of a legal contract between individuals, Root said that a 'sincere and genuine common purpose to do the thing to which the contract might relate is as efficient without the seal and the writing as it would be with it'.[29] Other parts of the speech that were underlined included Root's recognition that there remained points of divergence between the US and Canada, which he identified as including the questions over the boundary line and north-eastern fishing rights. Root also regretted that the Alaskan boundary dispute had created 'much hard feeling'. Somewhat disingenuously – given his central role in arguing the US case during the 1903 tribunal – Root blamed the US Congress for not carrying out a survey of the borderline sooner, meaning that it had needlessly developed into a 'most critical situation'. Root's speech was a delicate mixture of careful diplomacy, platitude, and pointed remarks. He argued that 'the progress, the growth, the glory, of England is at every step a gain to every man who speaks the English tongue, who has formed his character and his customs upon English law and the genius of English institutions'. Yet in addition to highlighting the need for cooperation between Britain and Canada, and the US, and arguing that this needed no formal alliance, he also said that with 'every country that seeks to attain the purpose that dwells in all the highest ideals and the noblest purposes of the American people there is an alliance effective and perpetual'. This section of Root's speech, which did not speak to notions of a unique cultural affinity between the British Empire and the US, and which instead made clear that other nations could join in friendship with the US too, was not underlined by the Foreign Office staff.[30] Apparently pleased with Root's more hopeful sentiments, however, the British highlighted the section of his speech in which he said that

> dealing with all the questions that exist to-day, and all the questions to arise, our people have resting upon them the duty to be just, to be considerate – not grasping and arrogant – and to deal with other peoples as a just and kindly man would deal with his neighbour.[31]

The Foreign Office would have taken this as an indication that the Secretary of State was committed to a conciliatory approach to international relations, but also as an articulation of Root's desire that Britain and Canada should do likewise. If all parties shared this commitment, Root said that 'never shall we have to blush for our failure to live up to our high ideals'.[32]

Root's speech was of great interest, both to the press and to the British government. In a letter to the Foreign Secretary, Ambassador Durand confirmed that Root's words had 'aroused some interest' in the US and that the speech was of 'considerable importance'.[33] The *New York Times* described Root's speech as 'notable', while a *Washington Post* report from London said that the Pilgrims dinner and 'Secretary of State Root's speech, has attracted more attention here than any other topic during the week'. According to the *Post*, the *Spectator* had opined that Root's speech was evidence that the US had 'gradually acquired the benignity and wisdom which belong to maturity'. The *Pall Mall Gazette*, meanwhile, regarded the event as a 'landmark in the history of the relations between the two branches of the Anglo-Saxon race'. Moreover, it was impressed by the fact that '[w]ords were spoken, and spoken deliberately and officially, which would have been impossible of utterance only a few years ago'.[34] The *Times* correspondent also picked up on the official nature of Root's speech, writing that it was all the more significant for having been 'spoken as with the tongue of the President himself'.[35]

The 'high ideals' about which Root had spoken were articulated by Earl Grey during his own address to the assembled Pilgrims. The Governor General said that 'although Canada and the United States are ruled by different constitutions, the beat which proceeds from the one great Anglo-Saxon heart which is common to us both, makes itself felt in all our veins'.[36] He believed, no less, that the 'coming solidarity and unification of the Anglo-Saxon race' would provide for the 'future peace and hope of the world'.

It was the 'proud mission of the Anglo-Saxon race to maintain and to advance the cause of civilization', of which the 'peoples of the United Kingdom, of the self-governing nations of the British Empire and of the United States are joint trustees'. Then, and even though Grey acknowledged that there were 'several questions outstanding between the Dominion of Canada and the United States which have been left open too long and which call for settlement', he said that he was sure that the Canadian and US governments desired to 'take advantage of the opportunity which the present feeling of amity between the two countries affords'.[37] With an added significance for having been delivered by a high-ranking British official to an American audience which included the US Secretary of State, Grey finished with a statement clearly designed to communicate Britain's desire for cooperation with the US:

> England thankfully recognizes that your desire to cooperate with her in this beneficial work, and the knowledge that the Stars and Stripes and the flag of England stand in all the gateways of the world, as on these walls, their varying colors draped together . . . as the joint emblems of freedom, righteousness and duty, may well cause us all to rejoice and to feel proud, first, that we have an imperial mission to perform, and secondly, that, so long as we are true to each other and to ourselves, we shall have strength, as well as the will, to accomplish the noble purposes of our joint and splendid destiny.[38]

According to a despatch from Sir Percy Sanderson – the British Consul-General in New York, who was also a founding member of the Pilgrims – Grey was 'extremely well received' by his audience.[39] Likewise, the former Foreign Secretary, Lord Lansdowne, later told Grey that, having read the speech in the press, he had found it 'excellent in form and substance', and remarked that it had been 'very favourably commented upon' in Britain. This is significant as it demonstrates that the Society had influence in Britain.[40] Meanwhile, Canadian press coverage – as the London *Times* and the *Pall Mall Gazette* had done in relation to Root's speech – focused on the significance of the official utterances made at the Pilgrims dinner. In Toronto, *The Globe* felt that the event was notable 'not merely because of the high standing and wide celebrity of both the hosts and the guest, but because it was calculated and intended to foster the growth of kindly relations between Canada and the United States', while the Tory *Mail and Empire* was impressed that '[n]ever before did statesmen of the two pow-ers express more unreservedly the respect, admiration, and liking of the one for the other'.[41]

The Pilgrims dinner was not, however, 'favourably com-mented upon' everywhere. The New York-based, Irish-American newspaper, the *Gaelic American*, regarded it as a 'demonstration organized by the pro-British toadies and sycophants of New York to boom the Anglo-American alliance'. The newspaper believed that this was a formal alliance to which Theodore Roosevelt had 'given some kind of assent', and blamed the 'nondescript aggre-gation of degenerate Americans, Britishers and Jews' who appar-ently constituted the Pilgrims Society. The presence of the Irish Catholic Archbishop of New York and the Irish-American busi-nessman John D. Crimmins was an additional 'regrettable and painful incident in the latest Pilgrims fiasco'.[42] The *Gaelic Ameri-can* supported Irish independence and was edited by a County Kerry-born man named Michael O'Reilly, who had first arrived in the US in 1887. O'Reilly had founded the Friends of Irish Free-dom and was a member of both Clan-Na-Gael and the American Irish Historical Society.[43] Clan-Na-Gael had replaced the Fenian Brotherhood as America's principal Irish revolutionary organisa-tion during the course of the late nineteenth century and later, during the First World War, would seek German support for an uprising in Ireland.[44] As an explicitly imperialist and pro-British organisation, the Pilgrims Society was anathema to O'Reilly. It is therefore unsurprising that the *Gaelic American* was so sharp in its criticism of the Earl Grey dinner. Nevertheless, the response of O'Reilly's paper is instructive of the fact that the Pilgrims Soci-ety was regarded as a bastion of the Anglo-American establish-ment and was evidently considered significant enough to warrant such a vociferous attack. The *Gaelic American*'s criticism of the Earl Grey dinner is also an early example of some of the con-spiracy theories that have surrounded the Pilgrims Society right up until the present day. Such theories typically suggest that the Society operates as a sinister network of elite men with great influence and control over world affairs.[45] While this book does make a case for the significance and relative influence of the Soci-ety, these other theories are part of a wider tradition of 'new world order' conspiracies of the type that highlight the omnipres-ent power that people like the Rothschilds allegedly hold over world finance. The focus on the Rothschilds – who were, in fact, represented in the Pilgrims' membership in 1909 by James A. De Rothschild – is occasionally anti-Semitic, an element also evident in the *Gaelic American*'s 1906 portrayal of the Pilgrims.[46] In the case of the *Gaelic American*, this spoke to a wider trend of Western anti-Semitism that had emerged from the nineteenth century, in which Jews were held responsible for much that was wrong with the world. As Eric Hobsbawm has written, 'Jews were almost universally present' and 'could serve as symbols of the hated capitalist/financier' or the 'revolutionary agitator'.[47]

The dinner for Earl Grey held a wider significance for this analysis of the Pilgrims Society beyond simply the strong reaction it precipitated amongst proponents and opponents of Anglo-American friendship. The significance of the event lay in its facilitation of elite networking. Importantly, Earl Grey's visit to the US included a trip to Washington. According to George T. Wilson, the Society was 'instrumental' in organising all of Earl Grey's travel arrangements, 'both between Ottawa and New York and New York and Washington'.[48] After he left New York following the Pilgrims event, Grey and his wife spent a night at the White House, where he was entertained at a large dinner with Theodore Roosevelt, members of the US Cabinet and the Speaker of the House of Representatives. He later wrote to Roosevelt to thank him for his hospitality, 'particularly our breakfast with you' which 'will always occupy a bright and honoured place in our recollections'. According to a letter written by Grey to Lord Elgin, the Colonial Secretary, Roosevelt had joined them for breakfast at 8.15 a.m. and had talked almost the entire time 'at full gallop' until 9.30 a.m.[49] Grey was also touched by a visit to George Washington's home at Mount Vernon and by a story he was told about the origins of the tradition of ships on the Potomac sounding their bell as a mark of respect as they passed the estate. According to a member of Grey's party, this was first done by the captain of a British merchant ship in 1813, 'notwithstanding the fact that the two countries were at war'. For Grey, there was a 'pretty touch of sentiment about this which cannot fail to touch the hearts of 2 (sic) nations whenever it is brought home'.[50]

There was, however, more to Grey's Pilgrims-assisted visit to Washington DC than simply pleasant breakfasts and day trips. Before returning north, Grey also spent two nights with Durand at the British Embassy, during which time he had a discussion with the British ambassador and Root 'regarding the relations of Great

Britain and the United States'.[51] In the immediate aftermath of the Pilgrims dinner, Grey had felt that the 'iron is malleable' and that the time was ripe to finally address those Canadian–American differences that stood in the way of Anglo-American rapprochement. Writing to Lord Elgin, Grey explained that Roosevelt and Root were 'both very anxious for a treaty . . . to settle all outstanding questions between Canada and the US', but said that, following his discussions with the president, he believed that Roosevelt was focused more on that year's congressional elections. Grey said that he feared that Roosevelt would 'subordinate' Canadian–US relations to electoral considerations and implied that Roosevelt would take a hard line in any negotiations between the two countries in an effort to curry favour at home. Grey said that Roosevelt was 'an impulsive fellow and I cannot forecast what consideration may weigh with him'. It was, however, with Root that Grey had the most diplomatically significant contact while in Washington, for instance when Grey and Durand met with the Secretary of State to 'discuss informally the whole position'. This meeting between the three men had been organised at Root's request and resulted in a decision to drop any notion of reconvening the 1898 Joint High Commission. Rather, a commitment was made to conduct Canadian–American diplomacy through the Secretary of State and the British ambassador. Then, at the start of May, Root sent to Ambassador Durand a document outlining his position on sixteen matters for US–Canadian negotiation, including the fisheries.[52] Further to these discussions, Grey invited Root to visit Ottawa in January 1907.[53] In accepting this invitation, Root attended a number of public functions, including at the Golf Club and the Canadian Club, and reportedly 'charmed everyone by his attractive personality', going some way to rehabilitate his reputation amongst those Canadians who had resented his role in the Alaskan negotiations in 1903.[54] The value to Britain and Canada of Root's trip to Ottawa was articulated by Sir Edward Grey in a letter to Earl Grey. According to the Foreign Secretary, 'the important thing is to make Root feel on his visit that Canada is as desirous as he is of an amicable settlement'.[55]

The significance of the Pilgrims dinner and the importance of sociability for official negotiations was also perceived by the *Boston Evening Transcript* ahead of Root's trip to Ottawa. The paper wrote that even though it had been 'officially stated that the visit is purely social, there is no question here that its real purpose is to settle all of the pending questions between the United States and Canada'. Importantly, the paper understood that it was because Grey and Root had met at the Pilgrims dinner in March 1906 that the Ottawa trip in January 1907 was possible, writing that a 'mutual regard resulted from that meeting which is expected to go far toward smoothing the way to the settlement of all frictional points between the two countries'.[56] It is clear that the Pilgrims event, by bringing statesmen together and allowing them to give expression to notions of Anglo-American friendship, was regarded as having made a measurable contribution to the improvement of official diplomatic relations. Writing again to Lord Elgin, Grey himself said that he felt that the 'Pilgrims dinner was a really great success' and that 'the representative and influential character of the assemblage made the banquet almost a "record"'. Even though the audience at the dinner was entirely made up of elites and was not, in fact, 'representative' of wider American public feeling, Grey felt that its success was 'evidence of the extremely friendly attitude of the US to Canada and the UK'.[57]

As successful as Grey's and Root's respective trips clearly were, it is equally important not to accept at face value the positive presentations of the event given by some of the contemporary press reports and items of correspondence. Behind the public speeches at the Pilgrims dinner, the hard realities of diplomacy and national interest were still apparent in other examples from the correspondence of the principal actors. As discussions about the North Atlantic fisheries and pelagic sealing rolled into the rest of 1906, Grey felt that if 'Root and Roosevelt really wish to clean the slate the means of doing so is to their hand'.[58] Writing in January 1907 to Esmé Howard, who was Britain's acting-ambassador in Washington during the handover period between the tenures of Mortimer Durand and James Bryce, Grey also said that, unless the US was more willing to compromise, he could 'foresee the prospect of prolonged and fruitless controversy. The probability of the United States and England arriving at any settlement of a question which has been the subject of controversy for nearly 100 years is I fear very small.'[59] Revealing a frustration both with Root and with Newfoundland, Grey told Durand that he could 'not understand Root's position. He does not seem to have realized that he can obtain everything he has asked for by giving to Canada the same rights qua Atlantic fish that his Government is prepared to give to Newfoundland.'[60] Nevertheless, the evidence surrounding Grey's trip to Washington and Root's trip to Ottawa shows that the Pilgrims dinner had clearly offered an environment conducive to the friendly and collegiate communication of outstanding diplomatic matters. British and American political elites had been able to give expression to their respective countries' position, while at the same time articulating the underlying ideological reasons for why these positions need not undermine Anglo-American friendship. This much was recognised by Louis Hay, who wrote to George Wilson to congratulate him on the success of the Grey dinner, noting that the Pilgrims were becoming 'world-wide in reputation and their dinners the occasion for official declarations'.[61] By making such significant speeches at a Pilgrims function, Grey and Root contributed to the Society's growing reputation, importance, and influence. At the same time, however, the existing prestige of the Pilgrims – which originated in its links to the upper-class associational cultures of London and New York, and in the elite networking underpinning its exclusive membership – lent weight and legitimacy to the statesmen's speeches. This process was assisted by having held the dinner at the Waldorf-Astoria, a prestigious hotel symbolic of the absolute height of New York high society. Following recent disputes and amidst ongoing discourses involving Canada, the Pilgrims dinner was also an opportunity to provide reassurance and affirmation of the state of the 'great rapprochement' between Britain and the US. The Pilgrims facilitated official negotiations in much more direct ways too: Earl Grey was in the US in the first place because of Joseph Choate's invitation on behalf of the Pilgrims, and had had his transport to Washington largely arranged by the Society. The elite and influential nature of the Society's membership – like former Ambassador Choate – had ensured that the Society had itself become influential enough to play so central a part in this instance of British–Canadian–US diplomacy. In all of these ways, the Pilgrims Society had shown itself to be more than just a banqueting club and had demonstrated the ways in which it acted as a conduit for, and between, official and unofficial actions and actors. People like Choate acted under its auspices in an effort to facilitate official diplomatic contact. As Root himself said in a letter to Grey at the end of April 1906, the Pilgrims dinner 'besides being agreeable will do some good'.[62] The next section of the chapter will look at the some of the other ways in which this was so.

The significance of the dinner, II: public diplomacy

If the Pilgrims dinner in New York helped facilitate official negotiations, it was also an effort to improve wider public sentiment
between Britain, Canada, and the US. The Pilgrims was not only
a conduit between official actors, but its profile meant that it was
also a conduit between policy-making elites and the wider public. Earl Grey, for one, was alive to the public relations – or public diplomacy – potential of the Pilgrims dinner. Firstly, Grey's
public diplomacy was an example of 'advocacy diplomacy', by
which is meant the 'creation and dissemination of information
materials to build understanding of a policy'.[63] To this end, Grey
sought printed copies of Root's speech for circulation in Canada,
both amongst policy-makers and the wider public, explaining
that the 'more it is read here the better'. Agreeing with a similar
statement from Root, Grey wrote that 'I realise with you that the
public on both sides will be required to be educated' if the process of '"cleaning the slate" may be accomplished'. He told Root
that he was 'approaching the Canadian Press with a request that
they shall give your speech the fullest possible honours, and call
the attention of their readers, not only to its contents, but to the
tone and spirit which animated it from start to finish'.[64] In a letter to Lord Elgin, meanwhile, Grey explained that Root's speech
was important because of 'what he says, how he says it and who
says it'.[65] By attempting to have the Root speech inserted in as
many newspapers as possible, Grey was clearly attempting to
influence public opinion and trying bring it into line with his and
other elites' desire for British–Canadian–American friendship.
There was indeed interest in Canada in the Pilgrims dinner, as
shown by the passages from *The Globe* and the *Mail and Empire*
quoted earlier. Even so, while Alberta's *Daily Herald* reported on
18 April on one aspect of Earl Grey's US trip, it did not mention
Root's speech. With the massive earthquake in San Francisco the
headline news event that day, and for days later, it is evident
that the Root speech was lower down the news agenda than it
might otherwise have been.[66] Grey's actions nevertheless provide
evidence of some of the new ways in which international relations were thought about at the turn of the nineteenth and twentieth centuries. Mass-circulation newspapers had only come to
prominence in Europe in the 1870s and 1880s, while the 1890s

had seen the rise of the so-called 'yellow press' in the US. As a result of this larger reading public, and the concomitant belief that public opinion could impact upon official relations, diplomats and other actors in international relations realised that it was important to engage with a wider constituency than just fellow statesmen.[67] By courting widespread coverage for Root's speech, Grey evidently felt that wider positive public sentiment was an important part of improving British–Canadian–American relations.

The second way in which Grey was conducting what would now be termed public diplomacy was in his use of 'cultural diplomacy'. This cultural diplomacy was couched by the content of the speeches made at the Pilgrims dinner, particularly those parts which highlighted the purported commonalities between British and American conceptions of peace, freedom, imperialism, and civilisation. There was, however, another element to the event that provides an even clearer example of cultural diplomacy in action. In the context of what was a high-profile affirmation of Anglo-American cultural affinity, Grey used the Pilgrims banquet – which coincided with the bicentenary of the birth of Benjamin Franklin – to announce the symbolic gift to the 'American people' of a portrait of Franklin. This was a private undertaking on the part of Grey, but it also had the support of his superiors in the British government. For example, Lord Elgin, the Colonial Secretary, wrote to Grey ahead of the US trip to say that he hoped that it would 'be successful and pleasant and I look forward especially to the account of the presentation of the portrait'.[68] This demonstrated that Grey believed that culture was a relevant factor in international relations. As the remainder of this chapter will argue, such cultural diplomacy was demonstrative of some of the ideas that underpinned the Pilgrims Society's conception of Anglo-American rapprochement.

According to George Wilson, Grey had been 'induced' by the Pilgrims to publicly make the announcement at the Waldorf-Astoria, having initially planned on doing so later in April at another event.[69] The painting had been on display in his Northumberland mansion, and had come into the Grey family's possession after it was taken from Franklin's home in Philadelphia by British forces under Major-General Sir Charles Grey, the 1st Earl Grey, during the American War of Independence. Grey told the Pilgrims that he made the gift because:

my sense of equity tells me that there are higher laws than the law of possession, and because I believe that neither England nor America can fulfil their high mission unless we approach the consideration of every problem affecting our relation to each other, not from the narrow, selfish and provincial standpoint of what America and England can each of them do for themselves alone, but from the higher standpoint of what we all can do for England, America and the world.[70]

It is unlikely, however, that the idea for the gift originated with Earl Grey. A Philadelphian lawyer named Francis Rawle had written to Grey in December 1905 to enquire about the picture, having been informed by Joseph Choate that it was in Grey's possession. Rawle did not explicitly ask for the painting's return, but he did remind Grey of the looming bicentenary celebrations and asked 'whether you will tell me what is known of the history of this portrait before it came into the possession of your family and since'. In his reply to Rawle, Grey made no mention of returning the painting, only noting the 'tradition in my family that Franklin referred with regret to the loss of his portrait on the ground that it was generally admitted to be a very faithful likeness'.[71] Indeed, an untitled newspaper clipping amongst Grey's personal papers shows that Grey was originally 'of the opinion that the picture was entailed in his family and that it would be impossible to return it to the people of the United States'.[72] Yet something had clearly changed by February 1906, when Grey wrote to Theodore Roosevelt to tell the US president that '[a]s your English friend I desire to give my prisoner, after the lapse of 130 years, his liberty'. Grey explained to Roosevelt that Choate had suggested the Franklin bicentennial celebrations on 20 April 1906 as a 'fitting opportunity for restoring to the American people a picture which they will be glad to recover'.[73] Meanwhile, after he had written to Grey in 1905, Rawle had contacted Dr Silas Weir Mitchell – a Philadelphian polymath and friend of Grey's – in an effort to bring pressure to bear on Grey to return the portrait ahead of the bicentenary.[74] Regardless of whether it had been Choate, Rawle, or Weir Mitchell – or a combination of all three – who had encouraged Earl Grey to return the painting, the gift evidently pleased President Roosevelt. Following a meeting with Roosevelt and Root at the start of March 1906, Choate said that both men were 'very enthusiastic about the portrait, particularly the President'.[75] Then, in a letter to Grey, Roosevelt said that he regarded the painting as a 'thoughtful and generous gift'. He promised to formally and publicly thank Grey, but also wanted to 'say privately how much I appreciate not only what you have done but the spirit in which you have done it adds to the generosity of the gift itself'. He promised, as per Grey's request, to keep the painting at the White House, where, indeed, it remains today.[76] The portrait arrived in New York on 15 April 1906 addressed to Roosevelt and with a note attached for the benefit of the customs officers saying that it had 'no definite monetary value, but that from a sentimental standpoint it was priceless'.[77] It was sent on to Washington DC, but was then returned northwards to Philadelphia for temporary exhibition during the city's Franklin celebrations.[78]

Despite the US president's official and unofficial expressions of gratitude for the return of the Franklin portrait – and even though Grey had believed that the success of the Pilgrims dinner was a proof of a widespread desire for British–US–Canadian friendship – the wider press response to the gift was mixed. Unsurprisingly, the *Gaelic American* mocked the Pilgrims for their 'wild applause' of Earl Grey's announcement at the banquet at the Waldorf-Astoria and sardonically noted that the 'return of the stolen goods was hailed as an act of extraordinary generosity'. A correspondent to the letters pages, meanwhile, juxtaposed the Pilgrims' veneration of the 4th Earl Grey with the fact that the 1st Earl Grey – in addition to having stolen the Franklin portrait in the first place – was also responsible for the 'massacre of Paoli' in 1777, when British forces were alleged to have attacked American revolutionary forces in cold blood.[79] Newspapers with less of an intrinsic anti-British bias also picked up on the notion that Earl Grey was simply returning a stolen item to which he had no rightful claim of ownership. Suggesting a difference between British and American press attitudes towards rapprochement – or at the very least, a difference in perceptions about the significance and underlying merits of Grey's gift – not all newspapers in the US supported the *Pall Mall Gazette*'s belief that the portrait 'must have touched American hearts as nothing else could have done'.[80] For example, the *Buffalo Commercial* wrote that while 'it would not be gracious to speak of it as a bit of loot come back . . . that is what it is', and wondered about the 'extent, value and historic significance of the rest of the "loot"' acquired by means of the 'world-wide military campaigning of our British cousins'.[81] The *Philadelphia Inquirer*, meanwhile, was unhappy that the portrait was to be kept at the White House, wanting it returned instead to the city 'from whence it was looted'.[82] In truth, newspaper coverage was predominantly positive, with Earl Grey's gift described elsewhere as 'handsome' and 'graceful'.[83] The *New-York Tribune* was particularly fulsome in its description of the gift as an 'incident at once significant of the cordial relations between America and the Mother Country'. Unlike some of the other American newspapers, it did not depict the portrait as loot, noting instead that it was 'naturally prized as one of the "spoils of war"' by the 'distinguished general', the 1st Earl Grey.[84] The paper was owned by Whitelaw Reid who, as serving US ambassador to Britain, had received the portrait at his Embassy in London before sending it onwards to the US in advance of the Franklin bicentennial.[85] For that reason, it is unsurprising that the *Tribune* regarded the portrait's repatriation as the Grey family's most recent contribution to the English-speaking world.[86]

As shown by the admittedly mixed press response, Earl Grey's decision to return the portrait was not unproblematic. With the Pilgrims Society and some journalists promoting an idealised vision of the past and present Anglo-American relationship in order to promote a better future, other elements in the press ensured that the reality of the previous 130 years was not entirely forgotten. The tension between these two competing narratives speaks to the existence of something of a watershed in attitudes to Anglo-American relations. Whereas the Pilgrims sought to couch remaining sources of friction – like the Canadian and Newfoundland fishery disputes – in the language of rapprochement, others remained unwilling to absolve the Grey family and the British of their past actions. A lingering bitterness over the injustices inflicted on America by the British sat uneasily alongside the officially friendly tone of Anglo-American relations as articulated by Earl Grey and Elihu Root at the Pilgrims banquet at the Waldorf-Astoria. The contradictory reaction to the event and to Earl Grey's gift was very much a sign of the times.

Whatever the various responses, Earl Grey's gift of the Benjamin Franklin portrait to the American people, via the White House, was an act of public diplomacy. If Grey's dissemination of Elihu Root's speech was evidence of the 'advocacy' stage of public diplomacy, then his gift of the Franklin portrait, along with some of the content of the speeches at the Pilgrims event, were examples of 'cultural diplomacy'. Earl Grey's position as Governor General of Canada, together with Elihu Root's presence at the Pilgrims dinner, provided the occasion with an official quality, even though the Pilgrims were themselves a private organisation. While Earl Grey's gift was ostensibly a private act – in that the portrait was Earl Grey's private property, and in that he was under no official obligation to make the gift – it was designed to promote the idea of Anglo-American friendship and was undertaken by a man involved in the official pursuit of such an aim. It was also an act supported by Lord Elgin, the Colonial Secretary. The Pilgrims provided a milieu in which official and unofficial aims and activities merged. Announced at the Pilgrims dinner and widely reported in the press, the gift became a public act with the aim of cultivating popular and elite opinion in favour of good Anglo-American relations. This was public diplomacy as part of an effort to solidify the acceptance of a set of political and cultural ideas that apparently connected Britain and the US and which underpinned the rapprochement between the two countries. What these ideas were is examined below.

The culture of the Pilgrims' cultural diplomacy

Like his fellow Founding Father Thomas Jefferson, Benjamin Franklin has served as a symbol of American national identity in the centuries since his death. For much of the nineteenth century, popular images of Franklin on everyday material items such as coins, stamps, and tokens meant that his legacy was accessible to poorer Americans and immigrants, and could thus act as an emblem for social inclusion. According to Carla Mulford, however, by the end of the nineteenth and the start of the twentieth centuries, US imperialism in places like Cuba and the Philippines, but also on the Western Frontier, meant that Franklin also 'served as a vehicle for messages about American identity, American progress, and American prowess'.[87] Alongside the statue-building of the 1890s, the renewed scholarly and literary interest in Franklin at the start of the twentieth century – which, in the case of a 1907 essay written by Annie Russell Marble, highlighted the essential Englishness of his writing and its absence of 'uncouth' Americanisms – was an attempt by American elites to institutionalise him as a symbol of the 'on-going hegemony of Anglo-America'.[88] This was also shown by Frank Strong's 1898 biography of Franklin, which highlighted that Franklin came from 'good English stock', through his father, who was born in Northamptonshire.[89] In addition to courting wider public sentiment through 'advocacy' public diplomacy, it was this elite aspect of American national identity, and its affinity with Benjamin Franklin, to which Earl Grey appealed when he returned the portrait in 1906 in an act of cultural diplomacy.

The appropriation and reimagining of the British and American past in an effort to inject the early twentieth-century rapprochement with shared meaning was characteristic of the Pilgrims Society's methods. As shown by the idealised treatment of the Franklin portrait's provenance, the Pilgrims encouraged the sifting out of unsavoury aspects of the Anglo-American historical memory in order to present a more hopeful vision of its future. This was what Robert Hendershot has described as 'Anglo-American sentimentality', and by which he more specifically means the 'perception of cultural affinity' that was primarily evident 'amongst the Anglo-American foreign policy élite'. As Hendershot also argues in relation to the post-Second World War special relationship, this perception of cultural affinity was often a 'chimera' that obscured the real nature of Anglo-American relations.[90] The Pilgrims and Earl Grey conveniently ignored some recent geopolitical events that presented Britain and the US in a negative light, including the tensions in the North Atlantic triangle relationship relating to the Alaskan boundary and to the fisheries. They also ignored other recent events that jarred with their positive self-perceptions, including the grubby incident at Chumik Shenko in Tibet in March 1904, when British imperial forces on their way to Lhasa massacred 500 Tibetans, and the suppression of the 1906 Zulu rebellion in Natal.[91] This irony was not lost on the *Gaelic American*. In its coverage of the Earl Grey dinner, it explicitly linked the Pilgrims with the worst excesses of British imperialism, though not, it seems, American imperialism. The paper described the London branch of the society as the 'cosmopolitan gamblers who brought on the war for the destruction of the two Boer Republics and the hideous slaughter in Tibet', noting how appropriate it was that Lord Roberts – 'the Butcher of South Africa' – was the branch's president. It also wrote that the 'foreign, colonial and Indian policy, which the Pilgrims represent, and for which they seek American support' was 'revealed by the slaughter in Natal the other day of twelve Kaffirs'.[92] It might also have been pointed out that Adna Chaffee, the US Army General who had played a prominent role in the violent suppression of the Filipino rebellion at the turn of the century, was a founding member of the

US Pilgrims.[93] Clearly this representation of the Pilgrims' imperialism did not chime with the society's own conceptions of the values underpinning the Anglo-American relationship, even if Earl Grey's speech at the Waldorf-Astoria in March 1906 had been thick with imperialist rhetoric. Grey, of course, believed that his imperialism was civilising and democratic. He regarded British and American imperial activity as a benign, freedom-giving, and improving influence upon the world, particularly through the exporting of the apparently unique English propensity for self-government.[94] Some of this was made much more explicit at the London Pilgrims dinner for Lord Curzon the week after the Grey banquet in New York. Curzon used part of his speech in London to articulate the ideas that underpinned his own imperialism, and why he believed these ideas were applicable for the rest of the British Empire and for the US too. He explained that Britain was

> not in India or in any foreign place, any more than the Americans are in the Philippines, for the benefit of what in diplomacy is called your own 'nationals.' You are there for the benefit of the people of the country.[95]

He took the success of the Pilgrims as evidence of the success of Anglo-American imperialism:

> Wherever the unknown lands are waiting to be opened up, wherever the secrets or treasures of the earth are waiting to be wrested from her, wherever peoples are lying in the backwardness of barbarism, wherever new civilizations are capable of being planted or old civilizations of being revived, wherever advance is possible and duty and self-sacrifice call – there is, as there has been for hundreds of years, the true summons of the Anglo-Saxon races. May we hope, in this assemblage of Englishmen and Americans, that neither of the two great branches of the Anglo-Saxon race, now so happily reunited, may ever fall below the dignity of our high calling.[96]

Such imperialistic ideas sat comfortably alongside the Pilgrims' perception of the Anglo-American past, present, and future. Just as Anglo-Saxonist ideas helped justify Britain and the US's imperial duty to school native peoples about self-government, so too did themes of Anglo-American cultural affinity allow the Pilgrims Society to reconcile the turbulent past of the Anglo-American relationship with their hopes for its future.[97] The Pilgrims did all of this by articulating certain political and cultural ideas that they believed connected Britain and the US. As a white, self-governing dominion, Canada was also included.

Importantly, ideas about peace, democracy, liberty, civilisation, and imperialism – each with an Anglo-Saxonist tinge – constituted the 'culture' which characterised the Pilgrims' cultural diplomacy. Canada was indeed a part of this, with Earl Grey telling the Pilgrims that the 'throne which Canada has built for the Goddess of Liberty is not less comfortable than that which the character of your people and your political constitution have built for her in the States'.[98] Ideas about the rule of law contributed to a wider North American identity which focused on the English underpinnings of notions of British justice. This was the case in both the US and Canada, though in the latter country it was manifested not only via ideological and cultural affinities, but also by the extant constitutional connection between Canada and Britain.[99] In a general sense, to groups like the Pilgrims, Anglo-American cultural affinity was enshrined in English-speaking freedoms symbolised largely by institutions and principles such as parliamentary democracy, self-government, the rule of law, Magna Charta, and *habeas corpus*. This was what Elihu Root had meant when he told the Pilgrims that 'the progress, the growth, the glory, of England is at every step a gain to every man who speaks the English tongue, who has formed his character and his customs upon English law and the genius of English institutions'.[100] Indeed, it was precisely for these reasons that Earl Grey and the Pilgrims Society were able to make diplomatic, cultural, and political capital out of returning a portrait of Benjamin Franklin which had been stolen from Franklin's home by the British during the American Revolution. Ideas about the perceived English aptitude for liberal democracy and self-government – which had been spread by the Pilgrim Fathers in the seventeenth century and by the apparently civilising influence of the British Empire ever since – were now extended to include the United States. This Anglo-American cultural connection circumnavigated problematic historical and contemporary realities, including the memory of the Revolution, right up to recent Anglo-American disagreements relating to Canada and Newfoundland, and also some inconvenient truths about British and US imperial activity in Tibet, South Africa, and the

Philippines.[101] Thus the image of Franklin was ironically appropriated as a symbol of Anglo-American rapprochement. It served as a vehicle for Earl Grey and the Pilgrims' cultural diplomacy, which was itself an effort to highlight the underlying comity of British and American democracy and civilisation.

Conclusion

The 1906 dinner for Earl Grey is instructive about the Pilgrims Society on a number of counts. The Benjamin Franklin celebrations in 1906 provided the unofficial, public, and cultural opportunity to appeal to Anglo-American affinity. By gifting the Franklin portrait to the US, and by making the announcement to the Pilgrims, Earl Grey was partaking in what would now be termed public diplomacy. In particular, this was an act of cultural diplomacy. This demonstrated that Grey believed culture could play a role in international relations and that the Pilgrims could support that role. Elites who favoured improved relations between Britain and the US chose to ignore the circumstances under which the Grey family had acquired the painting, and instead used the occasion of the gift to tap into notions of the shared heritage of the 'English-speaking peoples'. With Choate commissioning a copy of the Franklin portrait for Grey, and with the British king receiving an honorary degree from Pennsylvania University as part of Philadelphia's Franklin celebrations, it is clear that Grey's gift was reciprocated.[102] The Pilgrims Society also offered an unofficial locus for the communication of official messages. After the 1906 dinner, for example, press reports highlighted the fact that Root had been speaking with the 'tongue of the President himself'.[103] Impressed with the content of Root's speech, and with its significance, Grey was motivated to attempt to disseminate Root's speech amongst the Canadian newspapers. This is an example of the 'advocacy' stage of public diplomacy. Pilgrims Society functions frequently enjoyed press coverage and provided a high-profile platform for speakers to advocate their position both to the reading public and in a more targeted fashion to influential people among the Society's assembled guests. More than that, however, the exclusivity of the Pilgrims lent legitimacy and prestige to the public utterances of statesmen like Root and Grey. Simultaneously, by such utterances having been made at its functions, the Society was itself further legitimised as a high-status, elite organisation.

The event also demonstrates the extent of the Society's ambition. Through a combination of a favourable diplomatic environment and an increased awareness on the part of statesmen like Root and Grey of the networking and publicity potential of the Society, the Pilgrims were increasingly able to have a direct impact on official and public diplomacy. With Root having drafted proposals for the settlement of Canadian–American differences in May 1906, just over a month after the Pilgrims banquet in March, it is clear that the Pilgrims Society was able to facilitate contact amongst diplomatic elites already predisposed to its message of Anglo-American amity. As such, it had served as a conduit for the agency of official actors, and had acted as a conduit through which its (unofficial) members could influence official diplomatic relations. This contributed to the development of the Society's semi-official status. One obvious example of this was the Society's involvement in the travel arrangements for Grey's trip to the White House to meet Theodore Roosevelt. More significantly, however, the Pilgrims had provided an opportunity for a meeting between Grey and Root. This much was noted by the press, for example when the *Boston Evening Transcript* wrote that 'a mutual regard' between Grey and Root had resulted from the Pilgrims dinner. The good feeling elicited by the Pilgrims event was 'expected to go far toward smoothing the way to the settlement of all frictional points between the two countries'. The Pilgrims Society was evidently considered to have facilitated official diplomatic contact.[104] It is clear that the speeches at the 1906 dinner were well received in Britain – including by the former Foreign Secretary Lord Lansdowne – and that the Franklin portrait enjoyed widespread press coverage in the US. As such, this act of public diplomacy succeeded in reaching out to wider publics. For one, the vehemence of the attacks on Grey and the Pilgrims from the Irish-American press suggests that the opponents of Anglo-American friendship felt that the Society's activities were both significant and successful. Meanwhile, George T. Wilson believed that the Grey dinner was 'the most successful function in the history of the American Pilgrims'.[105]

The Pilgrims Society had proven that it was more than just a banqueting club. The elite associational culture of which it was a key part facilitated diplomatic contact and networking, and provided a conduit for public diplomacy. Grey's Franklin portrait was a private act with a public and official motivation. In the person of Lord Elgin, the Colonial Secretary, it also had wider official support. This was not the sort of official sponsorship and funding enjoyed by public diplomatists in the 1930s and 1940s, but the Pilgrims' activities in this earlier period demonstrate both the nineteenth-century roots of its largely private activism and an increasing understanding amongst some diplomats and statesmen at the start of the twentieth century, like Earl Grey, that an engagement with public opinion was potentially useful in international relations. Grey evidently saw a semi-official use for the ostensibly private Pilgrims Society. As a result, the Pilgrims Society had contributed to the circumstances that allowed Ambassador Durand to report at the end of 1906 that the 'old enmity is dead, and the Americans would not be easily stirred up against us as in former times'.[106] While ill-feeling and diplomatic disagreements between the two countries were by no means extinguished in 1906, it is true that the later 1900s witnessed an improved relationship compared with the earlier period. Accordingly, the next major developments in Anglo-American relations, and the Pilgrims Society's next noteworthy public diplomacy interventions, would come with the First World War.

Notes

1. Nicholas, *The United States and Britain*, p. 58; Tony McCulloch, 'The North Atlantic Triangle: A Canadian Myth?', *International Journal*, Vol. 66, Issue 1 (Winter 2010–11), p. 200; John Bartlet Brebner, *North Atlantic Triangle: The Interplay of Canada, the United States and Great Britain* (New Haven, 1945); David G. Haglund, 'Brebner's *North Atlantic Triangle* at Sixty: A Retrospective Look at a Retrospective Book', *The London Journal of Canadian Studies*, Vol. 20 (2004–5), p. 124; this triangle was also an economic one of 'buying and selling, investing and dividend-paying, migration and production. See Brebner, *North Atlantic Triangle*, p. 225, and p. 192 for the 1871 treaty and the fisheries; Burk, *Old World, New World*, p. 257 and p. 274.
2. Sir Mortimer Durand to Sir Edward Grey, 22 January 1906, TNA, FO371/158/203.
3. Adams, *Brothers Across the Ocean*, pp. 123–34; Peter Neary, 'Grey, Bryce, and the Settlement of Canadian–American Differences, 1905–1911', *The Canadian Historical Review*, Vol. XLIX,

No. 4 (1968), p. 358; the French claim to access to the waters was settled in 1904, an agreement that paved the way for the Entente Cordiale between Britain and France. See Burk, *Old World, New World*, p. 432; the Canadian and Newfoundland aspects of the North Atlantic fisheries dispute could not be solved separately. See Alvin C. Gluek, 'Pilgrimages to Ottawa: Canadian–American Diplomacy, 1903–13', Canadian Historical Association, *Historical Papers* (1968), p. 73.

4. Adams, *Brothers Across the Ocean*, pp. 123–50; for Root's biography, see Warren Zimmermann, *First Great Triumph: How Five Americans Made Their Country a World Power* (New York, 2004), pp. 123–48; as Secretary of War and as Secretary of State, Root was responsible for far-reaching modernisation reforms to the government departments under his charge. See Herring, *From Colony to Superpower*, pp. 348–50.

5. Neary, 'Canadian–American Differences', pp. 365–6; Adams, *Brothers Across the Ocean*, p. 149.

6. Elihu Root to Durand, 3 May 1906, Office of the Governor General of Canada Mss, Library and Archives Canada [LAC], RG7, 98 192F pt.1c; Gluek, 'Pilgrimages to Ottawa', p. 73; Neary, 'Canadian–American Differences', p. 358 and pp. 362–3; Tilchin, *Roosevelt and the British Empire*, p. 55; *The Times*, 14 July 1898; Baker, *Pilgrims of Britain*, p. 178.

7. John Herd Thompson, 'Canada and the "Third British Empire", 1901–1939', in Philip Buckner (ed.), *Canada and the British Empire* (Oxford, 2010), p. 93.

8. Durand to Sir Edward Grey, 31 August 1906, TNA, FO371/158/327; Gluek, 'Pilgrimages to Ottawa', p. 72.

9. Gluek, 'Pilgrimages to Ottawa', pp. 65–83.

10. Durand to Grey, 28 February 1906, Governor General Mss, LAC, R977-1312-2E; Grey to Durand, 19 February 1906, Grey Papers, DU, File 247/4; Gluek, 'Pilgrimages to Ottawa', pp. 74–5.

11. Grey to Elgin, 9 March 1906, Governor General Mss, LAC, R977-1312-2-E.

12. 'The Pilgrims List of Members and Bye-Laws', 1909, Brittain Papers, BLPES, Box 5; *New York Times*, 6 December 1912.

13. Earl Grey to the Earl of Elgin, Colonial Office, 8 February 1906, TNA, FO371/158; it has not been possible to uncover primary source material in FRUS relating to the Earl Grey dinner.

14. Colonial Office Minutes, 15 February 1906, TNA, FO371/158/635.

15. Gluek, 'Pilgrimages to Ottawa', pp. 74–5.

16. Lawrence Martin, *The Presidents and the Prime Ministers: Washington and Ottawa Face to Face – The Myth of Bilateral Bliss, 1867–1982* (Toronto, 1982), pp. 64–5.

17. Laurier's approach to Canadian–British and Canadian–American relations was a complex one. Up until 1908, he had taken a lenient approach to the US's gradual infringing of the 1817 Rush–Bagot agreement, an agreement regarding the number and size of naval ships on the Great Lakes. Likewise, for all his unhappiness with the US in the aftermath of Alaska, Laurier would later support a form of Canadian–US trade reciprocity. Indeed, it was partly this issue that ensured his defeat during the election of 1911, when Robert Borden replaced him as prime minister following a campaign which portrayed Laurier as anti-British and pro-American. See Gluek, 'The Invisible Revision of the Rush–Bagot Agreement, 1898–1914', *Canadian Historical Review*, Vol. 60, Issue 4 (1979), p. 474–82; Thompson, 'Canada and the "Third British Empire"', p. 94.

18. The Waldorf-Astoria Archive, <http://www.waldorfarchive.org/> (last accessed 9 May 2014). See also Waldorf-Astoria website and history page, <http://www.waldorfnewyork.com/about-the-waldorf/hotel-history.html> (last accessed 9 May 2014). See also Homberger, Mrs. Astor's New York, p. 65.

19. Baker, *Pilgrims of the US*, p. 79 and p. 86; *New York Times*, 2 May 1929; 'The Pilgrims List of Members and Bye-Laws', 1909, Brittain Papers, BLPES, Box 5; as an interesting aside, the American Pilgrims donated $500 to the New York Mayor's *Titanic* relief fund and £100 to the London Mayor's fund and joined 'hands and hearts in sincerest Anglo-American sympathy over the great tragedy of the sea'. See Minute Book 2, 25 April 1912, Pilgrims Mss, NYC.

20. Paul Groth, *The History of Residential Hotels in the United States* (Berkeley, 1994), p. 37.

21. Joseph Choate to Grey, 6 March 1906, Governor General Mss, LAC, R977-1311-0-E.

22. Minute Book 1, 5 March 1906, Pilgrims Mss, NYC; *Washington Post*, 1 April 1906.

23. 'Dinner Given by the Pilgrims of the United States to His Excellency the Right Honorable Earl Grey', 31 March 1906, TNA, FO371/158; *Washington Post*, 2 June 1906.

24. *Washington Post, Boston Daily Globe, New York Times*, 1 April 1906; *Review of Reviews*, 1 September 1906.

25. Temperley, *Britain and America*, p. 80; Adams, *Brothers Across the Ocean*, p. 136; in any case, Newfoundland was regarded by both the British and the Canadians as a colony of lesser importance, compared with Canada. See James K. Hiller, 'Status Without Stature: Newfoundland, 1869–1949', in Buckner (ed.), *Canada and the British Empire*, pp. 127–39; for Grey's criticisms of Newfoundland's approach, which he felt stood in contrast to Canada's conciliatory attitude, see Grey to Durand, 27 December 1906, Grey Papers, DU, File 247/8.

26. 'Dinner Given by the Pilgrims of the United States to His Excellency the Right Honorable Earl Grey', 31 March 1906, TNA, FO371/158.
27. *The Evening Statesman* (Walla Walla, Washington), 31 March 1906.
28. 'Dinner Given by the Pilgrims of the United States to His Excellency the Right Honorable Earl Grey', 31 March 1906, TNA, FO371/158.
29. 'Dinner Given by the Pilgrims of the United States to His Excellency the Right Honorable Earl Grey', 31 March 1906, and *New York Times*, 1 April 1906, within TNA, FO371/158; it is not apparent who highlighted the Grey speech, or in which government department this was done. The primary source document has simply been marked up in blue pencil without any additional information as to why this was done, or whom it was done for.
30. 'Dinner Given by the Pilgrims of the United States to His Excellency the Right Honorable Earl Grey', 31 March 1906, TNA, FO371/158; between 1904 and 1905 Root had negotiated arbitration treaties – albeit of limited scope – with each of the European powers, and also with Japan. Anglo-American arbitration, for instance regarding Alaska, was therefore part of a wider international trend during the 1900s. See Herring, *From Colony to Superpower*, p. 358.
31. 'Dinner Given by the Pilgrims of the United States to His Excellency the Right Honorable Earl Grey', 31 March 1906, TNA, FO371/158.
32. Ibid.
33. Durand to Sir Edward Grey, 9 March 1906, TNA, FO371/158/650.
34. *New York Times*, 1 April 1906; *Washington Post*, 8 April 1906; *Pall Mall Gazette*, 2 April 1906.
35. *The Times*, 2 April 1906.
36. 'Dinner Given by the Pilgrims of the United States to His Excellency the Right Honorable Earl Grey', 31 March 1906, TNA, FO371/158.
37. Ibid.
38. Ibid.
39. Sir Percy Sanderson to Durand, 2 April 1906, TNA, FO371/158/644.
40. Lansdowne to Earl Grey, 30 April 1906, Grey Papers, DU, File 207/4.
41. *The Globe* and the *Mail and Empire*, 29 and 21 June 1906; Gluek, 'The Rush–Bagot Agreement', p. 478.
42. *Gaelic American*, 7 April 1906; *Gaelic American*, Chronicling America, Library of Congress, <http://chroniclingamerica.loc.gov/lccn/sn83045246/> (last accessed 14 May 2014).
43. For O'Reilly's obituary, see *Washington Post*, 3 August 1942.
44. F. S. L. Lyons, 'The Revolution in Train, 1914–1916', in Vaughan (ed.), *A New History of Ireland*, p. 191; R. V. Comerford, 'Isaac Butt and the Home Rule Party, 1870–77', in Vaughan (ed.), *A New History of Ireland*, p. 22.

45. Institute for the Study of Globalization and Covert Politics, 'The Pilgrims Society: A Study of the Anglo-American Establishment', <http://wikispooks.com/ISGP/organisations/Pilgrims_Society02. htm> (last accessed 14 May 2014).

46. 'House of Rothschild Controls Our Lives', <http://www.realjew-news.com/?p=14> (last accessed 14 May 2014); 'The Pilgrims List of Members and Bye-Laws', 1909, Brittain Papers, BLPES, Box 5.

47. Hobsbawm, *The Age of Extremes: The Short Twentieth Century 1914–1991* (London, 1994), p. 119.

48. Wilson to Brittain, 2 April 1906, Pilgrims Mss, LMA/4632/ A/05/002/01; Grey had travelled into the US on the Montreal Express, to which his private railway carriage, *Victoria*, had been attached. While in New York, Earl Grey and his wife stayed with Joseph Choate at his home on East Sixty-Third Street. See *Washington Post*, 31 March 1906; Pilgrims accommodated visiting guests in their homes on other occasions, as shown by a note in the London branch's minutes in 1929 to the effect that the 'Honorary Secretary [John Wilson Taylor] has also privately entertained visiting Americans associated with the Pilgrims of the United States'. See Minutes, 22 July 1929, Pilgrims Mss, LMA/4632/ A/01/001.

49. Grey to Theodore Roosevelt, 10 April 1906, Grey Papers, DU, File 247/5; Grey to Lord Elgin, 5 April 1906, Governor General Mss, LAC, R977-10-3-E.

50. Grey to Roosevelt, 10 April 1906, Grey Papers, DU, File 247/5.

51. 'Dinner Given by the Pilgrims of the United States to His Excellency the Right Honorable Earl Grey', 31 March 1906, TNA, FO371/158; Durand to Sir Edward Grey, 9 March 1906, TNA, FO371/158/650.

52. Grey to Elgin, 5 April 1906, Governor General Mss, LAC, R977-10-3-E; Root to Durand, 3 May 1906, Governor General Mss, LAC, RG7, 98 192F pt.1c; Gluek, 'Pilgrimages to Ottawa', pp. 75–7; Neary, 'Canadian–American Differences', p. 358.

53. Gluek, 'Pilgrimages to Ottawa', p. 77.

54. Neary, 'Canadian–American Differences', p. 363; *Chicago Daily Tribune*, 20 January 1907; *New York Times*, 22 January 1907; Gluek, 'Pilgrimages to Ottawa', p. 77.

55. Edward Grey to Grey, 12 January 1907, Grey Papers, DU, File 247/9.

56. *Boston Evening Transcript*, 18 January 1907.

57. Grey to Elgin, 3 April 1906, Governor General Mss, LAC, R977-1318-3-E.

58. Grey to Elgin, 26 October 1906, Grey Papers, DU, File 247/7.

59. Grey to Esmé Howard, 12 January 1907, Grey Papers, DU, File 247/8.

60. Grey to Durand, 27 December 1906, and Grey to Howard, 12 January 1907, Grey Papers, DU, File 247/8; such an attitude towards Newfoundland's actions during the fisheries dispute, combined with perceptions of its relative insignificance, may partly explain why the Pilgrims dinner did not especially address the Newfoundland aspect of relations between the US and British North America.
61. Hay to Wilson, 5 April 1906, Pilgrims Mss, LMA/4632/C/05/034.
62. Root to Grey, 29 April 1906, Grey Papers, DU, File 247/5.
63. Cull, *American Propaganda and Public Diplomacy*, p. xv.
64. Grey to Root, 19 April 1906, Grey Papers, DU, File 247/5; Grey to Root, 5 June 1906, and Root to Grey, 2 June 1906, Grey Papers, DU, File 247/6.
65. Grey to Elgin, 5 June 1906, Governor General Mss, LAC, R977-1325-0-E.
66. *Daily Herald* (Calgary), 18 April 1906. See the Alberta Heritage Digitization Project, <http://www.ourfutureourpast.ca/newspapr/brwsindx.asp?code=n1x> (last accessed 16 May 2014).
67. Geppert, 'The Public Challenge to Diplomacy', pp. 133–8; Herring, *From Colony to Superpower*, p. 311.
68. Elgin to Grey, 22 March 1906, Governor General Mss, LAC, R977-1314-6-E.
69. Wilson to Brittain, 2 April 1906, Pilgrims Mss, LMA/4632/A/05/002/01.
70. Grey to Mr Mansfield, 8 February 1906, Grey Papers, DU, File 285/3; 'Dinner Given by the Pilgrims of the United States to His Excellency the Right Honorable Earl Grey', 31 March 1906, TNA, FO371/158; the portrait was painted in 1759 by the artist Benjamin Wilson (b.1731–d.1788). See Charles Henry Hart, 'The Wilson Portrait of Franklin: Earl Grey's Gift to the Nation', *The Pennsylvania Magazine of History and Biography*, Vol. 30, No. 4 (1906), pp. 409–16.
71. Francis Rawle to Grey, 14 December 1905, and Grey to Rawle, 20 December 1905, Grey Papers, DU, File 278/7.
72. Clipping from an unknown newspaper, 21 April 1906, Grey Papers, DU, File 278/7.
73. Grey to Roosevelt, 7 February 1906, Grey Papers, DU, File 278/7.
74. Clipping from an unknown newspaper, 21 April 1906, Grey Papers, DU, File 278/7; Nancy Cervetti, *S. Weir Mitchell, 1829–1914: Philadelphia's Literary Physician* (University Park, 2012), p. 3.
75. Choate to Grey, 6 March 1906, Governor General Mss, LAC, R977-1311-0-E.
76. Roosevelt to Grey, 12 February 1906, Grey Papers, DU, File 278/7; 'Portrait of Benjamin Franklin (Wilson-White House), 1759', <http://www.benfranklin300.org> (last accessed 19 July 2013);

Harvey Rachlin, *Scandals, Vandals and da Vincis: A Gallery of Remarkable Art Tales* (London, 2007), p. 78.

77. *New York Times*, 16 April 1906.
78. *Washington Post*, 16 April 1906.
79. *Gaelic American*, 7 April 1906.
80. *Pall Mall Gazette*, 2 April 1906.
81. *Buffalo Commercial*, 5 April 1906.
82. *Philadelphia Inquirer*, 17 April 1906.
83. *Knoxville Sentinel*, 4 April 1906; *Telegraph* (Macon, GA), 5 April 1906.
84. *New-York Tribune*, 3 April 1906.
85. *The Sun* (New York), 4 April 1906.
86. *New-York Tribune*, 3 April 1906.
87. Carla Mulford, 'Figuring Benjamin Franklin in American Cultural Memory', *The New England Quarterly*, Vol. 72, No. 3 (September 1999), p. 435; Merrill D. Peterson, *The Jefferson Image in the American Mind* (Charlottesville, 1998).
88. Mulford, 'Figuring Benjamin Franklin', pp. 437–41.
89. Frank Strong, *Benjamin Franklin: A Character Sketch* (New York, 1898), p. 5 and p. 111; Mulford, 'Figuring Benjamin Franklin', p. 435.
90. Hendershot, 'Cultural Sinews', p. 52 and pp. 55–6.
91. Charles Allen, 'The Myth of Chumik Shenko', *History Today*, Vol. 54, Issue 4 (2004), pp. 10–17; Denis Judd, *Empire: The British Imperial Experience, from 1765 to the Present* (London, 1997), p. 239.
92. *Gaelic American*, 7 April 1906.
93. Indeed, the *Gaelic American* could also have recalled that in 1902 Elihu Root, then Secretary of War, had been heavily criticised by American anti-imperialists for wilfully ignoring evidence of American atrocities in the Philippines. See Michael Patrick Cullinane, *Liberty and American Anti-Imperialism, 1898–1909* (London, 2012), pp. 120–1 and pp. 141–5; Baker, *Pilgrims of the US*, p. 154.
94. Jack P. Greene, 'Introduction: Empire and Liberty', in Greene (ed.), *Exclusionary Empire: English Liberty Overseas, 1600–1900* (Cambridge, 2010), pp. 23–4; for Greene, British liberty was 'exclusionary' because, for much of the eighteenth and nineteenth centuries, political and civic participation was restricted to a property-owning elite both in Britain and in the Empire, and because self-government was denied to large swathes of the imperial and colonial population. This also speaks to the tension inherent in Earl Grey's perception of Britain's civilising mission and the violent reality of the Tibetan example.
95. *The Times*, 7 April 1906.
96. Ibid.

97. Kramer, 'Empires, Exceptions and Anglo-Saxons', pp. 1315–53; Kramer, 'Race, Empire, and Transnational History', in Alfred W. McCoy and Francisco A. Scarano (eds), *Colonial Crucible: Empire in the Making of the Modern American State* (Madison, 2009), p. 204.

98. 'Dinner Given by the Pilgrims of the United States to His Excellency the Right Honorable Earl Grey', 31 March 1906, TNA, FO371/158.

99. Philip Girard, 'British Justice, English Law, and Canadian Legal Culture', in Buckner (ed.), *Canada and the British Empire*, pp. 259–77.

100. Ibid. pp. 259–77.

101. Greene, 'Introduction: Empire and Liberty', p. 23.

102. *New York Times*, 19 May 1906; Sir Mortimer Durand to Sir Edward Grey, Despatch No. 74, 30 April 1906, TNA, FO371/159.

103. *The Times*, 2 April 1906.

104. *Boston Evening Transcript*, 18 January 1907.

105. Wilson to Brittain, 16 January 1907, Pilgrims Mss, LMA/4632/A/05/002/01.

106. 'Report on the United States of America for the Year 1906', Durand to Sir Edward Grey, 28 December 1906, TNA, FO881/8834.

4 The Pilgrims and the First World War

> ... I have now seen the US come into the war, having done all the little that I could do to bring that about; and I have seen the welcome and done all that I could to take advantage of it for the complete understanding of the two peoples . . .
> (Walter Hines Page)

On the night of 20 July 1917, thousands of miles from the mud- and blood-splattered reality of war on the Western Front, over 11,000 people crammed into New York's Madison Square Gardens for a rally to encourage Americans, and Britons living in the US, to enlist for military service. Three months after American entry into the war, and with conscription having already been introduced in Britain and the US, the British Recruiting Mission and the Mayor's Committee on National Defense used the Madison Square Garden event to tap into feelings of English-speaking patriotism. With British, Scottish, Canadian, and American flags flying, the 236th Battalion of the Canadian Expeditionary Force marched around the hall accompanied by a pipe band. The Marine Band of the Brooklyn Navy Yard also performed, and the American singer Sophie Braslau urged everyone to 'Pack Up Your Troubles in Your Old Kit Bag'.[1] Representatives of the Pilgrims Society were amongst the attendees, with the Society having paid $25 for tickets to listen to two of their own – Lord Northcliffe and James Beck – address the audience.[2]

Northcliffe was in the US between May and November 1917 as head of the official British War Mission, in which capacity he toured various cities in an effort to improve political, military, and economic cooperation between Britain and the US.[3] Beck – a conservative Republican who went on to become President Warren Harding's solicitor general – also had experience of undertaking international tours in support of the war effort. Unlike Northcliffe's official visit to the US in 1917, however, Beck's trip had been a semi-official one coordinated by the Pilgrims Society. He was a long-standing supporter of the Pilgrims and an Anglophile who in 1914 had published *The Evidence in the Case*, a book outlining his interpretation of why Germany was to blame for starting the world war. In 1916 he visited Britain as part of a speaking tour in an attempt to ease tensions surrounding the US's continued neutrality. This followed on from a tour of the US that Harry Brittain had made in 1915. Utilising the Pilgrims' unofficial networks and reporting back to the British ambassador, Cecil Spring-Rice, and to officials at the Royal Colonial Institute, Brittain travelled across the US – from the East Coast all the way to Los Angeles – measuring the extent of German propaganda in the US.[4] The Pilgrims' presence at Madison Square Garden in 1917, together with the Beck and Brittain trips in 1915 and 1916, demonstrates that the Society was not a passive observer of the First World War.

The Beck and Brittain trips – which have been covered extensively elsewhere – show that the Pilgrims Society actively pursued a public diplomacy programme during the early years of the war. This was even more the case later in the conflict. As this chapter will show, the Society operated with varying levels of complicity with the state, resulting in its public diplomacy role taking on what would now be regarded as a propagandistic complexion. Indeed, the First World War contributed to the process of 'propaganda' becoming a pejorative term associated with subversive and covert influences. In the view of some isolationist Americans in the 1920s, such influences included the Pilgrims Society. The increasingly negative perception of the term 'propaganda' meant that it later had to be replaced in official discourses by the term 'public diplomacy'.[5] In truth, it remains difficult even today to differentiate between 'public diplomacy' and 'propaganda'. The Pilgrims, however, did not use the former term, while some amongst the Society were comfortable with the latter.[6] It is, moreover, partly because of the merging of state–private interests in support of Allied and US war aims after April 1917 that comparisons can be drawn between the Pilgrims' activities in this period and the development of state-sponsored cultural diplomacy programmes from the 1930s onwards. The nineteenth-century roots of the Pilgrims' earlier form of public diplomacy were still evident in the First

World War, but now the Society's activities meshed more closely than ever before with the interests of the state. The Pilgrims was not the British Council of the 1930s, nor was it the United States Information Agency of the 1960s. Yet neither was its activity the same as the public diplomacy of nineteenth-century world's fairs and expositions.

This chapter has three sections. The first section details the Pilgrims' experience of the war up until the end of US neutrality in April 1917 and will establish the context for the Society's activities thereafter. As the chapter's second section shows, the Society's network was utilised in the services of the National War Aims Committee and in the creation of the American Officers' Club in London. Both of these ventures relied on cooperation with officialdom. The contention here is that the First World War offered a new opportunity for the Pilgrims Society to pursue, and to implement, its agenda of Anglo-American friendship. The chapter's third section will show that this continued in the immediate aftermath of the conflict through the heavy involvement of the Society's network in the US's coordinated public celebration of Anglo-American wartime cooperation on Britain's Day in December 1918.

The Pilgrims and the end of US neutrality

While the Pilgrims Society had a role to play in helping to address transatlantic misunderstandings regarding US neutrality, the New York branch was itself placed in a difficult position by Woodrow Wilson's announcement upon the commencement of hostilities in Europe in 1914 that Americans – many of whom, not least the Anglo-Saxonist Pilgrims, shared cultural, ethnic, and political affinities with the warring nations – should remain 'neutral in thought as well as in action'.[7] George Wilson wrote to Harry Brittain that the New York committee, with one unnamed exception, was 'heart and soul with the Mother Country'. Wilson himself said that he was 'entirely in consonance with the idea that it is indeed a war of Liberty, and I hope with all my heart that the Dove of Peace will soon prevail over the Prussian Eagle of destruction. That's my vintage of "neutrality".' Nevertheless, the US Pilgrims did not immediately agree upon the 'advisability of an official expression of sympathy' for Britain and its allies, according to Wilson because of a 'desire to obey the injunction of the President to maintain strict neutrality in word and deed'.[8] Whether or not to officially support Britain was a matter of some debate for the Society, with other members feeling that 'some expression' by what was an 'Anglo-American Society organized for the purpose of promoting Anglo-American friendship ... would be most appropriate and could not be misinterpreted'. As a result, a sub-committee was appointed in November 1914 to write a draft resolution.[9] The resolution that was ultimately sent to the London Pilgrims combined a restrained message of support for Britain's war effort with words of condolence for the death of Lord Roberts, the president of the London branch who had died of pneumonia that month while in France in his capacity as colonel-in-chief of the empire forces.[10]

It is self-evident that the Society was predisposed to supporting the British war effort even though some in the New York branch felt unable to make that support entirely explicit. The need for tactfully worded resolutions like the one quoted above was, however, removed once the US entered the war in April 1917. In the first few months of 1917 it became increasingly difficult for Woodrow Wilson to keep the US out of the war in Europe. German submarine attacks on American shipping continued, while the British had intercepted the explosive Zimmerman Telegram in February.[11] It was for these reasons that George Wilson wrote to Brittain at the end of March exclaiming that '[t]hings are moving – aint they?' He described a Union League Club (ULC) meeting he had recently attended at which were adopted a number of resolutions arguing that the US and Germany were practically at war and calling for the US government to act accordingly. Wilson had been on the 'Committee on Immediate Defense and National Security' which had presented these resolutions to the ULC meeting and which was backed by prominent Republicans like Theodore Roosevelt, Elihu Root, Joseph Choate, and Charles E. Hughes. The Pilgrims chairman was then appointed to a special committee established to communicate these resolutions to the White House. Also at the ULC meeting, Roosevelt had, according to Wilson, 'thundered out with all the earnestness of his nature' his idea of 'sending an expeditionary force over, so that the Stars and Stripes will mingle with the Union Jack and Tri-Color on the battle plains of France'.[12] Roosevelt wanted to raise a volunteer force similar to his Spanish-American War 'Rough Riders' and was in the process of outlining how his scheme would work. Roosevelt approached the president with his plans after the US entered the conflict, but was prevented by Woodrow Wilson from implementing them. The two remained political rivals and the Democratic president was concerned that the glory accruing to Roosevelt by active involvement in the fighting would provide the Republicans with political capital. Notwithstanding the political considerations, there was a real concern that Roosevelt's amateur army would only get in the way of the professional forces. With this in mind, 57-year-old insurance broker George Wilson's contention that 'I'd like to go with him!' was surely rhetorical.[13]

After US entry into the war in April, meanwhile, Cecil Spring-Rice wrote of how struck he was at 'how small the visible effect of war is'. He noted that it was possible to travel long distances in a railway carriage and not hear any passengers talk of the war, while the 'luxury of hotels, the number of automobiles' and 'the extravagance of dress have not diminished'.[14] The US's physical distance from the conflict meant that the American population's experience differed from that of the European peoples, for whom the war effort had greater immediacy. It took a great degree of governmental intervention to mobilise the US's people and economy for war, for example through the introduction of conscription (and the concomitant challenges of quickly training and transporting the soldiers: by the end of the year only 175,000 soldiers had arrived in France, a contrast with the 2 million that had arrived by the end of the war), federal control of the railways and, of course, the use of propaganda.[15] The war visited the Pilgrims in a number of ways too; trivially in January 1918, when the New York branch resolved 'that no champagne should be served by the Society at any functions during the remainder of the War', and more seriously in March when some of George Wilson's paperwork and correspondence was stolen by a German agent who was working in his office as a clerk. It had become apparent to Wilson that – since the arrival into the US in April 1917 of Arthur Balfour's official British War Mission, the precursor to Lord Northcliffe's – Harry Brittain and others in Europe were not receiving his letters. Wilson explained to Brittain that his 'desk had been ransacked in my various absences, and the carbon copies of letters filched therefrom'. He felt that this was unusual, as his correspondence apparently 'contained nothing that would have been of benefit to the enemy'. Wilson had nevertheless informed the authorities, who – as he told Brittain – had asked him 'not to speak of the affair' to anyone.[16] Even though Wilson was surprised that he was targeted by the Germans, it is not difficult to see why they had taken an interest in his correspondence. Wilson was a well-known member of the city's foremost British–American association. Indeed, had their agent acted two years previously, the Germans would have discovered that Wilson was indeed in favour of Britain's war effort when the US was still neutral, and that he had worked with figures in Britain to organise James Beck's visit to Europe. As Wilson's office clerk clearly suspected, and as the remainder of this chapter will show, the Pilgrims continued to play an active role in the First World War after the US entered the conflict.

US entry into the First World War was a signal event for the Pilgrims Society. Though the US had declined to enter a formal alliance with Britain and France and was instead an 'associated power', the events of April 1917 provided vindication for the Pilgrims of the work it had been undertaking since the Society's founding in 1902. More than that, US belligerence was regarded as representing a measurable outcome of the Society's efforts. So much so, an internal memorandum from the London Society's business secretary, Mrs Welsh-Lee, said that with 'the entry of the United States into the war, Part 1 of the history of the Pilgrims was brought to a successful conclusion'.[17] It was proof, in Harry Brittain's words, that 'since the famous gathering at Ghent a hundred years ago, we have been engaged in writing out a preface to the story of the English-speaking world'. Calling upon his characteristic flair for expression and hyperbole, Brittain wrote that US entry into the First World War 'turned a life's dream into an assured reality, a reality the stupendous size of which one barely grasps in outline through the mists of kaleidoscopic days'.[18] Two days after Woodrow Wilson's war address to Congress, Brittain telegraphed the New York Pilgrims on behalf of the British branch in 'grateful recognition of [the] services to our common humanity and our love [of] freedom so splendidly asserted by Choate and [the] Pilgrims [of the] United States'. Brittain said that the British Pilgrims perceived a 'dawning of [a] new day not merely in Anglo American relations but in human history' and that they believed that the Monroe Doctrine was safeguarded, as a result of which so was the 'liberty and security

[of] all peoples great and small'. Paraphrasing 'The Battle Hymn of the Republic', Brittain said that 'as Christ died to make men holy let us die to make men free'. 'It is in that spirit we welcome our new and splendid Ally in the sternest of all struggles for the freedom of the world.'[19] Joseph Choate reciprocated on behalf of the US Pilgrims a few days later with the message that the US was going to war in defence of 'the highest ideals of English and American liberty'.[20] Then, on 12 April, the Pilgrims hosted a dinner for Walter Hines Page at the Savoy in London, at which the US ambassador described Anglo-American wartime cooperation as the 'supreme political event of all history'. According to the *New York Times*, the banquet was marked for its 'profusion of flags and cheering such as dignified assemblages in Great Britain rarely indulge in'. Earlier in the day, the American Luncheon Club had held another event at the Savoy to celebrate the US's entry into the war. Page also attended this as the guest of honour, as did the Prime Minister David Lloyd George.[21] US entry into the war was a truly momentous development, not just for the significant military advantage that it undoubtedly gave the Allies, but also because it seemed to have realised the aims of the Pilgrims Society and the other associations that been formed around the turn of the century to promote Anglo-American rapprochement.[22] Indeed, some of these other societies – including the American Society – joined with the Pilgrims in marking the occasion, for instance at a service at St Paul's Cathedral on 20 April. The British king and queen attended, as did Page, while representatives from the Pilgrims Society, the American Society, and the American Luncheon Club sat alongside US Embassy and consular staff. American members of the Atlantic Union had also been encouraged to attend what was a ticketed event organised 'under the auspices of the American Embassy and Consulate-General and all the American organizations in London'.[23]

Even though Britain and the US were by no means irrevocably set on the path towards the 'special relationship' of the later twentieth century, US entry into the war represented a watershed in Anglo-American relations. Not only was the US participating in a European conflict, itself an important departure from the traditional ideal of exceptionalism, but it was doing so on the side of its traditional enemy; a country with whom official relations had remained problematic right up until Woodrow Wilson's decision to enter the conflict.

The idea that the aims of the proponents of Anglo-American amity had been accomplished with the US entry into the war was also articulated by Ambassador Page. Five months after the US entered the First World War, Page – who has been described by one writer as 'extravagantly pro-British'– wrote an entry in his personal diary which reflects many of the characteristics of the Anglo-American wartime relationship from the perspective of a man tapped into its official and unofficial elements:

> I cannot keep from wondering now whether my job here may not already have been done. I kept the sea as smooth as possible during the dangerous days of neutrality (and what anxious times did come then!); and I have now seen the US come into the war, having done all the little that I could do to bring that about; and I have seen the welcome and done all that I could to take advantage of it for the complete understanding of the two peoples.[24]

Page's remarks also speak to another aspect of the Pilgrims' approach to the First World War, namely the efforts of people like Harry Brittain to utilise US belligerence in an effort to promote their ideas of Anglo-American friendship. As will be argued in the next section of the chapter, US involvement in the First World War ensured that the Pilgrims Society, its ideas, and its networks became yet more relevant to the Anglo-American relationship.

The Pilgrims, the NWAC, and the American Officers' Club

In the first two years of the war it had been more important for Britain to push the agenda of Anglo-American friendship than it was for the US. Britain had an urgent wartime need for American financial aid and, eventually, for military support. Then by 1917, the British government needed to address a rising feeling of war-weariness amongst its people. In relation to public morale in particular, and with American support for the Allies now a tangible reality, the US and ideas about Anglo-American amity were used in the British domestic context more explicitly than ever before. Equally, the US's status as an 'associated power' – while unimportant to the Pilgrims – meant that Britain and the US were perhaps not as close as they might have been had they officially become allies. As such, there was still public diplomacy work for the Pilgrims Society to do in support of Anglo-American friendship. This section looks at some examples of this work.

Harry Brittain remained the most prominent, influential, and proactive member of the Pilgrims Society during the First World War. This means that a consideration of his wartime activities sheds light on those of the Society. The London Pilgrims' chairman occupied three principal roles in relation to the war from 1917 until the end of the conflict. He was a committee member of the newly formed domestic propaganda organisation, the National War Aims Committee (NWAC); he served a spell as Director of Intelligence for Neville Chamberlain's National Service Department; then, under the auspices of the Pilgrims Society, he formed the American Officers' Club in London. His time in the National Service Department was relatively short, similar in that respect to Chamberlain's brief tenure as the Department's Director-General. The Department had been established in December 1916 in an effort to oversee the efficient organisation and distribution of the country's resources, but Chamberlain resigned in August 1917. Brittain appears to have left the Department at the same time as Chamberlain, perhaps out of loyalty to a man whose family he had known since Joseph Chamberlain's tariff reform campaign at the turn of the century.[25] His job as Director of Intelligence principally involved dealing with the press and was essentially a propaganda role. This was something in which he had expertise, not only through his organisation of the Imperial Press Conference in 1909, but also earlier in the war when he had opened his London home to American journalists as the 'common meeting-place for the scribes and men prominent in British political life'. 'Over social tea the chroniclers of British life for American publications' met with elites such as Arthur Balfour, Earl Grey, and Andrew Bonar Law.[26] This technique of meeting socially with journalists continued in his work with the National Service Department, with a memorandum written in March 1917 for the British Cabinet explaining that a number of 'Leading Newspaper Proprietors and Editors' had recently been 'entertained to lunch' by Harry Brittain. This was an event that was 'expected' to 'result in a more friendly tone in the Press' towards the Department.[27] Indeed, Chamberlain later thanked Brittain for having agreed to join the Department 'at a time when we had many difficulties with the press . . . But your tact and your wide circle of acquaintances among journalists of all descriptions enabled you to put things right in a wonderfully short time.'[28]

The American Officers' Club, meanwhile, was founded in the autumn of 1917. Located within the salubrious Mayfair townhouse of Lord Leconfield, the Club was set up by Harry Brittain as a free social club for American military officers arriving in Europe on their way to the front. It was run in close conjunction with the Pilgrims, and members of the Pilgrims Society were initially given automatic membership, while the Duke of Connaught simultaneously served as president of both organisations. Likewise, Brittain was chairman of both, whilst the Pilgrims business secretary, Mrs Welsh-Lee, undertook a similar function with the American Officers' Club. As the new club was, according to Brittain, 'so thoroughly organised and run with such clockwork', he was able to leave it largely in the hands of the Pilgrims treasurer, John Wilson Taylor, and a number of other colleagues.[29] No specific information is given as to why it was thought best to create the Club as a quasi-separate entity and not simply to offer American officers membership to the Pilgrims Society. One possible explanation is that the Pilgrims did not have a clubhouse and was not, as such, in a position to play the role of a social club. The American Officers' Club also had a narrower and more temporary focus than did the Pilgrims: namely, the hosting of US servicemen during the war. Its separate existence enabled it to maintain this focus. As Brittain explained, he was motivated by the belief that the American officers 'should have a place of their own, run as far as possible on American lines, with every attention paid to their wishes and to American ideas'.[30] The Club was officially opened on 20 November 1917 by the Duke of Connaught in a ceremony attended by notable guests such as Walter Hines Page, James Bryce, and Sir Eric Geddes, the First Lord of the Admiralty.[31] The club held dinners and organised sports days and visits at British country retreats, including to Brittain's cottage in Surrey. A lecture series was also arranged, with speakers including Arthur Balfour and Lord Reading. Brittain's self-appointed role as host to American officers in Britain was also given official backing and he was later appointed to committees which had been formed at the Ministry of Information and the Royal Air Force to help cater for the visiting US forces.[32] The Ministry of Information's so-called 'Committee for Entertaining

American Forces' had the assistance of other organisations too, including the Atlantic Union and the British–American Fellowship, and so the American Officers' Club was just one of many British efforts to accommodate American troops. Over 300,000 US soldiers were arriving monthly in France by mid-1918 and a number of London inns and golf clubs offered the visiting forces use of their facilities. An article in the London *Times* noted that, compared with the inns, the American Officers' Club had the 'reputation of being "rather more staid"'.[33] Even so, state support for the American Officers' Club went beyond that given it by the Ministry of Information. For example, Brittain had approached the Treasury seeking financial assistance for the club and was subsequently given £3,000 'towards preliminary expenses', though this was £2,000 less than he had asked for. He also managed to persuade the local authority that the Club's work 'would have far reaching effects, and was much more of a national institution than a Club' and that, as a result, it should receive a tax rebate.[34] Similarly, Mrs Welsh-Lee later described the Club as an 'opportune mixture of hospitality and indirect propaganda'.[35] These statements show that Brittain and Welsh-Lee were looking beyond the Club's immediate wartime application and regarded it as an exercise in informal public diplomacy. Though the club closed once the war had ended and the US military had returned home, Brittain saw it as a 'gift from Britons, who, through that gift, might show their friendship and appreciation' to the Americans for having entered the war. It was also hoped that the club's events would 'bring Britons and Americans into a more enlightened relationship . . . than has been done by any other plan ever devised'.[36] As *The Times* noted approvingly, every American officer who had used the Club would 'remember with unquenchable gratitude the countless delightful experiences that were his' and would become a 'protagonist of Anglo-American fraternity who will not easily tire of acclaiming the virtues of Old England, for it was his happy lot to be the beneficiary of one of the finest of them'.[37] With Americans receiving exposure to ideas of Anglo-American friendship in the hope that they would return to the US to promote such ideas there, the American Officers' Club was an example of the 'exchange' element of public diplomacy. In short, it was another effort by the Pilgrims Society and Harry Brittain to establish connections between Britain and the US and to promote friendship between the two countries in what had become the relatively favourable circumstances of the war. On this occasion, they were given significant official backing.

If the American Officers' Club was an example of state-supported, though privately executed, public diplomacy, then Brittain's work with the NWAC is instructive of the new ways in which cultural ideas about Anglo-American friendship were deployed after April 1917 and provides further evidence of the continued wartime role played by the unofficial Pilgrims Society network. The NWAC was established in June 1917 and followed on from a reorganisation of the British propaganda bodies in January and February which had resulted in the creation of a newly centralised Department of Information. This reorganisation had not accounted for domestic propaganda, a gap which the NWAC aimed to fill. The NWAC was a cross-party, semi-official body, initially part-funded by private donations. Its chairman was Frederick Guest, David Lloyd George's chief whip in the House of Commons, while its vice-chairman was Robert Sanders, the Tory whip. Its executive committee was primarily made up of parliamentarians and it utilised the constituency organisations of the three main parties to create local War Aims Committees across the country. The NWAC aimed to counteract the pacifism of anti-war and anti-conscription socialists and shop stewards – especially in light of revolutionary events in Russia – and to boost the morale of a war-weary civilian population, doing so by means of patriotic pamphlets, lectures, rallies, and films. It focused its work in places where radical dissent was particularly strong, including in Glasgow, Wigan, and Hull. As was the case with other outlets of British propaganda, the NWAC portrayed exaggerated examples of German 'atrocities', for instance in a calendar that it produced depicting a different German war crime for each month of the year, including the *Lusitania* sinking and the killing of the nurse Edith Cavell. It also occasionally distributed less truthful messages, for example in its portrayal of Bolshevism as a Jewish conspiracy. It was some of these methods that contributed to 'propaganda' becoming a pejorative term in the years following the First World War.[38]

David Monger has, meanwhile, successfully shown that the NWAC used ideas of 'supranational patriotism' to compare Britain to its principal ally France and, once it had entered the war, the US. According to Monger, this 'transcended a simply "national" approach to patriotism' and involved identifying shared attributes between the Allied and Associate nations in their collective fight against Germany.[39] For example, propagandists highlighted to the British public the sacrifices made by French workers and quoted pro-war comments made by Samuel Gompers, the American labour leader. Similarly, in the context of what Monger terms 'proprietorial patriotism', the NWAC highlighted to the British public the Allies' apparently unique devotion to such core values as liberty, democracy, honour, and justice and argued, by extension, that they were the defenders of civilisation. These values of course chimed with those of the Pilgrims Society, with the Chicagoan journalist Edward Price Bell writing in 1918 that 'what the Pilgrims stand for essentially – a free, progressive and honour-loving civilisation – is the very thing that practically the whole non-Germanic world is now praying for, if not fighting for'.[40] Likewise, ideas of civilisation often had a Christian underpinning in NWAC propaganda. This was something that was also evident in the quote from 'The Battle Hymn of the Republic' used by Harry Brittain in his telegram to the US Pilgrims in April 1917. Since the NWAC was able to call upon the existing supranational patriotism of Anglo-Saxonism, the wider significance of the US's entry into the war was more readily communicated than were ideas about British–French commonality.[41] It did this not only by highlighting the impressive contribution and effort that it felt the US would inevitably bring to the war, but by using familiar cultural tropes to promote ideas of Anglo-American friendship. Comments made by Woodrow Wilson comparing George Washington to the Barons of Runnymede were published repeatedly by the NWAC, as was the president's phrase that the war was about 'making the world safe for democracy'.[42] 'Democracy' was evoked alongside 'liberty', in conjunction with the now familiar suggestion that both concepts had their roots in medieval England and had since been transferred to the rest of the English-speaking world, especially to America. This had been a common refrain since the 1890s, throughout the period of the 'great rapprochement', and was a central component of Pilgrims Society rhetoric.[43] Moreover, in the NWAC's *Reality* pamphlet, Winston Churchill had written that Magna Charta, the US Declaration of Independence, and the Bill of Rights were the three 'title-deeds' of English-speaking freedom.[44]

Yet, there was a certain irony to invoking liberty while the state was simultaneously encroaching upon civil liberties, for instance through the provisions of the Defence of the Realm Act (DORA) in Britain and the Espionage Act in the US.[45] By its concerted efforts to overcome domestic dissent – efforts that included liaising with the police and the Home Office to arrange counter-demonstrations against pacifists – the NWAC was itself a subversive and sinister element in the suppression of civil liberties, 'inconsistent with liberal inhibitions'.[46] Propagandists addressed this inconsistency by suggesting that only a victorious end to the war could guarantee the restoration of freedom, while also highlighting the perceived benefits to the working classes and the efficiencies which had been created by the increased wartime role of the state. This spoke to a wider debate over the potential benefits of state involvement, for example in industry through the Ministry of Munitions, which some people – including socialists like Henry Hyndman – felt was a step in the right direction towards socialism. There were similar developments in the US, where the federal government had taken control of the railways and where some progressives expressed the hope that the war would help engender a renewed spirit of civic duty and social efficiency.[47] Thus the war was presented as a battle in defence of liberty and liberalism, while it was also used to suggest that benign collectivistic state intervention – itself 'illiberal', in some senses of the word – was perhaps possible in peacetime. 'Liberty' and 'liberalism' had been appropriated by Anglo-American elites, propagandists, and warmongers. The terms were devoid of any clear meaning beyond the idea that they were somehow 'good', intrinsically English, British, American, and, for now, French, and that they were worth fighting for.

The NWAC was deliberately given the appearance of operating at arm's length from what was supposed to be a liberal state, even though it had the support of the government and eventually received official funding. For some in officialdom, including Frederick Guest, it was important that the NWAC did not appear linked to the government. It was believed that this lent its output greater plausibility.[48] Harry Brittain was particularly adept at operating within the nebulous boundaries of such a state–private network.[49] With Brittain a member of the NWAC's executive committee, the British state had access to the Pilgrims and to the conduit that the Society provided to elite figures in the US. Demonstrating that he was at the forefront of the NWAC's efforts to bring American pro-war speakers to Britain, Harry Brittain exchanged a number of letters on the subject with

Walter Hines Page and Nicholas Murray Butler in mid-June 1917. The US ambassador had requested a membership list of the New York Pilgrims 'in order to turn over in [his] mind the names of one or two who might be persuaded to come over to this side for the purpose of letting a few of our British audiences know something of the USA'. As evidence that there was indeed some concern about war-weariness in the UK, and demonstrating that the value of Beck's trip the year before only went so far, Brittain reported that he had recently returned from a visit to parts of the North of England 'intensely impressed with the necessity of placing clearly before my fellow-countrymen some of the great ideals for which America stands'.[50] Brittain explained to Murray Butler that a 'Committee has recently been formed under the auspices of your Embassy and our Foreign Office to make clear to Englishmen, particularly in the great industrial sections of the North, what America stands for'. The hope was to 'arrange a series of lectures and addresses during the autumn, and shall have, I trust, various speakers from your side of the water'. In addition to utilising members of the Pilgrims Society, Brittain envisaged calling upon elements in the YMCA.[51] The NWAC was not at this stage fully formed, so it would appear that Brittain was referring to the so-called 'Anglo-American Committee'. This group predated the NWAC by a few months and had the approval of John Buchan's Department of Information. It met at least once in Brittain's Westminster home but was eventually disbanded and subsumed by the NWAC.[52] Brittain appears to have himself made the suggestion to merge the two bodies in an effort to 'save Government expense and also prevent over-lapping'.[53] With the Department of Information more focused on foreign propaganda, the aims of the Anglo-American Committee as outlined by Brittain were, in any case, more suited to a domestic organisation like the NWAC, even if the Anglo-American Committee was inevitably internationalist in tone. Nevertheless, Brittain was 'very willing to help in any way the National War Aims Committee and particularly the American end', and admitted that he was well placed to organise speaking engagements for visiting Americans. Those who did not officially make their arrival known to the British authorities – as the 'better known a man is in America the more quietly he will slip away, for obvious reasons' – Brittain said that he could find out about such people by other means:

[t]he arrival of most of these men is made known to me in one way or another, either through the Pilgrims of New York, through the American Embassy, or American correspondents here, or through the pretty considerable mail which I receive by every boat from America.[54]

Thus it was under the auspices of the NWAC that Brittain, as 'liaison officer' to the US, along with Guest, took a number of American speakers, including the New York journalist Irving Bacheller, to Blackpool in July to articulate the 'full meaning of mutual cooperation' before an audience of 'thousands of visitors, and good sterling munition workers who had come from all parts of the Midlands and the North [of England]'.[55] Indeed, the NWAC had drawn up plans for an 'American Educational Campaign', with the aim of enabling

the British public to realise the fundamental unity between the British and American people, to appreciate the causes which made the present Anglo-American unity of purpose possible and the desirability of establishing a still better understanding between the two nations when the war is over.[56]

Brittain was once again demonstrating his desire to use the war to further his aim of Anglo-American friendship. The 'causes which made the present Anglo-American unity of purpose possible' – namely German militarism – were outlined in other examples of his writing, for instance when he said that the 'German mentality is a thing beyond the comprehension of the Anglo-Saxon'. He believed that, for Britain and the US, '[m]utual trust, mutual reliance, mutual sacrifice, as the war runs on to final victory, will create a bond which no co-operation in peace could accomplish with such complete effectiveness'.[57]

Like other aspects of the NWAC's work, the American Educational Campaign was to include the publication of written material and the delivery of lectures, in this case by 'accredited American representatives'. This was a form of advocacy diplomacy. Before undertaking this work, these Americans were to be given an 'opportunity of seeing what the old country is doing', with a draft itinerary suggesting day-long visits to the centres of munitions production in Glasgow, Gretna, and Sheffield. Time was also set aside to visit some hospitals and the naval fleet, while an additional five days were to be spent in France. This was a form of exchange diplomacy.[58] The explicit desire to link immediate wartime aims with the longer-term goal of Anglo-American friendship demonstrates the influence of the Pilgrims chairman. The NWAC visit to Blackpool should be seen in the context of the ideas which lay behind this detailed scheme. Similarly, there was a variety of other speaking engagements made by Americans in Britain on behalf of the NWAC, including by the Chicagoan judge Henry Neil.[59] For example, speaking at an event in Wolverhampton in July 1918 – where some of the employees of the city's Team Department were on strike – Neil said the US had entered the war to fight for the universal right to self-determination.[60] Then in May 1918, Brittain was asked by the Ministry of Information to host a delegation of American labour leaders. Along with his Pilgrims colleague and fellow propagandist Sir Campbell Stuart, and Geoffrey Butler from the Ministry, Brittain accompanied the American representatives as they delivered lectures to British munitions workers and visited the king and queen at Buckingham Palace. They also travelled to the Western Front for a few days and had an extended stay in Paris to meet pro-war individuals, as 'many French Ministers thought that the Pacifist and Socialistic groups had been getting at the Labour delegates'.[61]

Brittain and the Pilgrims Society were participating in a great transatlantic discourse which had taken on a new urgency amidst the pressures of war. Their efforts to foster Anglo-American friendship remained largely unofficial, though in 1917 and in the context of the NWAC these efforts were also state-sponsored. With US belligerence now assured, this transatlantic discourse became increasingly reciprocal. In another example of Anglo-American cooperation in the realms of propaganda and intelligence, Brittain had the Committee of Public Information – the US equivalent of the NWAC – send him examples of their own propaganda materials.[62] In all of these ways, the cultural affinities of the Anglo-American rapprochement – exhibited by elements in Britain and the US across the two decades prior to the First World War – helped condition the attitudes towards, and interpretations of, the US's intervention in the First World War. Just as some on the British left regarded the increased wartime role of the state as a step in the right direction towards socialism, so did people like Harry Brittain see the US's entry into the war as a means by which to further their aim of Anglo-American friendship.

The Pilgrims continued to hold events throughout the war and continued their monthly committee meetings. The British Pilgrims held a lunch for James Beck at the American Officers' Club at the start of November 1918 and at the end of that month marked the close of the war with a Thanksgiving dinner, while the New York Pilgrims marked their fifteenth anniversary in March 1918 with a dinner for the Archbishop of New York.[63] There had, however, been unease amongst some of the Society's members about the appropriateness of holding certain functions during the period of international crisis. In March 1917, in the days leading up to the president's war address, George Wilson declined the New York committee's offer of a function in his honour because he felt that a 'public festivity' was 'out of place and inadvisable' in those 'strained and anxious days'.[64] Likewise, twelve months later – when the idea of marking the anniversary of US entry into the conflict was raised – the New York executive committee was 'unanimously of the opinion that the time for The Pilgrims to celebrate this historic day would be after the war is over and not during it'. George Wilson wrote to Harry Brittain that while 'it may be perfectly all right for you on your side to celebrate it a number of the Committee expressed the opinion that it might not be so here'. Brittain had hoped to mark the anniversary in the form of an 'Inter-Dependence Day', but, in the end, nothing happened in either London or New York.[65]

Britain's Day

Though there was no gushing celebration of Anglo-American 'inter-dependence' during the war, such an event was held after the end of the conflict, as George Wilson had suggested.

December 1918 witnessed the period's most significant outward display of Anglo-American friendship: 'Britain's Day'. An exercise in cultural public diplomacy conceived by some of the elites associated with the British–American clubs in the US as a nationwide celebration of Britain's contribution to the war, Britain's Day was in fact held across the weekend of 7 and 8 December. It was principally and widely celebrated with banquets, public meetings, pageants, and church services, with a memorandum from the Foreign Office to the British Cabinet indicating that it had been marked in 'at least 3,000 localities' across the US.[66] In addition to events in New York, Washington, and Philadelphia, the occasion was celebrated in Boston, San Francisco, Los Angeles, Atlanta, Cleveland, Detroit, and Michigan. Many of these events were religious in character, for instance in Denver, where activities were 'largely confined to church services' – though this was partly because mass meetings had been restricted in an effort to combat the spread of the post-war global flu pandemic.[67] There were no such restrictions in Minneapolis, where a crowd of 3,000 listened to a naval band, while in Boston the crew of the British navy ship the HMS *Devonshire* – which had travelled to the city especially – were honoured by an event in the Symphony Hall. Seattle marked the occasion by welcoming military personnel from British Columbia, which demonstrates the wider North American appeal of Anglo-Saxon patriotism.[68] Britain's Day on the Pacific Coast was – according to the *Christian Science Monitor* – characterised by the 'idea that through the experiences of the war the British and American peoples have become indissolubly united and that they will face the future with common aims'. As has been shown, this attitude had always been a part of the Pilgrims Society's interpretation of the significance of the US's entry into First World War. The lineage of these ideas of Anglo-Saxon rapprochement as displayed during Britain's Day was further evident in Los Angeles, where organisers distributed copies of the Treaty of Ghent.[69]

The distribution of the Treaty of Ghent speaks to the involvement of the Sulgrave Institute. The Sulgrave Institute had grown out of the movement to mark the centenary of the signing of the Treaty of Ghent and the end of the War of 1812, which was supposed to have been celebrated in 1914 by a variety of activities, including lectures and the distribution of educational materials to schoolchildren. The outbreak of war, however, disrupted the celebration. The plans for the centenary were coordinated in the US by the 'National Committee for the Celebration of the One Hundredth Anniversary of Peace among English-Speaking Peoples' and in Britain by the British Peace Centenary Committee. An important element to the celebrations was the purchase in 1914 of Sulgrave Manor in Northamptonshire, which was regarded as the ancestral home of George Washington, and which gave the Sulgrave Institute both its name and its focal point. In light of the redundancy of the peace centenary celebrations, the Peace Committees were superseded by the Sulgrave Institute.[70] The British Peace Committee and the Sulgrave Institute were also closely associated with the Anglo-American Society, which was founded in 1918 and which eventually had branches in British cities other than London, including Southampton, Sheffield, Liverpool, and Manchester. Both organisations had links to the Pilgrims Society, including through Harry Brittain – who chaired the British Committee's Dominions sub-committee – and John A. Stewart, a New York businessman and Republican who was the driving force behind the American organisation and who was a member of the Pilgrims from 1912.[71] After the First World War, the Sulgrave Institute and the Anglo-American Society – the full name of which was the 'Anglo-American Society for the Celebration of the Tercentenary of the Pilgrim Fathers, 1920, and for Fostering Friendship between the British and American Peoples' – focused on the celebration of the tercentenary of the landing in America of the Pilgrim Fathers.

Figures associated with Sulgrave were primarily responsible for the original idea for Britain's Day. The Pilgrims Society was also involved in organising the events, with George Wilson attending a November meeting of the Britain's Day committee and pledging $266 from the Society towards the underwriting agreement for the celebrations. The National Security League – an organisation formed in 1914 to campaign for military preparedness, and whose leading members were Pilgrims, including Stanwood Menken, James Beck, and Joseph Choate – was among the other organisations with an interest in the arrangements, while Sulgrave and the Pilgrims' John Stewart, Charles W. Eliot (president emeritus of Harvard University), and Alton B. Parker (judge and Democratic presidential candidate in 1904) sat on the Britain's Day national committee.[72] An earlier Foreign Office memorandum to David Lloyd George's Cabinet in November had noted that this 'unique pro-British demonstration' was 'entirely American in its conception' and that it would perhaps be a good idea if the British government could send some high-profile political or military figures to the US in support of this friendly gesture.[73] The most significant event of the weekend was a large rally of 5,000 people in New York's hippodrome, at which messages of support were read on behalf of Woodrow Wilson, the British King George V, the French Prime Minister Georges Clemenceau, the British Field Marshall Douglas Haig, Herbert Asquith, James Bryce, Arthur Balfour, Theodore Roosevelt, the US General John Pershing, and H. G. Wells. Charles Evans Hughes, Republican presidential candidate in 1916 and honorary vice-chairman of the Britain's Day committee, paid tribute to Britain's military contribution and said that America had taken 'from the people of Great Britain and their historical struggle our lessons in political liberty. We have written Magna Charta into our constitutions.'[74] Meanwhile, in Washington DC – where government employees were given a half-day holiday on Saturday 7 December for Britain's Day – Porter McCumber, senator from North Dakota, told an audience at the Central High School that 'the American may well be proud that Britain was not only the birthplace of his fathers but also the source of his ideals'.[75] This rhetoric echoed what Winston Churchill had said about the three title-deeds of the English-speaking world in his article for the NWAC and is further evidence of the supranational patriotism evident in some aspects of the Anglo-American wartime relationship. Much of the speechifying during Britain's Day was couched in terms of Anglo-Saxonism, the umbrella concept under which ideas about liberty and democracy existed.[76] Such was the success of Britain's Day that one observer felt that it should be repeated every year as Magna Charta Day, not least because victory in the First World War was a victory for 'all the fundamental things for which Magna Charta stands'.[77] The Pilgrims were at the heart of this success, with the *New York Times* reporting that '[n]owhere was the expression of good will between the two nations more enthusiastic and more visible' than at the Pilgrims' Britain's Day banquet at the Ritz-Carlton.[78]

As an elite-led flaunting of the dominant white, Anglo-Saxon and Protestant cultural tropes of American identity, Britain's Day was also a manifestation of domestic Americanism in the face of allegedly un-American historical developments. This was also true in relation to the US preparedness movement before April 1917, which Priscilla Roberts has regarded as partly 'an attempt by old-stock Americans to reassert their dominance over the newer immigrant elements of the population'. Anglo-Saxon rhetoric served this purpose by highlighting the US's allegedly longstanding English traditions to which many of the policy-making elite subscribed and with which they wanted immigrants to assimilate.[79] More specifically, Britain's Day should be regarded in the context of the US's post-war Red Scare. By the end of the war, anti-German feeling merged with anti-Bolshevik sentiment – partly in reaction to Russia's separate peace with Germany, made earlier in the year – to create a renewed fear of the 'other' amongst an American population particularly receptive to such anxieties following the wartime anti-German propaganda of the Creel Committee. Industrial disputes (1917 had already witnessed the highest-ever number of strikes in America) and the economic consequences of military demobilisation – including high unemployment – combined to create a potent mix of fears about socialists, immigrants, and blacks.[80] These fears could spill over into violence, for instance the lynching and castration of a member of the International Workers of the World in Washington State in November 1919, while the authorities acted to suppress radical activity, for example through the so-called 'Palmer Raids' ordered by the Attorney General later in 1919 and 1920. Patriotic, right-wing organisations like the National Security League and the Ku Klux Klan were complicit in much of this anti-socialist activity.[81] Even though Britain's Day occurred slightly before the Red Scare took hold more firmly in the American imagination in the spring of 1919 – when a number of bombings and attempted bombings across the US were attributed to anarchists – already in December 1918 there was evidence of anxiety amongst some elites about the radical threat. For example, in November the Mayor of New York had prohibited the public flying of the red flag as he believed it was 'repulsive to ideals of civilization and the principles upon which our Government is founded'.[82] The beginnings of the Red Scare were also evident during at least one Britain's Day event, with the English poet Alfred Noyes asking the National Special Aid Society at New York's Delmonico's restaurant why 'we are trying underlings for placing explosives on ships and for murder' while letting 'those in high places who gave the orders go free', thus allowing 'the Bolsheviki' to 'cry that only under the red flag justice will be meted out? We need the voice of Uncle Sam to aid us in making this impossible.'[83] It is unclear to which violent attacks Noyes was referring, though he may have been recalling the trial and conviction in January and February 1918 of a number of German spies accused of conspiring to bomb Allied ships sailing out of New York.[84] In any case, he was arguing that the US justice system should act to ensure that perceptions of leniency did not encourage or add to the appeal of Bolshevism.

In all of these ways, Britain's Day was more than simply a celebration of Britain's military victory against Germany. Just as propagandists had presented the war as a battle in defence of the ideas of liberty, democracy, and civilisation, so was Britain's Day presented as a celebration of the victory of these ideas. This victory was not simply against Germany, but had also been won by overcoming problems in the Anglo-American relationship, including concerns about the destabilising influence in both countries of pacifists, socialists, and a war-weary public. Likewise, and with a view to the longer-term evolution of the Anglo-American relationship, Chauncey Depew used Britain's Day to highlight the centenary of peace between Britain and the US, noting that it was all the more remarkable for having been achieved in spite of 'many causes for irritation and anger'.[85] With Philadelphian schoolchildren being asked to write essays on 'subjects relative to England', and with their parents being fed information about the British military, Britain's Day was a public diplomacy effort to consolidate this apparent victory.[86] Events in the 1920s – including international disputes concerning war debt and naval disarmament – meant that this was by no means the beginning of the Anglo-American special relationship, but it was a carefully coordinated culmination of efforts made by elements in both countries to spin a narrative emphasising the Anglo-American comity of interest.

Conclusion

For the Pilgrims Society, the First World War provided a chance to solidify the rapprochement of the 1890s. Amidst flourishes of Anglo-American triumphalism, US entry into the conflict in April 1917 was regarded as an event of huge significance. Its significance was anticipated before it happened, and articulated afterwards, by means of a mix of official and unofficial propaganda. The Pilgrims, and ideas about Anglo-American cultural affinities, were central components of that mix. The Pilgrims' activity during the First World War blurred the lines between official and unofficial action, and between propaganda and public diplomacy. The 1920s would see the London Pilgrims become a venue for official policy announcements by US ambassadors, which meant that that decade provided a middle ground between the more state-sponsored approaches to public diplomacy of the 1930s and the Cold War and the more private nature of such activity in earlier years. The First World War, meanwhile, provided a further developmental link in the chain between these periods. The Pilgrims' wartime activities were mostly private in conception and in practice, but they utilised and solidified the connections between the Society and officialdom. While some of the activities undertaken by the Pilgrims – including those associated with the National War Aims Committee and the Creel Committee – contributed to 'propaganda' becoming a pejorative term and led to its phasing out in the 1930s by organisations like the British Council in favour of terms like 'cultural diplomacy', the Pilgrims' approach during the First World War was essentially a form of public diplomacy, including its advocacy, exchange, and cultural elements.[87] The Pilgrims' various activities during the First World War were also an extension of late nineteenth- and early twentieth-century concepts of international activism. This development witnessed a shift from the private activism of the world's fairs, but also from the less proactive approach taken by the Pilgrims through its hosting of banquets, like that in 1906. More than that, and with varying and increased degrees of cooperation with the state at a time when national state interests were more acutely at stake than ever before, such concepts were put to new and more complex uses between 1914 and 1918.

Notes

1. *New York Times*, 21 July 1917.
2. Minute Book 3, 17 July 1917, Pilgrims Mss, NYC; *New York Times*, 21 July 1917.
3. Burk, *Sinews of War*, pp. 99–138; J. Lee Thompson, '"To Tell the People of America the Truth": Lord Northcliffe in the USA, Unofficial British Propaganda, June–November 1917', *Journal of Contemporary History*, Vol. 34 (1999), p. 258; Thompson, *Politicians, the Press and Propaganda: Lord Northcliffe and the Great War, 1914–1919* (Ashland, OH, 1999), pp. 151–68.
4. Stephen Bowman, 'An Englishman Abroad and an American Lawyer in Europe: Harry Brittain, James Beck and the Pilgrims Society During the First World War', *Journal of Transatlantic Studies*, Vol. 12, No. 3 (2014), pp. 258–81.
5. Taylor, *Projection of Britain*, pp. 1–4; Justin Hart argues that cultural diplomacy moves along the 'dissemination-exchange spectrum' and that US cultural diplomacy ultimately 'moved ever-closer to the propaganda end' of that spectrum. In his view, the realisation in official circles that foreign policy and foreign relations were inseparable contributed to the process by which the US government

took responsibility for public diplomacy away from private organisations in the 1930s and 1940s. In turn, this made cultural relations synonymous with propaganda. This view is a logical one, but the contention here is that neither propaganda nor public diplomacy need rely on government involvement. In any event, the Pilgrims demonstrate that government interest in semi-official public diplomacy and propaganda, including cultural diplomacy, occurred in an earlier period than that identified by Hart. See Hart, *Empire of Ideas*, p. 42 and p. 63.

6. Even after the war, Harry Brittain was happy to describe the Pilgrims' activities as 'more or less propaganda'. Brittain to Wilson, 25 September 1920, Pilgrims Mss, LMA/4632/A/05/002/01. This was also shown by Welsh-Lee's plans for a Propaganda Sub-Committee.

7. Nicholas, *The United States and Britain*, p. 62.

8. Wilson to Brittain, 6 October [presumably 1914], Pilgrims Mss, LMA/4632/A/05/002/01.

9. Minute Book 2, 5 November 1914, Pilgrims Mss, NYC.

10. Minute Book 2, 20 November 1914, Pilgrims Mss, NYC; Robson, 'Frederick Sleigh Roberts'.

11. Herring, *From Colony to Superpower*, p. 409.

12. Wilson to Brittain, 23 March 1917, Pilgrims Mss, LMA/4632/A/05/002/01; *New York Times*, 21 March 1917; Wilson's attendance at the ULC meeting speaks to the Republican proclivities of the New York Pilgrims. The Pilgrims had close links with the ULC, which was a pro-Republican club founded during the Civil War. Wilson had been, for example, president of the ULC, while the Pilgrims occasionally used the ULC as a venue for functions. This link is further indicated by people like Chauncey Depew, Joseph Choate, and James Beck. See *New York Times*, 5 May 1913, 25 April 1915, and 1 January 1918. See also Joanne R. Reitano, *The Restless City: A Short History of New York from Colonial Times to the Present* (New York, 2010), pp. 72–7; incidentally, it could not be argued that the London Pilgrims had proclivities towards any one British political party.

13. David M. Kennedy, *Over Here: The First World War and American Society* (Oxford, 2004), pp. 148–9; John Milton Cooper, Jr., *The Warrior and the Priest: Woodrow Wilson and Theodore Roosevelt* (Cambridge, MA, 1983), pp. 323–6; Wilson to Brittain, 23 March 1917, Pilgrims Mss, LMA/4632/A/05/002/01.

14. Spring-Rice to Balfour, 19 October 1917, Arthur Balfour Papers, BL, 49740.

15. Robert H. Zieger, *America's Great War: World War 1 and the American Experience* (Lanham, 2000), pp. 57–78; Kennedy, *Over Here*, p. 169.

16. Minute Book 3, 7 January 1918, Pilgrims Mss, NYC; Wilson to Brittain, 14 March 1918, Pilgrims Mss, LMA/4632/A/05/002/01; Burk, *Sinews of War*, pp. 99–138.

17. 'Suggestions for the immediate re-organisation and for the future of the Pilgrims' Society', July 1919, Pilgrims Mss, LMA/4632/A/05/004. This document outlined a programme for the Society's future – 'Part 2' of the Pilgrims' existence – and was examined in greater detail in Chapter 2.

18. 'America, Ourselves and the War: What it means to the English-speaking world', undated notes, Brittain Papers, BLPES, Box 7.

19. Telegram from Harry Brittain to the Pilgrims of the US, 4 April 1917, Minute Book 3, 22 May 1917, Pilgrims Mss, NYC.

20. Telegram from Joseph Choate to the Pilgrims of Great Britain, 11 April 1917, Minute Book 3, 22 May 1917, Pilgrims Mss, NYC.

21. *New York Times*, 13 April 1917.

22. Jim Beach, 'Origins of the Special Intelligence Relationship? Anglo-American Intelligence Co-operation on the Western Front, 1917–18', *Intelligence and National Security*, Vol. 22, No. 2 (April 2007), p. 245.

23. *The Times*, 12 April 1917; *New York Times*, 21 April 1917.

24. Nicholas, *The United States and Britain*, p. 62; Personal Diary, 24 November 1917, Walter Hines Page Papers, Harvard University Houghton Library [HL], bMS Am 1090.5.

25. David Dilks, *Neville Chamberlain, Vol. 1, 1869–1929* (Cambridge, 1984), p. 215.

26. *Detroit Free Press*, 5 January 1919, within Butler Papers, CUBL, Box 50.

27. 'National Service Department No. 8 Report for Week Ending 15th March, 1917', TNA, CAB24/8.

28. Neville Chamberlain to Brittain, 30 August 1917, Brittain Papers, BLPES, Box 8; the idea that 'intelligence' and 'propaganda' work go hand in hand was itself a product of the experience of British propaganda during the First World War, when publicity material was produced in response to information about prevailing American public opinion. As has been seen, Brittain played a role in gathering this information. See also Sanders and Taylor, *British Propaganda During the First World War*, p. 168.

29. Brittain, *Pilgrim Partners*, pp. 116–25; 'To Members of the Pilgrims who have not joined this Club', undated, Brittain Papers, BLPES, Box 7; Brittain to John Barrett, 30 March 1918, Brittain Papers, BLPES, Box 7.

30. Brittain, *Pilgrim Partners*, p. 117.

31. 'The American Officers' Club in London', Edward Price Bell, 1918, Brittain Papers, BLPES, Box 7.

32. Brittain, *Pilgrim Partners*, p. 122; 'Sir Harry Brittain: A short epitome of personal effort to further a closer Anglo-American understanding', undated, Brittain Papers, BLPES, Box 7.

33. Zieger, *America's Great War*, p. 96; *The Times*, 16 August 1918.

34. Minutes, 18 and 24 July 1917, Pilgrims Mss, LMA/4632/A/01/001.

35. 'Suggestions for the immediate re-organisation and for the future of the Pilgrims' Society', July 1919, Pilgrims Mss, LMA/4632/A/05/004.

36. Brittain, *Pilgrim Partners*, p. 117; 'The American Officers' Club in London', Edward Price Bell, 1918, Brittain Papers, BLPES, Box 7.

37. *The Times*, 23 April 1919.

38. Report from Ministry of Labour for the War Cabinet, week ending 9 January 1918, TNA, CAB 24/38; Sanders and Taylor, *British Propaganda During the First World War*, p. 67 and p. 141; David Monger, *Patriotism and Propaganda in First World War Britain: The National War Aims Committee and Civilian Morale* (Liverpool, 2012), pp. 28–30 and p. 269; Cate Haste, *Keep the Home Fires Burning: Propaganda in the First World War* (London, 1977), pp. 41–2; David Welch, 'Introduction', in Mark Connelly and David Welch (eds), *War and the Media: Reportage and Propaganda, 1900–2003* (London, 2004), p. xi.

39. Monger, *Patriotism and Propaganda*, pp. 92–3.

40. 'The American Officers' Club in London', Edward Price Bell, 1918, Brittain Papers, BLPES, Box 7.

41. Monger, *Patriotism and Propaganda*, p. 140, pp. 146–7 and pp. 102–3.

42. Ibid. p. 145, p. 157 and p. 165.

43. *New York Times*, 21 July 1917; MacRaild et al., 'Interdependence Day and Magna Charta', pp. 140–62; Jessica Bennett and Mark Hampton, 'World War 1 and the Anglo-American Imagined Community: Civilization vs. Barbarism in British Propaganda and American Newspapers', in Joel Wiener and Mark Hampton (eds), *Anglo-American Media Interactions, 1850–2000* (New York, 2007), pp. 155–75.

44. Monger, *Patriotism and Propaganda*, pp. 162–3.

45. Ibid. pp. 162–3.

46. Brock Millman, *Managing Domestic Dissent in First World War Britain* (London, 2000), pp. 245–6 and p. 230; Haste, *Home Fires*, pp. 170–1.

47. Monger, *Patriotism and Propaganda*, p. 162; Haste, *Home Fires*, p. 41; James Hinton, *The First Shop Stewards' Movement* (London, 1973), pp. 43–6; Kennedy, *Over Here*, p. 44; Zieger, *America's Great War*, p. 2.

48. Sanders and Taylor, *British Propaganda During the First World War*, p. 70.

49. The term 'state–private network' has been more commonly utilised in the study of networks in the Cold War era. See the work of Inderjeet Parmar, for example 'Conceptualising the State–Private Network in American Foreign Policy', in Helen Laville and Hugh Wilford (eds), *The US Government, Citizen Groups and the Cold War: The State–Private Network* (London, 2005), pp. 13–27.

50. Millman, *Domestic Dissent*, p. 231; Brittain to Walter Hines Page, 19 June 1917, Page Papers, HL, bMS Am 1090.1 (214).

51. Brittain to Murray Butler, 30 June 1917, Butler Papers, CUBL, Box 50; Brittain to Page, 28 June 1917, Page Papers, HL, bMS Am 1090.1 (214).

52. Brittain to Page, 23 July 1917, Page Papers, HL, bMS Am 1090.1 (214); Monger, *Patriotism and Propaganda*, p. 41.

53. Undated notes, Brittain Papers, BLPES, NWAC folder.

54. Undated notes, Brittain Papers, BLPES, NWAC folder.

55. Brittain, *Pilgrims and Pioneers* (London, 1946), pp. 164–6.

56. 'The American Educational Campaign', undated, Brittain Papers, BLPES, NWAC folder.

57. 'America, Ourselves, and the War: What it Means to the English-Speaking World, by Harry E. Brittain', undated, Pilgrims Mss, LMA/4632/A/05/002/02.

58. 'The American Educational Campaign', undated, Brittain Papers, BLPES, NWAC folder; it should be noted that no evidence has been found of the American Educational Campaign having been carried out.

59. Millman, *Domestic Dissent*, p. 236; Monger, *Patriotism and Propaganda*, p. 142.

60. *Birmingham Gazette*, 29 July 1918.

61. Brittain, *Pilgrims and Pioneers*, pp. 136–41; *The Times*, 17 May 1918; 'Visit of American Mission to France', undated report, Brittain Papers, BLPES, Box 7.

62. Brittain to Barrett, 30 March 1918, Brittain Papers, BLPES, Box 7; Nicholas Murray Butler, meanwhile, allowed the Committee of Public Information to base some of its staff in the headquarters of the Carnegie Endowment for International Peace, of which he was director. See Alan Axelrod, *Selling the Great War: The Making of American Propaganda* (New York, 2009), p. 69.

63. *The Times*, 7 November 1918; Baker, *Pilgrims of Britain*, p. 21; Baker, *Pilgrims of the US*, p. 162.

64. Wilson to Brittain, 23 March 1917, Pilgrims Mss, LMA/4632/A/05/002/01.

65. Wilson to Britain, 14 March 1918, Pilgrims Mss, LMA/4632/A/05/002/01; *Oil City Derrick* (Pennsylvania), 29 August 1928.

66. Western and General Report No. 98, 11 December 1918, Records of the Cabinet Office, TNA, Cab 24/150.
67. *Christian Science Monitor*, 9 December 1918.
68. *Boston Daily Globe*, 8 December 1918; *Christian Science Monitor*, 9 December 1918.
69. *Christian Science Monitor*, 9 December 1918.
70. T. G. Otte, '"The Shrine at Sulgrave": The Preservation of the Washington Ancestral Home as an "English Mount Vernon" and Transatlantic Relations', in Melanie Hall (ed.), *Towards World Heritage: International Origins of the Preservation Movement, 1870–1930* (Farnham, 2011), pp. 109–38; *The Times*, 4 July 1919; Robert M. Thompson to John A. Stewart, 10 May 1917, John A. Stewart Papers, NYPL, Box 1; Sulgrave Committee of Management Minutes, 9 March 1914, Sulgrave Mss, Sulgrave Manor Trust Archive, [SMTA]; some of the information concerning the merging of the Peace Committees, the Sulgrave Institute and the Anglo-American Society has been gathered from previously unpublished research undertaken by Dr Michael P. Cullinane.
71. Minute Book 2, 8 March 1912, Pilgrims Mss, NYC; Otte, '"The Shrine at Sulgrave"', p. 118; *The Times*, 4 July 1919; Anglo-American Society Minutes, 2 August 1918, and Sulgrave Committee of Management Minutes, 17 December 1919, Sulgrave Mss, SMTA.
72. *New York Times*, 9 November 1918; Minute Book 2, 5 November 1914, and Minute Book 3, 27 December 1918, Pilgrims Mss, NYC; *New-York Tribune*, 9 November 1918; *New York Times*, 9 January 1954; John Carver Edwards, *Patriots in Pinstripe: Men of the National Security League* (Washington, 1982), *passim*.
73. Western and General Report No. 95, 20 November 1918, Records of the Cabinet Office, TNA, Cab 24/150.
74. *New York Times*, 9 December 1918; for more on the symbolism of Magna Charta and its usage during Britain's Day, see MacRaild et al., 'Interdependence Day and Magna Charta', p. 148.
75. *Washington Post*, 9 December 1918; *New York Times*, 8 December 1918; Roberts, 'The Emergence of American Atlanticism', pp. 588–91; Edward McNall Burns, *The American Idea of Mission: Concepts of National Purpose and Destiny* (New Brunswick, 1957).
76. Western and General Report No. 98, 11 December 1918, Records of the Cabinet Office, TNA, Cab 24/150; *New York Times*, 8 December 1918.
77. *New York Times*, 21 December 1918.
78. *New York Times*, 8 December 1918.
79. Roberts, 'The Emergence of American Atlanticism', p. 594.

80. Todd J. Pfannestiel, *Rethinking the Red Scare: The Lusk Committee and New York's Crusade Against Radicalism, 1919–1923* (New York, 2003), pp. 1–9; Kennedy, *Over Here*, p. 56.

81. Kennedy, *Over Here*, pp. 290–1; Zieger, *America's Great War*, pp. 188–215.

82. Pfannestiel, *Rethinking the Red Scare*, p. 11; Zieger, *America's Great War*, pp. 195–6; *New York Times*, 19 November 1918.

83. *New York Times*, 8 December 1918.

84. *New York Times*, 25 January 1918.

85. *Washington Post*, 9 December 1918; *New York Times*, 8 December 1918.

86. *Evening Public Ledger*, 6 December 1918.

87. Taylor, *Projection of Britain*, p. 6.

5   The Decline of the Great Rapprochement

'I hate the English – Damn the Pilgrims' – 'To hell with Anglo-American friendship.'
(Anonymous member of the Pilgrims Society)

If the First World War had seen a change in the public diplomacy role of the Pilgrims Society compared with the banquets of the 1900s, then the decade following the end of the conflict witnessed further developments in how the Society related to more official channels of diplomacy. The war had also altered how Britain and the US related both to each other and to the rest of the world. Most obviously, Britain was now a debtor nation and the US a creditor. While Britain remained a great power and retained significant strategic influence – for instance through its prominent role in the newly created League of Nations, which gave it greater influence in Europe than that enjoyed by the US – the conflict had undermined its financial strength. By contrast, the post-war years witnessed a relative withdrawal from international interventionism on the part of the US, as shown, for instance, by its absence from the League of Nations. This isolationism paradoxically occurred alongside the increasing spread of American cultural values to Europe, partly on account of unofficial cultural and economic influences. The 'Americanisation' of Europe – through the appeal of jazz music, Hollywood films, technological advances, and mass consumerism – extended the US's sphere of influence in terms of what Joseph Nye would now call 'soft power' and in ways that brought into sharper focus the contrasting economic and commercial positions of Britain and the US.[1]

Some of the dichotomies in the Anglo-American relationship were mirrored in the contrasting fortunes of the two branches of the Pilgrims Society. As this and the following chapter will show, the London branch was more active in the 1920s than was the New York branch. Equally, however, American ideas – in the form of American political debates over issues such as the League of Nations and their impact on Anglo-American relations – provided the principal influences on the activities of the Society. Whereas the London Pilgrims hosted a number of distinguished speakers at a variety of high-profile functions, the New York branch struggled to organise a similarly strong programme of events. This contrasting level of activity was a product of a wider context in which the Anglo-American relationship was coming under increasing strain. Two of the most significant causes of this strain – namely the war debts and naval disarmament – were of direct relevance to the economic and strategic aspects of the Anglo-American relationship. They also impacted on wider public and cultural relations between the two countries and contributed to a period of resentment and misunderstanding. In particular, the underlying aims and objectives of the Pilgrims Society were challenged by a greater degree of American nationalist anti-British feeling. It is clear, however, that even though the ideals of the Society came under pressure in the 1920s, and even though the New York Pilgrims struggled to match their British counterparts' ability to maintain a strong programme of activities, the Pilgrims did not become an irrelevance. Rather, the opposite was the case: difficult international relations meant that there was an even greater need for the work of groups like the Pilgrims Society.

This chapter will examine the activities of the Pilgrims Society against the backdrop of official international relations in the 1920s. It will do so with particular reference to those Society events that directly impacted upon wider diplomatic relations and which are most instructive about the Society's self-described 'semi-official' status. The chapter has been divided into four sections. The first of these sections outlines in greater detail the complex geopolitical context of the 1920s, in particular events surrounding the League of Nations, the war debt, and naval disarmament, which fed into Anglo-American animosity. The second section discusses in detail the London Pilgrims' 1921 welcome for the new US ambassador in Britain, George Harvey. This event resulted in a controversial contribution to the American debate over membership of the League of Nations and also significantly raised the international profile of the Pilgrims Society and solidified its role as a public diplomacy actor. The third section of the chapter, meanwhile, traces in greater depth how Anglo-American ill-feeling was manifested within the Pilgrims Society, for example the surprising case of anti-Englishness directed at one of the leading figures in the New York branch, Frederick Cunliffe-Owen. The chapter's fourth section will examine the role the Pilgrims Society played in relation to the war debt question and the 1921 Washington Conference on naval disarmament, including further controversial inputs from Ambassador Harvey. This section also serves to demonstrate some of the ways in which the Pilgrims Society engaged with officialdom in this period. In sum, the Pilgrims' experience of the early 1920s is instructive about the development of the Society's public diplomacy role and also helps shed new light on another period in US history when some Americans retreated behind isolationism, protectionism, and self-interest.

'Damn the English anyway': Anglo-American relations in the early 1920s

The rise in anti-Britishness in the US was encapsulated by the Pilgrims' George Wilson, who told Harry Brittain in October 1922 that he had detected 'an increase in anti-British feeling – not only among the men in the street but among educated, cultured people'. Wilson was dismayed to find that the New York Yacht Club would not put on a function to welcome the new British Naval Attaché, as was customary, with one member having said, '"Oh damn the English anyway" – and he's a Pilgrim.'[2] American anti-British sentiment in the 1920s was fed by a combination of contemporary diplomatic issues and a traditional nationalist dislike of America's former colonial superior. It was symptomatic also of a desire amongst some in the US to distance the country from the Old World – which was often identified with dishonest statesmen – and to isolate it from a repeat of the sort of interventionism that led to its involvement in the First World War.[3]

With even members of the Pilgrims Society displaying anti-British sentiment, George Wilson blamed the so-called 'Balfour Note' of August 1922, which he said had 'rubbed us all the wrong way' and which he described as a 'faux pas, so far as the USA were concerned'.[4] Drafted by Arthur Balfour – acting Foreign Secretary (on account of the temporary absence of Lord Curzon through illness) and Lord President – the Balfour Note was the British government's response to the US's invitation to its debtors to come to an agreement to repay the money that was due following the First World War. Britain owed the US roughly £850 million, and was itself owed £1,825 million from its own European debtors. In the Balfour Note, Britain outlined its hope for the cancellation of both inter-Allied debts and German reparations. As the French would not agree to cancel reparations, the British were also hopeful that it could instead be agreed that Britain would pay the US simply what it received from its debtors. The US, however, did not accept this and saw no reason why Britain should not pay back the money it had loaned. This was agreed to, though the negotiations and their settlement caused bitterness in both countries.[5] Even George Wilson displayed a certain level of disapproval of the British stance in his explanation to Harry Brittain that any 'attempt to hold up America as a Shylock – or to put upon her the responsibility for the financial troubles of Europe, is bound to be resented over here'.[6] Wilson was articulating the feeling held by many Americans that the Balfour Note was a misguided attempt by the British to avoid their responsibilities as debtors, even though the war had cost Britain and its European allies significantly more in human and economic terms than it had the US. The ill-feeling surrounding this issue was at the heart of a public spat between Balfour and George Harvey following a Pilgrims event in London in February 1923 and will be returned to later in the chapter.

Anti-Britishness in the US was also put to domestic political usage. While many in the Republican Party – including those international bankers and businessmen to whom a constructive, if competitive, relationship with Britain was an economic necessity – were of Scottish or English descent and felt a sense of loyalty towards Britain, the Democratic Party attempted to make political capital out of wider anti-Britishness. This followed a realisation that the Democrats' defeat at the 1920 presidential election had partly been caused by its criticism of Warren Harding's German-American and Irish-American supporters. In addition, issues such as Irish independence, and to a lesser extent Egyptian independence, resonated with an American public traditionally suspicious of British imperialism.[7] Another contributor to American anti-Britishness was a growing awareness of the economic rivalry between the two countries.[8] While this resulted in resentment towards the US among Britain's commercial interest throughout the 1920s, at the start of the decade it primarily contributed to American suspicions that Britain was attempting to monopolise access to oil in Persia, for example through the Anglo-Persian agreement of 1919. This coincided with American concerns that the US would soon run out of oil should it rely on its existing sources. As a result, the oil lobby in the US, including Standard Oil, urged the State Department to protect the Open Door policy in the Middle East.[9]

American opposition to British imperialism was further evident, meanwhile, in some of the responses to the other great issue of Anglo-American diplomacy in the 1920s, namely naval disarmament. The Conference on Limitation of Armaments (referred to here as the Washington Conference) opened on 12 November 1921 and was designed to prevent a naval race between Britain and the US which neither country – with the exception of the naval interest in each – wanted nor could afford. Underlying the naval issue was the fundamental difference between each country's attitude to belligerent rights at sea and the notion of 'freedom of the seas'. Many Americans remembered and resented Britain's naval blockade during the US's period of neutrality during the First World War, while the British maintained that their status as a world power depended upon such blockades. The US was also uneasy about the Anglo-Japanese alliance, which it regarded as having the potential to draw the Royal Navy into conflict on behalf of the Japanese against American interests in the Pacific, and which was due to expire in 1922.[10] Britain welcomed the opportunity to improve Anglo-American relations without endangering its relationship with Japan and, along with Japan, France, and Italy, accepted the American invitation to convene in Washington to discuss naval limitation. While complete agreement was not reached, the conference did result in a series of important treaties, including the Five-Power Treaty. The outcome of the Washington conference helped improve Anglo-American relations in the mid-1920s, though by 1927 the naval rivalry between the two countries had again deteriorated. For now, however, the US could be pleased with a conference at which it had conceded less than the British and through which an arms race amongst some of the great powers had been prevented.[11] Yet the Four-Power Treaty between the US, the UK, France, and Japan – which, by putting in place a framework for consultation in the event of dispute or conflict in the Pacific, essentially replaced the Anglo-Japanese alliance – was criticised by some irreconcilable Republicans and, ironically, Wilsonian Democrats (who felt that it was a poor man's League of Nations). Importantly, however, both groups deployed anti-British arguments in criticism of the Treaty and questioned whether the US should so closely ally itself with the imperialistic British. Some Congressional critics, like Tennessee's John K. Shields, even perceived an attempt by pro-British Americans – including those who had participated in the Rhodes Scholarships – to forge a British–American union.[12] This would not be the last time in the 1920s that expression was given to fears about Anglo-American elites attempting to subvert the US's independence.

The Pilgrims, Ambassador Harvey, and the League of Nations, 1921

Many of the Pilgrims Society's most important functions in the 1920s catered specifically for new ambassadors. This was especially the case for the London branch, which welcomed four US ambassadors between 1921 and 1929. More than ever before, these events received a great deal of publicity. As a result, they are instructive of the Pilgrims' contribution to the history of public diplomacy as it developed in the 1920s and into the 1930s. The dinner for George Harvey in May 1921, when he arrived in London to replace John W. Davis as ambassador, demonstrates why this was the case. Harvey was a publicist, editor, and businessman who had originally been a Republican, before becoming a supporter of Woodrow Wilson as Governor of New Jersey. He returned to the Republicans ahead of the 1916 presidential election, partly as a result of his dissatisfaction with Wilson's policy of neutrality, but also because Wilson had previously sought to distance himself from Harvey on account of the latter's association with J. P. Morgan. Harvey went on to become a strong opponent of US membership of the League of Nations. He subsequently supported Warren Harding at the 1920 election, and it was his 'politically famous "hotel room filled with smoke"', as the *New York Times* described it, in which Harding's candidacy was decided upon at the Republican convention in Chicago. He served as ambassador in London until 1923, before becoming editor of the *Washington Post* for a time.[13] Harvey proved a divisive choice as ambassador, and was unpopular amongst some Republicans, who remembered criticisms he had made against Theodore Roosevelt – for instance against Roosevelt's alleged 'methodological attacks upon property, in appeals to envy and uncharitableness, in wanton extravagance, in the domineering characteristics of the Chief Executive'[14] – and many Democrats, who were embittered following his criticisms of Woodrow Wilson. Even Secretary of State Charles E. Hughes had expressed his opposition to Harding's wish to appoint Harvey. This was because Hughes had previously observed Harvey at a social function, during which Harvey drank too much and spoke too freely.[15] As Harvey's characterisation of Roosevelt shows, however, Harvey was the 'normalcy' ambassador for the 'normalcy' president. Like Harding, he favoured a retreat from the domestic and international interventionism of Roosevelt and Wilson.[16]

Harvey's selection was also the subject of a debate in the Senate in April 1921, during which his credentials for the post of ambassador were questioned, with Byron Patton Harrison, the Democratic senator for Mississippi and ally of Woodrow Wilson, noting that Harvey was a careerist and a 'past master in fomenting trouble and aggravating delicate situations'.[17] The Pilgrims' George Wilson was also unhappy that Harvey had been chosen as ambassador, writing Harry Brittain in May 1921 that he was 'dreadfully disappointed in the appointment'. Even though he was a Republican, Wilson regarded Harding's appointment of Harvey as a 'purely political one, and the first thing the President has done which has displeased a lot of us'. Wilson felt that Harvey 'lacks in representation, to use that word – meaning his physical appearance, personality' and that he was 'not in the class' of John Hay, Joseph Choate, Whitelaw Reid, Walter Hines Page, or John Davis. He was clearly concerned that Harvey's appointment was a slight to Britain and to Anglo-American friendship, and explained that he believed that the US 'should send our very best to the Court of St. James'.[18] Senator Harrison similarly felt that Britain deserved a better ambassador and, in Congress, questioned why 'no one in America could be found to represent this Government at London except one whose every talent has been employed against the League of Nations idea', especially as Britain was one of the most important members of the League.[19] Of course, Harding would have had no sense that Harvey's appointment was an insult to Britain. While the president did not regard Anglo-American friendship as the most pressing of issues, he neverthe-less considered himself a supporter of rapprochement between the two countries. Thus, an interpretation of Harvey's appointment as a political appointment of a man whose support the president clearly valued is stronger than any suggestion that Harding was indifferent to any perceived British opinions about the quality of the new ambassador.[20]

Throughout his time as ambassador, Harvey fulfilled the fears of George Wilson and Senator Harrison. Indeed, he immediately sparked controversy by delivering an unusually blunt speech at the Pilgrims Society's welcome banquet at London's Hotel Victoria on 19 May 1921. As had become traditional, this was the US ambassador's first public appearance in Britain. The Pil-grims went to great lengths to ensure that this was the case, and corresponded both with the British Foreign Secretary, Lord Cur-zon, and with the king's private secretary, Lord Stamfordham. Somewhat presumptuously, the secretary of the London Pilgrims, John Wilson Taylor, wrote to Stamfordham to remind Bucking-ham Palace that 'the Ambassador cannot appear at any public function until His Majesty has received His Excellency'. In a roundabout way of asking King George V to accept Harvey's cre-dentials as soon as possible so that the Pilgrims could be the first to entertain the new ambassador, Wilson Taylor explained the 'exigencies of the heavy preparation needed for such a function and the necessity of having it immediately after the ambassador's arrival are the reasons which I would ask you to accept as the excuse for my venturing to trouble you'.[21] Demonstrating that there was a degree of tension between the Society and the royal household – or at least an impatience with the Society's assertive-ness on the part of the latter, and thus a contrast between the Society's perceptions of its own importance and the perceptions of others – Lord Stamfordham somewhat curtly replied to say that the 'reception by the King of the new American Ambassador, when His Excellency presents his Credentials, is a matter which must be dealt with by the Foreign Office'.[22] Perhaps because he already knew that, Wilson Taylor had also written to Curzon, explaining that the Society was 'hopeful that His Majesty may receive the new Ambassador in time for the dinner to take place, and any assistance in your power to this end would be greatly appreciated'.[23] Curzon promised to do what he could to help expedite matters, and also said that he would 'make a point of being present' at the Pilgrims' welcome for Harvey.[24] This shows that the Foreign Office, if not Buckingham Palace, regarded the Pilgrims as an important part of what was a semi-official welcome to the new US ambassador.

Meanwhile, the British Pilgrims kept in communication with Harvey via the New York branch of the Society, with the American Pilgrims cabling their London counterparts in April for information as to how quickly they would be able to arrange a dinner, as Harvey had 'numerous pressing invitations but wishes to make his first appearance at Pilgrims dinner in accordance with custom'.[25] This process was eased by the fact that Harvey was a long-standing member of the Pilgrims.[26] He was evidently willing to keep in touch with the Society, just as the London and New York Pilgrims were willing to keep in touch with each other. As a result, it was a simple matter for the two branches to coordinate a welcome for the new ambassador. With the date set for 19 May, the US Pilgrims confirmed to the British branch that Harvey 'promises that it shall be the occasion of his first speech at any entertainment and that he will accept no invitation for any earlier date'.[27] Contacting the US ambassador before he left America via the New York Pilgrims – and specifically through the branch's well-connected chairman, Charles H. Sherrill, who was then in Washington – of course made logistical sense.[28] While the Society could alternatively have liaised with the US Embassy, Harvey's membership of the Society meant that he was familiar both with its personnel and its traditions. That is not to say that there was no contact between the US Embassy and the British Pilgrims. Indeed, ambassadorial staff sent Harvey's biographical details to Wilson Taylor, including information about his other club memberships, which included British ethnic societies like the St. George's Society, the Saint Andrew's Society and the Friendly Sons of St. Patrick.[29] The informal cooperation between Harvey, the Embassy, and the two Pilgrims branches – and indeed Curzon's willingness to expedite the acceptance of Harvey's credentials – confirms that the Society acted as a conduct and elite network between and amongst state and non-state actors.

The guests who assembled at the Hotel Victoria on 19 May 1921 to meet Ambassador Harvey were a distinguished group. Curzon did indeed attend, as did the Duke of York – on the condition that he did not need to make a speech – and David Lloyd George, the then British prime minister. It was Lloyd George's first time at a

Pilgrims dinner, but it was not that fact that led to the *Washington Post* writing that the event was 'enveloped in far deeper interest than usually attends a reception to a new ambassador by this international club'.[30] Instead, it was Harvey's speech that was of principal interest. The Pilgrims dinner came the month after Warren Harding's special address to Congress, in which the US president had explicitly and finally ruled out the possibility of US membership of the League of Nations.[31] This was a follow-on from the acrimonious nationwide debate about the US's place in the post-war world that had so marked the latter years of Woodrow Wilson's presidency. Wilson had been committed to the League of Nations and had outlined plans for such an organisation in his Fourteen Points statement in January 1918.[32] The debate over US involvement culminated in March 1920 when Congress voted against a version of the treaty which contained reservations diluting the US's commitment to collective security. In an all or nothing gesture, Wilson had instructed Democratic senators to reject the altered treaty.[33] Opposition to the president's version of the League centred on the figure of Henry Cabot Lodge, who was Republican chairman of the Senate's Foreign Relations Committee and whose own stance on the League could be described as 'strong reservationist'.[34] Reservationists, or 'limited internationalists', supported the US's involvement in the League provided alterations were made to Woodrow Wilson's original vision, in particular in relation to collective security. They wanted the US to become a member of the League, but on terms that did not compromise the country's independence in foreign policy, for example by rejecting or modifying any clauses in the Covenant of the League of Nations – like Article X – that they felt could potentially oblige League members to deploy military forces in defence of another League member. Limited internationalists included people like Elihu Root, Nicholas Murray Butler, and Charles Evans Hughes. Another strand of opposition to Wilson's League came from convinced isolationists and nationalists who did not support membership in any form, and included the so-called 'irreconcilable' senators like William E. Borah, Hiram W. Johnson, and James A. Reed.[35] George Harvey was amongst the latter group, saying in March 1919 that he was

> opposed to the covenant [of the League of Nations] as it stands. I am opposed to it as it may be amended. I am opposed to it in principle. I am opposed to it in theory. I am opposed to it in practice. I regard

it as the most un-American proposal ever submitted to the American people by an American president.[36]

Seen in this light, it is possible that Harvey's appointment as ambassador was an effort by Warren Harding to placate the irreconcilables in the Republican Party.[37] With Harding having expressed his wish to move on from what was regarded as a failed Wilsonian internationalism, Harvey used his Pilgrims speech to address anyone in Britain – where the government had strongly desired US membership – or in the US who was under the 'impression that in some way or other, by hook or by crook, unwittingly and surely unwillingly, the United States may yet be beguiled into the League of Nations'. To such people, he wanted to demonstrate 'how utterly absurd any such notion is'. The ambassador proceeded to inform the assembled Pilgrims that Warren Harding had been elected by a large majority on a mandate to ensure that the US would not have 'anything whatsoever to do with the League or with any commission or committee appointed by it or responsible to it, directly or indirectly, openly or furtively'.[38] Rev. Frederick Lynch – a Republican peace advocate who was part of the audience at the Hotel Victoria – later wrote to the *New York Times* an account of the Pilgrims' reaction to Harvey's speech.[39] This guest of the Pilgrims believed that '[n]o one who was not present at the dinner can have any idea of the consternation' that Harvey's words caused, explaining that the ambassador's declaration on the League of Nations issue fell 'like a thunderbolt' and was met with a 'dead silence'.[40]

The Pilgrims may well have been surprised, for Harvey's comments about Harding's mandate were not strictly accurate. Harding had deliberately been ambiguous about League of Nations membership, preferring to ensure that the Republican Party – with its competing irreconcilable and limited internationalist elements – remained united behind his candidacy.[41] This discrepancy was picked up on by the pro-League Lynch and by the *New York Times*. Both pointed out that Harvey's remarks – and indeed Harding's decision not to join the League – directly and publicly contradicted the position of high-profile, pro-League Republicans, including Secretary of State Hughes, the Secretary of Commerce Herbert Hoover, and the veteran statesman Elihu Root, who had all signed the so-called 'Appeal of 31 Eminent Americans' in October 1920 urging League membership with reservations.[42]

Similarly, a rector from Yonkers wrote in the letters pages of the *New York Times* in June describing Harvey's speech as an 'intolerable misrepresentation' as he had understood that US involvement in the League of Nations 'would be more probably and promptly ratified by the election of a Republican than Democratic executive'.[43] Echoing these sentiments, Mrs Ray Lyman Wilbur – the wife of the president of Stanford University, and a leader in the Women's League for the Peace Treaty – sent President Harding a telegram complaining that she felt 'grossly misrepresented' by Harvey's 'unauthorized statement' because she had felt 'assured by you in a pre-election telegram that the United States would enter an association of nations'.[44] The *New York Times* was also surprised that Harvey had used the forum provided by the Pilgrims Society – which, 'as we understand it, is not an official body' – to 'declare the political attitude of his Government in a manner commonly reserved for interviews with the Secretary for Foreign Affairs'. The paper criticised Harvey for speaking 'in a manner to convey the impression that the League is a disreputable organization', and for doing so in front of the prime minister and 'many leading public men of a great Power that is a member of the League of Nations'.[45] The *New York Times*' description of the Pilgrims and its comment on the propriety of making official policy announcements at the Society's functions is instructive on a number of counts. Crucially, it demonstrates that there was a growing public awareness of the Society as a semi-official, non-state actor, something that resulted in a questioning of exactly what the Society was for. The *New York Times* had regularly reported on Pilgrims events ever since it was founded, so the Society was not an unknown quantity for the paper. The Harvey dinner, however, clearly challenged existing notions of the Society as an elite dining club. Harvey had used his maiden speech in Britain to express a controversial policy position on behalf of the US and had done so in the knowledge that the location and venue – namely the Pilgrims Society – would generate greater interest around what he wanted to say. This was the Pilgrims Society acting as a tool for public diplomacy. Harvey wanted to advocate the US position on the League of Nations not only to the elites at the Pilgrims dinner – amongst whom was the British prime minister – but also to the wider British and American publics via the anticipated newspaper coverage. This represented a difference to earlier Pilgrims functions, for example the 1906 dinner in New York for Earl Grey. That too had presented a statesman with an opportunity to advocate a position both to another statesman and to the wider public and was, as such, an act of public diplomacy. The Harvey dinner in 1921 was, however, slightly different. Whereas Earl Grey and Elihu Root in 1906 had restricted their advocacy to general statements about Anglo-American cultural affinity, Harvey in 1921 outlined US foreign policy in a didactic and uncompromising fashion. As will become apparent, Pilgrims events later in the 1920s served a similar – though perhaps less bullish – function. The 1906 dinner had also presented an opportunity for Grey and Root to network privately, through which was facilitated a proactive discourse on specific Canadian–US differences. The Harvey dinner, by contrast, rather than facilitating an international conversation was characteristic more of the isolationist strand in the US's approach to foreign relations in the 1920s.

Harvey's speech provoked a public reaction from at least one British statesman. Lord Robert Cecil, who was the key British architect of the League, and who had worked closely with Woodrow Wilson to formulate plans for the organisation at the Paris Peace Conference, was motivated to write a letter to *The Times* in the days immediately following the Pilgrims banquet. While he did not specifically mention Harvey, Cecil noted that '[w]e have been authoritatively informed that the present Administration in the United States ... will have nothing to do, directly or indirectly, with the League of Nations'. He denied, however that this required Britain to 'modify our attitude towards the League or discourage us from giving it our utmost support'. He insisted that the League was a 'sober and serious attempt to safeguard mankind from a repetition of the horrors and destruction of the late war' and said that he hoped that the US, along with Germany and Russia, would eventually join: 'The sooner we can get their help the more effectually we could do our work.'[46] That Cecil felt the need to write this letter demonstrates that he believed that Harvey's Pilgrims speech had had sufficient reach and influence to potentially impact upon British elite and public opinion regarding the League. He evidently felt that he needed to act in order to offset any such impact. It was a tactful, though unambiguous, public repudiation of US policy by a British statesman made in response to Harvey's public diplomacy.

Even though the domestic US debate on the League of Nations was not as simplistic as Harvey had depicted, the ambassador was not saying anything contrary to the position of the president in May 1921. Harding had confirmed that the US would not join the League of Nations and Harvey was giving expression to that position. Other of Harvey's remarks, however, proved more problematical for the president, in particular those made in relation to the reasons for which the US had entered the First World War. Rather than upholding the Wilsonian notion that the US wanted to make the 'world safe for democracy', Harvey challenged the 'impression that we went to war to rescue humanity from all kinds of menacing perils'. He said that it was 'not a fact' that the US 'sent our young soldiers across to save this kingdom, France and Italy'. Rather, America 'sent them solely to save the United States of America, and most reluctantly and laggardly at that. We were not too proud to fight, whatever that may mean. We were afraid not to fight.'[47] According to Lynch, this resulted in a 'murmur of "Nays"' amongst the Pilgrims.[48] Though primarily motivated by a desire to attack Woodrow Wilson, Harvey's argument that the US had entered the First World War not for the benefit of civilisation but for essentially selfish reasons was contemporaneous with a developing revisionist interpretation of the conflict. Some American historians, including Charles A. Beard, had begun questioning whether Germany had indeed been primarily responsible for the outbreak of war in 1914.[49]

The war and the high-profile national debate on the League had awakened many more Americans to the importance of foreign affairs, a development that was evident in the interest shown in what had happened at the Pilgrims dinner.[50] Harvey's interpretation of the US's war aims in particular generated a great deal of comment in the US and his Pilgrims speech came to the notice of, and was criticised by, a wide variety of people. For the first time in any significant way, indeed more so than had even been the case with the Earl Grey dinner in 1906, the Pilgrims Society had come to the attention of the wider public. Press reports suggested that Harvey had 'aroused conflicting emotions in the minds of hundreds of thousands of Americans', particularly in relation to his remarks on the war. It was this matter that was 'emphasized in practically every letter and telegram of protest' – of which there were allegedly 'thousands' – sent to Harvey's Democratic enemies in the Senate. Senator Harrison reported that he had received 5,000 messages about Harvey's speech, the vast majority of which were critical of the ambassador. The senator was said to have 'great piles of letters and telegrams in his office from men and women in every walk of life' congratulating him on originally opposing Harvey's appointment. Many of these came from supporters of Woodrow Wilson, for example the Woodrow Wilson Club of New York University, whose message demanded that 'measures be taken forthwith to efface the stain thus ingloriously spread upon our escutcheon by one who has completely misconstrued the spirit of America'.[51] Back in the letters pages, the same Yonkers rector who had sought to highlight the subtleties of the League debate, and who was an enrolled Republican, 'as rector and friend of 145 boys who with knightly and generous purpose flung themselves into the war to end war, five of them making the supreme sacrifice', was further 'impelled to add my witness to the rising tide of protest against the bulk of Colonel Harvey's Pilgrim dinner speech', which he felt was 'an affront to the nobility and idealism of the American electorate and soldiery'.[52] Church ministers even criticised Harvey from the pulpit, with Reverend Dr William P. Merrill of Brick Presbyterian Church finding himself 'surrounded by his parishioners who congratulated him on his sermon, and said that he represented exactly their reaction toward Ambassador Harvey's words'.[53] Meanwhile, the mother of a soldier who had been killed during the war wrote to the *New York Times* that her son 'went to war eagerly, with the light of consecration in his face ... He knew that civilization was menaced, and he felt the privilege that was his in helping to save it.' The letter-writer focused on Harvey and not the administration, noting that 'President Harding doesn't belittle our dead.'[54]

Nevertheless, Harding was pressured to distance himself from Harvey's remarks. For example, Elisha Kent Kane, the owner of the Kushequa Route Railroad in Pennsylvania, wrote to the president urging him to 'degrade this man [Harvey] so promptly that his shame may not attach itself to your Administration'.[55] Press reports from Washington the day after the Pilgrims dinner noted, however, that '[c]omment at the White House and the State Department was withheld, but it is evident Colonel Harvey said nothing that is displeasing to President Harding and Secretary Hughes, and much that met with their approval'.[56] Criticism in the Senate largely came from pro-League Democrats, though Henry Cabot Lodge declined to comment, while the *New York*

Times noted that there had 'been comment, even on the Republican sides of the two Chambers'.[57] Amidst this atmosphere, there was considerable anticipation ahead of the president's appearance at a memorial service at Arlington Cemetery on 30 May. The *New York Times* noted that there was 'great eagerness to hear anything the President might say which might reflect his views upon the speech made by Colonel George B. Harvey . . . at the dinner given by the Pilgrims in London' and that 'attention was closely focused on Mr Harding's address to catch any intimation of his sentiments in this regard'. In the end, Harding did not explicitly touch on Harvey's speech, though he did contradict his ambassador by saying that the war was waged 'for humanity's sake'.[58] The previous day, at another event in Virginia, Harding was already reported as having made a speech 'in striking contrast' to Harvey's, in which the president said that

> America fought to preserve the rights of the Republic and to maintain the civilization which we had such a part in making, and in that service we have rendered tribute not only to that cause but also to the highest ideals of humanity.[59]

In truth, this was not the 'striking contrast' that it might have been. While Harding insisted that the US had wider reasons for going to war, he admitted first that it did so 'to preserve the rights of the Republic'. As such, the president was attempting to repair whatever damage had been done by Harvey, while at the same time seeking to avoid undermining him. Nevertheless, Tennessee's Senator McKellar believed that these two speeches 'prove that Colonel Harvey's utterances were repudiated by President Harding'.[60] Similarly, by June, the *New York Times* was explaining that there was a 'consensus of opinion' in Washington that Harding and Hughes had not known precisely what Harvey would say to the Pilgrims, even if they had discussed the address 'in a general way' before Harvey left for Britain. Even so, the paper reported that many people had come 'to the conclusion that portions of Mr Harvey's address would have given greater satisfaction if other phrases had been employed'.[61] In addition to Harding's Virginia speeches, Hughes had said that Americans had not gone 'forth to fight for this nation as one of imperialistic designs and cunning purpose . . . They offered their lives and all the energies of the country were harnessed in the supreme effort, because we loved the institutions of liberty.' According to the paper, this was evidence to many in Washington – in the absence of a direct statement from either Harding or Hughes – of the 'viewpoint of the executive branch of the Government to some of the statements in Ambassador Harvey's speech'.[62] Importantly, however, and even though Harding's public remarks in the weeks following Harvey's speech were interpreted as rebuking the ambassador, it appears instead that the president was not displeased. In a letter sent to Harvey at the beginning of June, Harding noted the 'little hubbub' that had been 'kicked up here over your speech at the Pilgrims' dinner', but explained that there was 'no suggestion that you have in any way distressed the world in general'. Rather, the president believed that 'the frankness of your expression has been very shocking to some of those who dwell in the clouds with the sponsors for the League of Nations' and that there was 'little if any criticism among those whose support you have a right to expect'.[63] Similarly, and though he did not mention that portion of Harvey's speech, it is unlikely that the president disagreed with his ambassador's interpretation of US war aims. In May 1917, when he was senator for Ohio, Harding had himself challenged the notion that the US had entered the war the month previously in defence of democracy. He said, for example, that he would 'rather have other nations of the world assume democracy by following America's example than have this form of Government forced upon them'. Rather than 'fighting to establish world democracy', Harding believed that it was 'none of our business what form of Government any nation has so long as it respects international law'.[64]

Whatever Warren Harding thought of it, George Harvey's inaugural speech to the Pilgrims in May 1921 was unlike any other made by an ambassador. It was a speech notable for the bluntness of its language and the assertiveness of its message. This message was directed as much towards the domestic audience in the US as it was to those in Europe who still hoped that the US might yet join the League of Nations, and it was in his homeland that Harvey's speech received the most attention. Importantly, however, the public response to elements of Harvey's speech – particularly from those Republican voters who felt betrayed by Harding's repudiation of League membership – demonstrates some of the subtleties of the American attitude towards international involvement in the 1920s. Moreover, it is of particular significance that Harvey had used the occasion of his Pilgrims speech to make such an important policy announcement. He clearly hoped that doing so at a high-profile function hosted by such a prominent Anglo-American association would attract greater attention. It also ensured that his controversial message was delivered in an environment otherwise conducive to international understanding. Indeed, the Society was relaxed about the controversial content of Harvey's speech. This is demonstrated by a letter from Wilson Taylor to Harvey in 1923, in which the Pilgrim said that he hoped that Harvey would make another speech to the Society which would generate similar levels of interest.[65] While the Society was impartial in its approach to the precise details of Harvey's speeches, it was evidently grateful for any publicity that served to highlight its general aim of Anglo-American friendship. Importantly, Harvey's speech to the Pilgrims was an example of 'advocacy' public diplomacy. With Harvey having helped establish the Pilgrims Society in this role – and having simultaneously raised the profile of the organisation in the US – his successors as US ambassador in London felt able to use the Society as a platform for statements of international significance. As will become clear in the next chapter, they did this during what was a continually difficult 1920s Anglo-American relationship.

The further development of anti-Britishness in the US, 1921–3

It is hard to imagine any of Harvey's predecessors speaking so bullishly to a Pilgrims audience. The 1920s, however, were different, and Harvey's assertiveness at the Pilgrims dinner matched the US's assertiveness with Britain during two of the main diplomatic events of the decade: namely, naval disarmament and the repayment of Britain's war debt to the US. This section will examine some of the ways in which animosity between Britain and the US developed as the 1920s wore on and will demonstrate what role the Pilgrims network played in these events.

It is noteworthy that the London Pilgrims were more successful than the New York Pilgrims in engaging with wider diplomatic developments. The New York Pilgrims found it difficult to attract high-profile guests to their banquets. In 1922, for example, the branch unsuccessfully attempted to arrange a function for Arthur Balfour, who prioritised the ESU over the Pilgrims. As a result, and 'in desperation, to show that the society was still in existence', they were obliged to arrange a second function for the British ambassador, Sir Auckland Geddes, in April 1922, in addition to the welcome banquet he had received two years previously. According to George Wilson, fewer than two hundred guests attended, making it 'the smallest dinner in the history of the Pilgrims'.[66] This was fewer than had attended Geddes's welcome banquet in May 1920, which was itself described by Wilson as the 'smallest dinner in seventeen years'.[67] Wilson partly blamed this on what he regarded as a dysfunctional committee in New York, which he in turn blamed on the figure of Frederick Cunliffe-Owen. Both branches of the Pilgrims Society had started the 1920s with new chairmen, with Harry Brittain and George T. Wilson each having resigned their positions by 1920, initially making way for Lord Desborough and Charles H. Sherrill respectively.[68] According to George Wilson, however, Cunliffe-Owen – who was one of the Society's vice-presidents – ran the Society in place of the absentee Chairman Sherrill.[69] Cunliffe-Owen was a writer, described in his *New York Times* obituary in 1926 as 'perhaps the best-known Englishman resident in the United States'.[70] He had worked for the British Foreign Office as a young man, before moving to America to become a journalist for the *New York World* and the *New-York Tribune* under Whitelaw Reid, through which one of his political columns became the US press's first syndicated column. According to a testimonial written by the Pilgrims Society, meanwhile, his 'close association with the British Embassy in Washington rendered his services in Anglo-American harmony most telling'.[71] Wilson frequently wrote to Brittain with updates on Cunliffe-Owen's performance, with Wilson's letters often tinged by an evident high opinion of his own tenure as leader of the American Pilgrims, and by his clear personal dislike of Cunliffe-Owen. This dislike partly stemmed from Wilson's belief that Cunliffe-Owen was 'seeking his own advancement and ends' – presumably meaning he felt that Cunliffe-Owen was using the Pilgrims' network for further social advancement – and also from the dispute with Lindsay Russell over the founding of the Society.[72] Not only had Cunliffe-Owen supported the readmission of Russell in 1913, but Wilson was also unhappy at Russell's suggestion in 1920 that Cunliffe-Owen had been involved with the Pilgrims in its formative years.[73] Wilson was further concerned that the executive committee was not meeting as regularly as it should (it had usually met once a month under Wilson, though not always), and was unhappy that Cunliffe-Owen had 'openly ridiculed' the idea of Harry Brittain potentially receiving an honorary degree from an American university.[74] According to Wilson, there were 'rumblings and mumblings in the membership, and I am repeatedly urged to take command of a revolution', though he declined to do so.[75] While Wilson suggested that other Pilgrims were also unhappy with Cunliffe-Owen, there was a clear personal element to his criticisms.

If Cunliffe-Owen's performance as leader contributed to the reasons for the small audience for the May 1920 event for Geddes, then other factors also played a part. Some Pilgrims pointed to the marked anti-British feeling in the US, which Wilson felt was 'more rampant than I have ever seen it'. Indeed, he told Brittain that 'there was one member on the Dinner Committee who had previously said "I hate the English – Damn the Pilgrims" – "To hell with Anglo-American friendship."' Wilson also, however, blamed Prohibition laws, 'as there are men who will not sit through a public dinner nowadays, on a dry basis'.[76] Another New York Pilgrims event in 1920, meanwhile, was described by Wilson as a 'frost'. After Chauncey Depew had made a speech at the function for members of the Sulgrave Institute, 'a large part of the feeders started to go out', requiring Sherrill to 'get up and bawl out a request to stay and to come up and fill the empty chairs in front!'[77] This relative lack of success stood in contrast to the London branch of the Society. While the British Pilgrims were able to arrange banquets for the British delegates to the naval disarmament conference in Washington in 1921, including Arthur Balfour, and for Stanley Baldwin in 1923 upon his return from the US at the conclusion of the debt negotiations, the only function linked to these geopolitical events that the New York Pilgrims organised was a dinner in October 1921 for the British admiral Lord Beatty, who was in the US to act as an adviser at the Washington Conference.[78]

The reasons for the contrasting fortunes of the two branches were located in the domestic American environment and mirrored the reality that the US – with its exporting of popular culture of music and film, not to mention tourists taking advantage of easier transport and a buoyant dollar – was increasingly capturing the imagination of Europe.[79] This was more conducive for the successful operation of a British-based pro-American organisation than it was for a US-based pro-British organisation. Unlike Britain, the US was a country in retreat from the international interventionism of its earlier political leaders. Indeed, the anti-British sentiment identified by Wilson within the Pilgrims Society took place amidst a wider context of nativism and isolationism in the US. Such nativism marked the post-war domestic environment with fear, uncertainty, and suspicion, and informed Warren Harding's normalcy agenda and the notion of 'America First'. These ideas were associated with the immigration restrictions introduced in an effort to keep out the large number of Southern and Eastern European migrants arriving in the US. Nativism was also evident in protectionist economic policies, and in the US's post-war Red Scare.[80] This doubt and uncertainty in the domestic setting meant that it was more difficult to mobilise a Society whose principal interest was the kind of active international friendship against which US isolationism was partly defined.

With members retreating from an interest in Anglo-American relations, as shown by the Pilgrim who had declared his wish for Anglo-American friendship to go 'to hell', it is clear that domestic trends were impinging on American engagement with international affairs. Like much of the American population, some members of the Pilgrims were evidently too distracted by the turmoil at home to focus on issues abroad. This offers one possible explanation for the low frequency of committee meetings under Cunliffe-Owen that Wilson had complained about. There was, however, an additional element to the opposition to Cunliffe-Owen. Intriguingly, some of Cunliffe-Owen's fellow New York Pilgrims took issue with a non-American having so much influence in the American branch of the Society. This was explained to Harry Brittain by George Wilson, who wrote in August 1920 that 'some members of the Committee are of the opinion that the American Pilgrims should not be run by an Englishman'.[81] According to Wilson, Cunliffe-Owen's leadership was 'as incongruous as if a fourth rate American in London were to run the affairs of the British Pilgrims!'[82] The notion that Cunliffe-Owen was unsuitable as leader of the New York branch because he was English was also demonstrative of wider American attitudes towards Britain in the early 1920s. Even though it would seem out of place in a Society aiming to further Anglo-American friendship, and was another example of internal divergence between Wilson and Brittain and Lindsay Russell, the opposition to Cunliffe-Owen was a mild form of American nativism. For those American Pilgrims opposed to Cunliffe-Owen on nativist grounds, the Pilgrims' notion of Anglo-American cultural, diplomatic, political, and commercial friendship was not more important than American nationalism, especially at a time when wider social tensions were forcing a reappraisal of what it meant to be American.[83] Moreover, the opposition to Cunliffe-Owen reflected the growing anti-British sentiment in the US which George Wilson had himself identified.

In addition to the rise in nativist sentiment, issues like Irish and Egyptian independence contributed to the anti-British feeling amongst an American public habitually distrustful of British imperialism.[84] An awareness of the commercial rivalry between the two countries also contributed to American anti-Britishness.[85] This was manifest during the early years of the 1920s in suspicions that Britain was monopolising access to oil in Persia.[86] Indeed, Sir Auckland Geddes had felt obliged to challenge such notions during his speech at his Pilgrims welcome banquet. Recognising that 'traditional hatreds and grudges died hard', the ambassador argued that 70 per cent of the world's oil output was American, compared with the British Empire's 2 per cent, and asked whether 'these figures suggest a monopoly for Britain?'[87] Perhaps feeling that his speech was overly focused on these wider issues at the expense of more positive sentiment, Geddes later wrote to Cunliffe-Owen to express his 'gratitude [for the Pilgrims' hospitality] which may have seemed somewhat absent in my speech'. More importantly, however, Geddes said that he appreciated the 'opportunity to say some serious things which appeared to me to be of paramount importance at the present time, and to say them to the body of men most suited to hear them and to see that they were emphasized in the right quarters'. The ambassador felt that '[a]ny influence that my words may have had depended largely on their setting, and I thank you very sincerely for all you personally, and those associated with you, did, to provide a setting so unique and so favorable'. Further demonstrating that he regarded the Pilgrims as a useful network for improving Anglo-American relations, Geddes finished by writing that the Society was a 'real inspiration to me and an encouragement to believe that a more real friendship between the English-speaking countries is within the bounds of practical politics, and not a dream'.[88]

Naval disarmament and war debt

The Pilgrims network as identified by Geddes was also utilised in the Society's engagement with the 1921 Washington Conference. The London Society arranged a banquet in October 1921 for the British delegates ahead of their departure for the US. Demonstrating that the Society was cognisant of the Japanese angle to the conference, one of the guests at the banquet was the Japanese ambassador, Baron Hayashi, whose attendance was secured partly with the cooperation of the Government Hospitality Fund. The involvement of the official government body responsible for overseeing the hospitality offered to foreign dignitaries is further evidence of the Pilgrims' state–private network. It also suggests that the British government hoped that, by involving Hayashi with the Pilgrims, the Japanese would not feel threatened by Anglo-American negotiations relating to the Anglo-Japanese alliance.[89]

The Pilgrims also held a dinner at the Hotel Victoria on 20 February 1922 for the return of Arthur Balfour and the other British delegates from Washington following the end of the conference. Balfour had returned to the UK amidst a general feeling that the outcome of the Washington conference boded well for the future of Anglo-American relations. The US Pilgrims, for example, cabled their British counterparts to 'rejoice with them that thanks largely to Anglo-Saxon cooperation in which Mr Balfour took so loyal a part the Washington conference has knit still closer the bonds of kinship and affection between the two great English-speaking nations'. At their annual general meeting in January, meanwhile, the New York Pilgrims noted that the conference was a recent example of a way in which the 'union of English-speaking nations as represented by The Pilgrims of the United States and Great Britain, has been emphasized recently', and recognised the 'wonderful way in which the Secretary of State, Mr Hughes, had brought to a quick and successful termination, negotiations which were usually long drawn out'.[90] As a result of the importance attached to the outcome of the conference, there was a great deal of interest when Balfour arrived back into Waterloo Station in London on 14 February. He was welcomed by a crowd that included Ambassador Harvey, most members of the British Cabinet, including David Lloyd George, and 'representatives of the Pilgrims'. Harry Brittain was also present and urged people to cheer as Balfour disembarked from the train.[91] Brittain had been tasked by the prime minister to help organise a welcome home dinner for Balfour on behalf of the government. This event took place on 16 February at the Hotel Cecil and was separate from the Pilgrims Society.[92] While the Pilgrims had hoped to be the first to entertain Balfour upon his return, Lloyd George told Brittain that he felt the government's event should take precedence. Brittain, however, would 'not do anything against my old and first love', and only agreed to help the prime minister when it transpired that the Pilgrims' banquet – which was originally supposed to be on 17 February – had been moved to 20 February.[93] That Brittain only accepted Lloyd George's request after he contacted the Pilgrims to make sure that their original plans had been changed suggests that the Society had first come under pressure from the prime minister. Certainly, the Society's office-bearers had been in touch with Lloyd George's office, for example on 9 February when they expressed the hope that the Pilgrims' 'arrangement meets with the Prime Minister's approval', while press reports explain that the Pilgrims had postponed the 17 February date 'in deference to the Government luncheon'.[94] The pertinent point, however, is that the Pilgrims were closely linked with the official welcome for Balfour upon his return from the Washington Conference. Not only were representatives of the Pilgrims present at Waterloo Station alongside the prime minister and the US ambassador, but the Society had arranged the date of its own banquet for Balfour in conjunction with Downing Street. It is also noteworthy that Lloyd George approached Harry Brittain, the vice-president of the Pilgrims, for help in organising the official government reception for Balfour. This demonstrates that both Brittain and the Pilgrims had a reputation for successfully hosting such important events and – in addition to Geddes' comment to the New York Pilgrims in relation to the Persian oil issue, and also the accommodation of the Japanese ambassador in London in October 1921 – is further evidence of the Society's state–private network, in particular the extent of its links with senior policy-makers.

With such interest in Balfour's return, it is not surprising to discover that the press was keen to cover the Pilgrims dinner. As was often the case with its events for high-profile individuals, the Society received a number of requests from newspapers seeking access to the dinner at the Hotel Victoria. Such newspapers included the *Chicago Daily Tribune* and the *Philadelphia*

Public Ledger, while the Press Association requested tickets for the admission of 'six relief reporters after dinner, in order that they may assist in the reporting of the speeches'.[95] The Pilgrims Society also benefited from its relationship with Sir Campbell Stuart, the managing director of *The Times* and managing editor of the *Daily Mail*. Stuart had joined the Society in 1918 and told Wilson Taylor that '[n]eedless to say I will see that a good report is given of the dinner'. The Pilgrims thanked Stuart for promising to provide such 'splendid publicity'.[96] This was another clear example of networking between the Pilgrims and journalistic elites.

George Harvey also made a speech at the Balfour dinner, though he avoided courting further international controversy. This did not, however, stop him – or indeed the Pilgrims Society – from receiving sharp criticism from anti-British figures in the US Congress. Poking fun at the Pilgrims Society, Senator James Reed explained to Congress that Harvey had made his speech 'in the presence of British nobles, amidst British beauties, at a banquet table in London, beneath the union jack'.[97] Whereas in 1921 Reed and Harvey had been joined in their opposition to the League of Nations (about which the senator was particularly vociferous, believing that American membership would tie the US to a 'British-dominated superstate'), the nationalistic Reed now attacked Harvey for hobnobbing with British elites. As a result of Harvey's contact with the Pilgrims, Reed publicly withdrew the support that he had given Harvey upon his appointment as ambassador. Displaying the anti-imperialist streak of American anti-Britishness, Reed went on to question whether American interests had been served by Britain's 'policy of blood and iron in Ireland', or by its policies in Egypt and, previously, in South Africa against the Boers. Reed also recalled Britain's tacit support for the Confederacy during the Civil War and questioned whether the two countries were 'united in spirit when, during the days of old Grover Cleveland – when, thank God, we had an American President – Great Britain proposed to invade Venezuela and to disregard the Monroe Doctrine'.[98]

While the naval disarmament question became a highly significant source of disagreement between the two countries later in the decade, the war debt issue proved more contentious during the earlier years. It is for that reason that the Pilgrims' functions for the Washington Conference passed without causing any great international controversy, whereas its engagement with the war debt question was more problematic. This was most obviously the case following the Society's dinner for Stanley Baldwin – who had become Chancellor of the Exchequer after the collapse of David Lloyd George's coalition government in October 1922 – upon his return to the UK following the war debt agreement between Britain and the US. Under Woodrow Wilson, the US had not pursued the wartime debt, instead focusing on the issue of the Treaty of Versailles, the League of Nations, and the 1920 presidential election. This changed in early 1922 with the creation by the Senate of the World War Foreign Debt Commission. Discussions between the governments on the issue remained cordial and low-key, until the publication of the controversial Balfour Note in August. Even though Britain and its European allies had made much the larger sacrifice during the First World War, many Americans regarded the Balfour Note as a condescending attempt by the British to avoid their responsibilities as debtors on what they regarded as spurious moral grounds. This much has already been seen in George Wilson's correspondence with Harry Brittain.[99] Baldwin and his delegation had arrived in the US in January 1923 to begin negotiations, with the two governments coming to an agreement at the start of February. President Harding signed the British Debt Agreement Act on 28 February, the same day as the Pilgrims' function in London for Baldwin, with Ambassador Geddes officially finalising the agreement on behalf of his government in June.[100] Though Baldwin had himself caused some controversy in the US by suggesting that too many Americans were insular in nature and were unable to see that international economic recovery was not best served by a tough debt settlement, the final agreement between the US and the UK did help improve Britain's image in America (even if Senator Reed was concerned that America's financial interest in British economic success meant that the US was tied to British imperialism).[101] Ahead of the Baldwin dinner, for example, the New York Pilgrims cabled the London branch to express 'profound congratulation to the entire Anglo-Saxon race that its two great Governments have so truly represented their peoples by their adjustment of this the largest international debt settlement ever negotiated'.[102] Yet Baldwin's remarks while in America revealed the British frustration towards the uncompromising approach taken by the US, and it was this frustration that Harvey aggravated during his Pilgrims speech.

The Pilgrims' banquet on 28 February 1923 at the Hotel Victoria was the first occasion on which Harvey had spoken publicly about the war debt, having previously mistakenly given the British government the impression that the US would accept an interest rate of 2 per cent, and not the 3.3 per cent that was expected.[103] Indeed, Harvey had taken a prominent role in urging Britain to take steps to come to an agreement with the US over the debt question. In July 1922 he accompanied William Taft, ex-US president and serving Chief Justice, at a meeting at Downing Street with Lloyd George and other senior Cabinet members at which the subject was broached.[104] Nevertheless, Harvey had assured Wilson Taylor that he would 'not make any utterance on the funding question until the Baldwin banquet', with the Pilgrims' secretary informing the ambassador that the Society hoped to 'hear from you one of those orations that always excite the deepest interest both in this country and America'.[105] On this occasion, however, Harvey's remarks contributed to the bad feeling that existed between the two countries on account of each other's contrasting expectations of the debt question, and resulted in a war of words with Arthur Balfour regarding his Note. During his speech to the Pilgrims Society on 28 February, Harvey outlined the terms of the loans given to Britain by the US as he understood them and argued that 'Surely the asking of repayment of such a loan could not rightfully be regarded as the act of a Shylock demanding his pound of flesh.' He went on to observe the perception that the US had 'singled out and "dunned" Great Britain', and insisted that '[w]e did neither the one nor the other'. The ambassador said that he was addressing the debt matter only because of the Balfour Note, which he argued had inaccurately suggested that the US only agreed to provide loans to Britain's wartime allies if Britain promised to secure the debt. In front of the assembled Pilgrims, Harvey urged the British government to 'remove the misapprehension created by this unfortunate allusion'. The press reported that Harvey's speech was 'listened to in almost complete silence' ('a profound and almost painful silence', according to Harvey's biographer), and that he 'got almost his first cheer' only when he suggested if 'Great Britain wished to refund to America part of her debt she knew where to get the cash'.[106] The *Washington Post* also reported that Harvey had caused 'displeasure in British official circles' and that, although the Foreign Office had 'declined to comment' on his Pilgrims speech, it was 'reliably stated that the Ambassador's remarks . . . were considered to be unusual for a foreign envoy'.[107] While the Foreign Office did not comment on Harvey's speech, Arthur Balfour – who was not then in government – did. Speaking in the House of Lords, Balfour defended the part of his Note which had argued that the US had 'insisted, in substance if not in form, that, though our Allies were to spend the money, it was only on our security that they were prepared to lend it'. He said that George Harvey regarded the 'financial arrangements between the partners in the great war as so many isolated undertakings, to be carried through one by one' and that this was based on a belief in the 'sanctity of contracts', but that he was 'inclined to take a somewhat less commercial view'.[108] For Balfour, the

> extraordinary circumstances of the war, the magnitude of the co-operative effort made by the Allied and Associated peoples . . . might seem to remove their financial arrangements into a sphere where the ordinary categories of debtor and creditor, though still valid, can hardly be deemed to be sufficient.[109]

Balfour's statement to the House of Lords and Harvey's speech to the Pilgrims demonstrated the fundamentally different approaches taken by Britain and the US towards the debt question. While Britain proceeded from the understanding that debts acquired between allies during wartime would be cancelled – partly to aid economic recovery, but also in recognition of the human cost of the conflict – the US's business culture meant that many Americans agreed with the sentiment expressed by Calvin Coolidge when he said that 'they hired the money, didn't they?'[110] It was left to another guest at the Pilgrims' Baldwin dinner, Montagu C. Norman – the Governor of the Bank of England, and who had been part of Baldwin's delegation to the US – to conclude his own speech to the Society with the remark that

> there were two societies on which they relied for the real peace and rehabilitation of the world, and the link between them was Great Britain. They were the League of Nations and the Pilgrims. If both were successful there would not be much to fear.[111]

In light of Harvey's war debt speech and his remarks in relation to the League of Nations two years previously, Norman's statement hints strongly at a dissatisfaction with the US's approach to international relations. It also, however, articulates the belief that the Pilgrims had a role to play in changing American attitudes, and that the Society offered an important conduit between the US and Europe in the absence of US representation in the League of Nations. The unofficial Pilgrims had certainly facilitated communication between the official figures of Harvey and Balfour, though on this occasion the exchange of words between these two British and American statesmen had been less than helpful.

George Harvey resigned from his post as ambassador in October 1923, having survived a number of unsuccessful calls in Congress across 1921 and 1922 to have him recalled, and finally left Britain in November. Rumours had circulated in the US that Harvey was returning to the US to help run Calvin Coolidge's 1924 presidential election campaign, but he appears to have had a wish to resign since before the surprise death of Warren Harding in August. According to press reports and to his biographer, Harvey was finding the cost of living too high in London and needed to settle a number of personal financial matters.[112] Just as the Pilgrims Society had welcomed this most controversial of US ambassadors to Britain in 1921, the Society organised a function to mark his departure from the country in 1923. This took place at the Hotel Victoria on 23 October. In making arrangements for the farewell banquet, the Pilgrims were in close touch with Downing Street, the Foreign Office, and Ambassador Harvey. As in 1921 – when they urged Buckingham Palace and the Foreign Office to expedite the acceptance of Harvey's credentials to ensure that the Society was the first to entertain the new ambassador – the Pilgrims were assertive in their dealings with officialdom. For example, upon learning from the press of Harvey's resignation, Wilson Taylor immediately wrote to the ambassador on behalf of the Society 'in the hope that you will reserve for them the same privilege (which they enjoyed when they received you) of being the principal semi-official body to entertain you'. Wilson Taylor went so far as to express the 'hope that you will so arrange your other engagements as to give our function its fitting prominence'.[113] This assertiveness – and description of the Society as a 'semi-official' organisation – was again evident in Wilson Taylor's letter to the Foreign Secretary. With Curzon unable to attend Harvey's farewell dinner due to illness, Wilson Taylor wrote him to say that the Society was 'rather at a loss to know whom to invite to represent the Government on this important occasion'. Wilson Taylor argued that it was 'essential that we should have someone representing the Government' because the Pilgrims Society's functions 'have come to be regarded – especially in America – as semi-official public functions'. The explicit use of the term 'semi-official' speaks to an increased awareness on the part of the Pilgrims about the nature of their relationship with officialdom. Clearly seeking official intervention, Wilson Taylor told Curzon that 'it would be presumptuous for me to do more than point this out to your Lordship, and I am emboldened to do so owing to your warm interest in our work'.[114] In the end, the Pilgrims got more than they might have wished for, with Stanley Baldwin, now prime minister, and Ambassador Geddes both attending the event. It seems unlikely, however, that Curzon played any role in securing the attendance of these two high-profile guests. In a letter to Wilson Taylor a few days before the banquet, the Foreign Secretary wrote that he did 'not regard it as necessary that whenever the American Ambassador comes or goes he shall be welcomed or speeded by a member of the govt'. He was concerned that this could 'add a new tenor to public life if it becomes the invariable practice here', which he felt was unnecessary, though he also recognised that the Pilgrims were free to independently invite official representatives if they wished.[115] This is instructive on a number of counts. Firstly, the letter implies that Curzon did not necessarily regard the Pilgrims Society as the semi-official body that Wilson Taylor argued that it was. This was slightly unfair on Curzon's part, particularly as the experience of the First World War had shown that the government had been willing to utilise for propaganda purposes the Society's semi-official status. Likewise, the Society had proven helpful in entertaining the visiting Dominion premiers in 1907 and 1911, and had also been used by Earl Grey in 1906 to conduct his semi-official cultural diplomacy in support of Canadian–American relations. The Society's links with the Government Hospitality Fund further demonstrate that this status was still recognised by some in officialdom. The Society did indeed play a semi-official role, something that – as the next chapter will go on to argue – became even more obvious later in the decade as the Society developed further as a precursor to cultural relations organisations like the British Council. Secondly, Curzon's letter supports the arguments made by Cameron Watt and Brian McKercher that Curzon, like Austen Chamberlain and David Lloyd George, approached Anglo-American relations without sentimentality for what others – including the later Labour

Prime Minister Ramsay MacDonald – regarded as the unique political, cultural, and diplomatic relationship between the two countries. To Curzon, good relations with the US were important, but no more important than those with other nations, particularly Britain's European neighbours.[116] This arguably accounts for his cool attitude towards the Pilgrims' links with the government: he did not agree with the Society that Anglo-American relations were of paramount importance. Thirdly, Curzon's note suggests that the British government – or at least the Foreign Office – was not necessarily unhappy to see Harvey leave, especially as the ambassador had been so outspoken at Pilgrims Society events in relation to sensitive British national issues like the war debt. Indeed, something of a negative attitude towards Harvey was evident in a note in 1925 from Robert Cecil, to the then Foreign Secretary, Austen Chamberlain, ahead of the arrival of one of Harvey's successors. There was a fear that the new ambassador, Alanson Houghton – who directly succeeded Harvey's replacement, Frank Kellogg – was also opposed to the League of Nations and might prove to be 'nearly as tiresome as Harvey'.[117]

Whatever Curzon's attitude to the semi-official status of the Pilgrims, Harvey – as a member of the Society – was happy to accept their invitation. He told Wilson Taylor that he was appreciative of the Pilgrims' offer of a dinner, in particular 'the spirit that prompted it', and was confident that together they could 'fix upon a feasible date as soon as I decide definitely when to sail'.[118] Even before he had written to Wilson Taylor, Harvey had met with two members of the Pilgrims' committee – J. Arthur Barratt and Sir John Henry – for lunch, at which he accepted the Society's invitation.[119] This demonstrates the informal nature of the Pilgrims' networking and also the way in which the Pilgrims' role as a conduit between the official and unofficial was partly dependent on the personal connections of its members. Such personal links aggregated for the benefit of the Society, which then provided a more effective conduit for the agency of those other individuals acting under its auspices. Henry had previously served as a link between the Society and officialdom. In a letter to Sir Auckland Geddes in response to the news that the British ambassador would attend the Harvey farewell banquet, Wilson Taylor expressed 'how very delighted the Committee were to learn from Sir John Henry, that you were so well recovered from your illness as to be able to accept the Pilgrims invitation'.[120] Likewise, ahead of the dinner for Harvey in 1921 Henry had personally visited

Downing Street and had 'conveyed the earnest hope of the Committee that the Prime Minister would attend the Pilgrims' banquet to the new American Ambassador', which, of course, Lloyd George did.[121] Henry was able to provide this function for the Pilgrims in large part because of the contacts created through his wartime role as a liaison officer between different government departments and because he had worked with Auckland Geddes both in the National Service Department and on the Board of Trade.[122]

In his final speech to the Pilgrims, which followed a toast led by the prime minister, Harvey spoke about the economic reconstruction of Europe and the role that he anticipated the US playing, especially in the context of the French and Belgian invasion of the Ruhr following Germany's default on its reparation payments: a situation that would result in the 1924 Dawes Plan.[123] Harvey also recalled his infamous first speech to the Pilgrims. With Stanley Baldwin 'puffing at his briar pipe throughout the address', Harvey insisted that his 1921 speech 'was a very good one'. Jokingly telling his fellow Pilgrims that 'Yes, I have made no mistakes', he said that his maiden speech was 'no less exemplary in substance and form than it proved successful in evoking quite unprecedented disapproval from the public prints of my native land'. He was glad, however, that since then 'much water has splashed over the dam' and that in his two and a half years as ambassador the Anglo-American relationship had benefited from the outcome of the Washington Conference, the settlement of the war debt question and the 'centuries-old problem in Ireland, whose satisfactory solution has become absolutely essential to the faith and friendship between England and America'.[124] With these words, Harvey covered some of the main issues around which Anglo-American relations had revolved in the early 1920s. In the case of the war debt, in addition to the debate over whether the US should join the League of Nations, Harvey's outspoken remarks at Pilgrims functions had ensured that the Society was at the centre of public attention, at least in the US, and at the centre of the tensions that existed between the two countries.

Conclusion

Reaction to George Harvey's maiden speech in London in 1921 had been particularly strong in the US due to the convergence of domestic politics and a high-profile national conversation in relation to America's place on the post-war international stage. The League of Nations debate meant that more Americans than ever before were aware of international politics and, in particular, Anglo-American relations. The response to Harvey's 1921 speech significantly raised the profile of the Pilgrims Society in the US, so much so that it – along with the other British–American associations – was accused later in the decade of acting as a subversive pro-British propaganda outfit. While the initial response to Harvey's 1921 speech was neither anti-British nor anti-Pilgrims Society, and was instead characterised by a concern that the ambassador was damaging the US's internationalist credentials, later perceptions of Pilgrims events centred more on fears about alleged moves towards some sort of British–American union. Some Americans were becoming less relaxed about the role of the Pilgrims Society as the 1920s wore on. There was an irony to this as Harvey used a later Pilgrims speech to indelicately criticise the British position on the war debt issue. As such, the Pilgrims could not win. They were suspected by some Americans of acting to undermine US independence, yet some of their public functions resulted in things being said – usually by George Harvey – that were distinctly unhelpful to Anglo-American relations.

While the semi-official role of the Society was occasionally questioned, for example by Curzon in 1923 and the *New York Times* two years previously, others readily accepted that the Pilgrims were a useful conduit for influencing official relations. Geddes, for example, explicitly acknowledged that his welcome dinner in New York in 1920 allowed him to make a number of vital points to influential people he regarded as 'most suited to hear them and to see that they were emphasized in the right quarters', specifically in relation to Anglo-American tensions over oil.[125] The pertinent point here is that the beginning of the 1920s witnessed the Pilgrims Society becoming heavily involved with many of the most pressing issues between Britain and the US. This simultaneously raised the profile of the Society and further consolidated its status as a public diplomacy actor. The Society was operating at a time at which its founding principles of Anglo-American cooperation were coming under increasing strain from an isolationist US, so much so that even some Pilgrims members articulated resentment towards the British. While this impacted negatively upon the success of the New York branch, this did not curtail the Society's contribution to the history of public diplomacy. The next chapter will show some of the reasons why.

Notes

1. B. J. C. McKercher, 'Wealth, Power, and the New International Order: Britain and the American Challenge in the 1920s', *Diplomatic History*, Vol. 12, Issue 4 (1988), pp. 411–41; John R. Ferris, '"The Greatest Power on Earth": Great Britain in the 1920s', *International History Review*, Vol. 13, No. 4 (November 1991), pp. 726–50; Nye, *Soft Power, passim*.

2. Wilson to Brittain, 14 October 1922, Pilgrims Mss, LMA/4632/A/05/002/01.

3. Michael E. Parrish, *Anxious Decades: America in Prosperity and Depression, 1920–1941* (New York, 1992), pp. 6–8; Moser, *Twisting the Lion's Tail*, p. 49.

4. Wilson to Brittain, 14 October 1922, Pilgrims Mss, LMA/4632/A/05/002/01.

5. Nicholas, *The United States and Britain*, pp. 82–3; Ruddock Mackay and H. C. G. Matthew, 'Balfour, Arthur James, first earl of Balfour (1848–1930)', *Oxford Dictionary of National Biography* (Oxford University Press, 2004), <http://www.oxforddnb.com/view/article/30553> (last accessed 31 January 2014); Robert C. Self, *Britain, America and the War Debt Controversy: The Economic Diplomacy of an Unspecial Relationship* (London, 2006), p. 40.

6. Wilson to Brittain, 14 October 1922, Pilgrims Mss, LMA/4632/A/05/002/01.

7. Moser, *Twisting the Lion's Tail*, pp. 17–20 and pp. 26–9; the Irish aspect of American anti-Britishness was demonstrated by an incident that occurred at Chicago's Carnegie Hall in 1920, during an event to celebrate the tercentenary of the landing of the Pilgrim Fathers. The event was disrupted by a group of people shouting 'Hurrah for America' and 'Down with England', and who argued that the Sulgrave Institute was behind a 'plot to make the United States a part of the British empire'. Some of the people involved in this incident were connected with a group called the American Women Pickets for the Enforcement of America's War Aims, an organisation which campaigned for Woodrow Wilson to recognise Irish independence, and which made particular reference to the president's ideas of self-determination. See *Chicago Daily Tribune*, 30 September 1920; Joe Doyle, 'Striking for Ireland on the New York Docks', in Ronald H.

Bayor and Timothy J. Meagher (eds), *The New York Irish* (Baltimore, 1996), pp. 361–2.

8. David A. Richards, 'America Conquers Britain: Anglo-American Conflict in the Popular Media During the 1920s', *Journal of American Culture*, Vol. 3, Issue 1 (Spring 1980), p. 96.

9. Ibid. p. 99; Marian Kent, *Oil and Empire: British Policy and Mesopotamian Oil, 1900–1920* (London, 1976); Donald Ewalt, 'The Fight for Oil: Britain in Persia, 1919', *History Today*, Vol. 31, Issue 9 (1981), pp. 11–16.

10. Burk, *Old World, New World*, pp. 465–7; David Dimbleby and David Reynolds, *An Ocean Apart: The Relationship Between Britain and America in the Twentieth Century* (London, 1988), p. 80; Nicholas, *The United States and Britain*, pp. 78–80; McKercher, *The Second Baldwin Government and the United States, 1924–1929: Attitudes and Diplomacy* (Cambridge, 1984), pp. 4–5.

11. Signed on 6 February 1922, the Five-Power Treaty accepted parity between the British and American navies, and established a capital ships ratio of 5:5:3:1.75:1.75 between the UK, the US, Japan, France, and Italy. Britain had also agreed not to renew its alliance with Japan – a 'real concession', according to Kathleen Burk – while all participants accepted a ten-year moratorium of capital ships production; Burk, *Old World, New World*, pp. 465–7; Dimbleby and Reynolds, *An Ocean Apart*, p. 80; Nicholas, *The United States and Britain*, pp. 78–80; Herring, *From Colony to Superpower*, pp. 453–6; Dobson, *Anglo-American Relations*, pp. 51–2.

12. Moser, *Twisting the Lion's Tail*, pp. 27–9; Nicholas, *The United States and Britain*, p. 79.

13. *Washington Post*, 21 August 1928; *New York Times*, 21 August 1928; *Boston Daily Globe*, 20 March 1921; Wills Fletcher Johnson, *George Harvey: 'A Passionate Patriot'* (Cambridge, MA, 1929).

14. *New York Times*, 20 March 1907.

15. *Washington Post*, 21 August 1928; *New York Times*, 21 August 1928; *Boston Daily Globe*, 20 March 1921; Niall Palmer, *The Twenties in America: Politics and History* (Edinburgh, 2006), p. 21; Betty Glad, *Charles Evans Hughes and the Illusions of Innocence: A Study in American Diplomacy* (Urbana, 1966), pp. 135–6.

16. Palmer, *The Twenties*, pp. 25–6.

17. *New-York Tribune*, 22 April 1921.

18. Wilson to Brittain, 2 May 1921, Pilgrims Mss, LMA/4632/A/05/002/01.

19. *New York Times*, 22 April 1921.

20. Benjamin D. Rhodes, 'The Image of Britain in the United States, 1919–1929: A Contentious Relative and Rival', in McKercher (ed.),

Anglo-American Relations in the 1920s: The Struggle for Supremacy (London, 1991), p. 188.

21. Wilson Taylor to Lord Stamfordham, 3 May 1921, Pilgrims Mss, LMA/4632/D/01/023.
22. Stamfordham to Wilson Taylor, 4 May 1921, Pilgrims Mss, LMA/4632/D/01/023.
23. Wilson Taylor to Earl Curzon, 3 May 1921, Pilgrims Mss, LMA/4632/D/01/023.
24. Curzon to Wilson Taylor, 5 May 1921, and Wilson Taylor to Curzon, 5 May 1921, Pilgrims Mss, LMA/4632/D/01/023.
25. Cablegram, Frederick Cunliffe-Owen to Lord Desborough, 28 April 1921, Pilgrims Mss, LMA/4632/D/01/023.
26. The Pilgrims List of Members and Bye-Laws', 1909, Brittain Papers, BLPES, Box 5.
27. Cablegram, Cunliffe-Owen to Lord Desborough, 8 May 1921, Pilgrims Mss, LMA/4632/D/01/023.
28. Cablegram, Charles H. Sherrill to Wilson Taylor, 4 April 1921, Pilgrims Mss, LMA/4632/D/01/023.
29. Arthur Bliss Lane to Wilson Taylor, 11 May 1921, Pilgrims Mss, LMA/4632/D/01/023.
30. *Washington Post*, 20 May 1921.
31. Palmer, *The Twenties*, p. 74.
32. Herring, *From Colony to Superpower*, pp. 412–13.
33. Robert K. Murray, *The Harding Era: Warren G. Harding and His Administration* (Minneapolis, 1969), p. 134; Cooper, *Warrior and the Priest*, p. 336; Patrick O. Cohrs, *The Unfinished Peace after World War 1: America, Britain and the Stabilisation of Europe, 1919–1932* (Cambridge, 2006), p. 66; William C. Widenor, 'Henry Cabot Lodge's Perspective', in Thomas G. Paterson (ed.), *Major Problems in American Foreign Policy, Volume II: Since 1914* (Lexington, 1989), pp. 93–108; Zara Steiner, *The Lights that Failed: European International History, 1919–1933* (Oxford, 2005), pp. 41–2.
34. Palmer, *The Twenties*, p. 17; unlike Wilson, Lodge believed that the US's international role was to serve as a good example to other countries, and to largely do so by not getting involved in entangling alliances. See Widenor, 'Henry Cabot Lodge's Perspective', p. 101.
35. Frank Costigliola, *Awkward Dominion: American Political, Economic, and Cultural Relations with Europe, 1919–1933* (Ithaca, 1984), pp. 32–3; Moser, *Twisting the Lion's Tail*, p. 10; Arthur S. Link, 'Woodrow Wilson's Perspective', in Paterson (ed.), *Major Problems*, pp. 83–5; Wilson's opponents criticised the notion that Article X was a 'moral obligation' and not a 'legal obligation'. Lodge and Root did not support an obligation of any variety being placed

on the US. Thus, as 'the success of a collective security organization would seem to rest on the absence of doubt as to the intentions of its members, that is, on the credibility of their commitments', opposition to moral or legal obligations to collective security 'was a denial of the theory on which collective security was based'. See Widenor, 'Henry Cabot Lodge's Perspective', pp. 105–6.

36.   *New York Times*, 18 March 1919.

37.   This was speculated by one correspondent of the *New York Times*. See *New York Times*, 27 May 1921.

38.   *The Times*, 20 May 1921; Watt, *Succeeding John Bull: America in Britain's Place 1900–1975* (Cambridge, 1984), p. 38; the Pilgrims as an organisation did not take a stance on US membership of the League of Nations. The New York branch was, however, lectured by Sir Henry Babington-Smith (a British civil servant, who was there as guest of the Society; for his obituary, see *The Times*, 1 October 1923) at its annual meeting in January 1919 on the international need for an effective League of Nations. Meanwhile, Charles Sherrill believed that Arthur Balfour's preference for attending ESU events over Pilgrims events was because the Society, unlike the ESU, had not openly supported the League. This, however, may simply have been because Balfour was the ESU's president in Britain. See Minute Book 3, 22 January 1919, Pilgrims Mss, NYC and Baker, *Pilgrims of the US*, p. 37; then, at a function in 1922, William Taft told the London Pilgrims that 'American membership in the League would have had to overcome a deep-seated popular conviction, confirmed by a century and a quarter's experience, of the wisdom of America's keeping out of European entanglements'. See *The Times*, 20 June 1922.

39.   Lynch was not a member of the Society, but had been given an invitation to the Harvey dinner following a request from the founder of the ESU, Evelyn Wrench, who knew that the Secretary of the Church Union of America was staying in the Hotel Victoria at the time. Wrench to Wilson Taylor, 13 May 1921, Pilgrims Mss, LMA/4632/D/01/023.

40.   *New York Times*, 12 June 1921 and, for Lynch's obituary, 20 December 1934; the information about Lynch being a Republican comes from Senator Harrison's contribution to 'Admiral Sims's Statement and Ambassador Harvey's Address', 13 June 1921, Congressional Record – Senate, 67th Congress, 1st Session, Vol. 61, Part 3, pp. 2482–6.

41.   Costigliola, *Awkward Dominion*, pp. 32–3; Moser, *Twisting the Lion's Tail*, p. 10; Link, 'Woodrow Wilson's Perspective', pp. 83–5.

42.   *New York Times*, 21 May 1921 and 12 June 1921; Costigliola, *Awkward Dominion*, p. 33.

43. *New York Times*, 5 June 1921.
44. *New York Times*, 25 May 1921.
45. *New York Times*, 21 May 1921.
46. *The Times*, 23 May 1921; Steiner, *Lights that Failed*, p. 33 and pp. 40–3.
47. *Washington Post*, 20 May 1921.
48. *New York Times*, 12 June 1921.
49. Moser, *Twisting the Lion's Tail*, pp. 38–41.
50. Herring, *From Colony to Superpower*, p. 428 and pp. 434–5.
51. *New York Times*, 26 June 1921.
52. *New York Times*, 5 June 1921.
53. *New York Times*, 30 May 1921.
54. *New York Times*, 5 June 1921 and 25 May 1921.
55. *New York Times*, 25 May 1921.
56. *New York Times*, 21 May 1921.
57. Ibid.
58. *New York Times*, 31 May 1921.
59. *New York Times*, 30 May 1921.
60. *New York Times*, 1 June 1921.
61. *New York Times*, 26 June 1921.
62. Ibid.
63. Johnson, *George Harvey*, p. 302.
64. *New York Times*, 31 May 1917.
65. Wilson Taylor to George Harvey, 30 January 1923, Pilgrims Mss, LMA/4632/D/01/034.
66. Wilson to Brittain, 10 September 1922, Pilgrims Mss, LMA/4632/A/05/002/01; Baker, *Pilgrims of the US*, p. 14, p. 37, and p. 163.
67. Wilson to Brittain, 3 June 1920, Pilgrims Mss, LMA/4632/A/05/002/01.
68. Minutes, 16 October 1919, Pilgrims Mss, LMA/4632/A/01/001; Sherrill was a New York lawyer, who was US ambassador to Argentina from 1909 until 1911, and who went on to become ambassador to Turkey between 1932 and 1933. See *New York Times*, 26 June 1936; Desborough was a politician and athlete, famous for his numerous ascents of the Matterhorn. See his obituary in *The Times*, 10 January 1945.
69. Wilson to Brittain, 10 September 1922, Pilgrims Mss, LMA/4632/A/05/002/01; it is not entirely clear what the arrangement of the American executive committee was at the start of the 1920s. While Anne P. Baker's official history of the Society indicates that Cunliffe-Owen became chairman in 1920 immediately after Wilson, and served for one year, the New York branch's minute book shows that it was Sherrill who replaced Wilson in March 1920, and that Sherrill

was re-elected in 1923. It is not easy to account for this discrepancy. See Minute Book 3, 15 March 1920 and 23 January 1923, Pilgrims Mss, NYC; Baker, *Pilgrims of the US*, p. 152.

70. *New York Times*, 1 July 1926; he was also a director of the St. George's Society of New York. See Baker, *Pilgrims of the US*, p. 52.
71. Minute Book 3, 3 November 1926, Pilgrims Mss, NYC.
72. Wilson to Brittain, 20 August 1920, Pilgrims Mss, LMA/4632/A/05/002/01.
73. Wilson to Brittain, 25 June 1913 and 28 February 1920, Pilgrims Mss, LMA/4632/A/05/002/01.
74. Wilson to Brittain, 20 August 1920, Pilgrims Mss, LMA/4632/A/05/002/01.
75. Wilson to Brittain, 10 September 1922, Pilgrims Mss, LMA/4632/A/05/002/01.
76. Wilson to Brittain, 3 June 1920, Pilgrims Mss, LMA/4632/A/05/002/01; Baker, *Pilgrims of the US*, p. 37.
77. Wilson to Brittain, 26 February 1921, Pilgrims Mss, LMA/4632/A/05/002/01; *The Sulgrave Review*, No. 5, February 1921, Sulgrave Mss, SMTA, Box 2.
78. *New York Times*, 28 October 1921. See also Minute Book 3, 1917–1927, Pilgrims Mss, NYC.
79. Nicholas, *The United States and Britain*, pp. 74–8.
80. Murray, *Harding Era*, pp. 265–7; Parrish, *Anxious Decades*, pp. 3–11 and p. 111; Palmer, *The Twenties*, p. 42; Roberts, 'The Emergence of American Atlanticism', p. 594.
81. Wilson to Brittain, 20 August 1920, Pilgrims Mss, LMA/4632/A/05/002/01.
82. Wilson to Brittain, 10 September 1922, Pilgrims Mss, LMA/4632/A/05/002/01.
83. Murray, *Harding Era*, pp. 265–6; Bethany Andreasen, 'Treason or Truth: The New York City Text Book Controversy, 1920–1923', *New York History*, Vol. 66 (1985), p. 413.
84. Moser, *Twisting the Lion's Tail*, pp. 26–9.
85. Richards, 'America Conquers Britain', p. 96.
86. Ibid. p. 99.
87. *New York Times*, 26 May 1920.
88. Sir Auckland Geddes to Cunliffe-Owen, 29 May 1920, Pilgrims Mss, LMA/4632/A/01/001.
89. Conway Davies, Government Hospitality Fund, to Wilson Taylor, 28 October 1921, Pilgrims Mss, LMA4632/D/01/026; *New York Times*, 1 November 1921.
90. Cablegram, Sherrill to Wilson Taylor, 19 February 1922, Pilgrims Mss, LMA/4632/D/01/027; Minute Book 3, 26 January 1922, Pilgrims Mss, NYC.

91. Moser, *Twisting the Lion's Tail*, p. 26; *The Times*, 15 February 1922.
92. Untitled and undated note, Pilgrims Mss, LMA/4632/D/01/027; *The Times*, 17 February 1922.
93. Brittain to Wilson, 22 February 1922, Pilgrims Mss, LMA/4632/A/05/002/01.
94. Pilgrims (unsigned) to J. T. Davies, 9 February 1922, Pilgrims Mss, LMA/4632/D/01/027; *The Times*, 14 February 1922.
95. John S. Steele (*Chicago Tribune*) to Wilson Taylor, 14 February 1922, N. W. Baxter (*Philadelphia Public Ledger*) to Wilson Taylor, 9 February 1922, and H. C. Robbins (Press Association) to Wilson Taylor, 16 February 1922, Pilgrims Mss, LMA/4632/D/01/027.
96. Sir Campbell Stuart to Wilson Taylor, 20 February 1922, and Wilson Taylor to Stuart, 20 February 1922, Pilgrims Mss, LMA/4632/D/01/027; 'Speeches at a dinner of the Executive Committee of the Pilgrims in honour of Sir Campbell Stuart', 23 October 1958, Brittain Papers, BLPES, Box 4; Haley, 'Stuart, Sir Campbell Arthur (1885–1972)'. Stuart later became chairman of the British Pilgrims. See Baker, *Pilgrims of Britain*, p. 178; Minutes, 27 June 1918, Pilgrims Mss, LMA/4632/A/01/001.
97. 'Treaty with Japan', 24 February 1922, Congressional Record – Senate, 67th Congress, 2nd Session, Vol. 62, Part 3, pp. 3008–12; *The Times*, 21 February 1922.
98. 'Treaty with Japan', 24 February 1922, Congressional Record – Senate, 67th Congress, 2nd Session, Vol. 62, Part 3, pp. 3008–12; *The Times*, 21 February 1922; Rhodes, 'Image of Britain', p. 192.
99. Rhodes, 'Image of Britain', pp. 195–7; Watt, *Succeeding John Bull*, p. 53.
100. *New York Times*, 1 March 1923; Rhodes, 'Image of Britain', pp. 197–8.
101. Moser, *Twisting the Lion's Tail*, pp. 32–3; Rhodes, 'Image of Britain', p. 198; *The Times*, 29 January 1923.
102. *The Times*, 1 March 1923.
103. John D. Hicks, *Republican Ascendancy, 1921–1933* (London, 1960), p. 138.
104. 'Note of a conversation at 10, Downing Street', 5 July 1922, Records of the Cabinet Office, TNA, Cab 23/36; Johnson, *George Harvey*, pp. 337–8.
105. Wilson Taylor to Lord Desborough, 6 February 1923, and Wilson Taylor to Harvey, 30 January 1923, Pilgrims Mss, LMA/4632/D/01/034.
106. *New York Times*, 1 March 1923; *The Times*, 1 March 1923; Johnson, *George Harvey*, p. 338.
107. *Washington Post*, 2 March 1923.

108. 'International Indebtedness', 8 March 1923, House of Lords Debate, Hansard, Vol. 53, cc 337–42.
109. Ibid.
110. Coolidge quoted in Burk, *Old World, New World*, p. 462; Temperley, *Britain and America*, pp. 117–18.
111. *The Times*, 1 March 1923; Philip Williamson, 'Norman, Montagu Collet, Baron Norman (1871–1950)', *Oxford Dictionary of National Biography* (Oxford University Press, 2004), <http://www.oxforddnb.com/view/article/35252> (last accessed 3 February 2014).
112. *Washington Post*, 4 July 1923; *New York Times*, 4 October 1923; Johnson, *George Harvey*, p. 391 and p. 408; 'Admiral Sims's Statement and Ambassador Harvey's Address', 13 June 1921, Congressional Record – Senate, 67th Congress, 1st Session, Vol. 61, Part 3, pp. 2482–6; *Chicago Daily Tribune*, 8 June 1921; *The Times*, 13 June 1921; *The Snyder Signal*, 17 June 1921; *Washington Post*, 29 September 1936; Moser, *Twisting the Lion's Tail*, p. 20; *New York Times*, 24 February 1922.
113. Wilson Taylor to Harvey, 4 October 1923, Pilgrims Mss, LMA4632/D/01/038.
114. Wilson Taylor to Curzon, 9 October 1923, Pilgrims Mss, LMA4632/D/01/038.
115. Curzon to Wilson Taylor, 19 October 1923, Pilgrims Mss, LMA4632/D/01/038.
116. Watt, *Succeeding John Bull*, p. 49; McKercher, '"The Deep and Latent Distrust": The British Official Mind and the United States, 1919–1929', in McKercher (ed.), *Anglo-American Relations in the 1920s*, pp. 210–17.
117. Robert Cecil to Austen Chamberlain, 22 April 1925, TNA, FO800/257; Martin Ceadel, 'Cecil, (Edgar Algernon) Robert Gascoyne- [Lord Robert Cecil], Viscount Cecil of Chelwood (1864–1958)', *Oxford Dictionary of National Biography* (Oxford University Press, 2004), <http://www.oxforddnb.com/view/article/32335> (last accessed 3 March 2014).
118. Harvey to Wilson Taylor, 9 October 1923, Pilgrims Mss, LMA4632/D/01/038.
119. Wilson Taylor to Harvey, 8 October 1923, Pilgrims Mss, LMA4632/D/01/038; Baker, *Pilgrims of Britain*, p. 53; 'The Pilgrims Dinner in Honour of His Excellency the American Ambassador', menu and committee list, 23 October 1923, Pilgrims Mss, LMA4632/D/01/038.
120. Wilson Taylor to Geddes, 17 October 1923, Pilgrims Mss, LMA4632/D/01/038.

121. Wilson Taylor to Davies, 6 April 1921, Pilgrims Mss, LMA/ 4632/D/01/023.

122. For Henry's obituary, see *The Times*, 24 December 1930; Keith Grieves, 'Geddes, Auckland Campbell, first Baron Geddes (1879– 1954)', *Oxford Dictionary of National Biography* (Oxford University Press, 2004), <http://www.oxforddnb.com/view/article/33359> (last accessed 11 February 2014).

123. *The Times*, 25 October 1925; Dobson, *Anglo-American Relations*, p. 54; Herring, *From Colony to Superpower*, pp. 458–9.

124. *Washington Post*, 24 October 1923.

125. Geddes to Cunliffe-Owen, 29 May 1920, Pilgrims Mss, LMA/ 4632/A/01/001.

6   Public Diplomacy Ascendant

> I cannot feel that the Pilgrims Society is only meant to articulate fine sentiments on sunshiny days and that it retires underground when the skies are darkened and the tempest is on.
> (Frederick R. Coudert)

At one of its dinners in London in 1926, the Pilgrims Society utilised some of the technological advances associated with the 'Americanisation' of Europe to send the world's first transatlantic commercial 'radio picture'. Unfortunately, due to 'static or other trouble' caused by a storm on the American side, the transmission of a photograph of the top table at the London event took nearly an hour and a half longer than expected to arrive at the New York offices of the Radio Corporation of America.[1] As the previous chapter demonstrated, this was not the first time that the image of the Pilgrims Society and the cause with which it was associated encountered difficulties while crossing the Atlantic. This chapter will demonstrate that nor was it the final time. The later 1920s were years of great flux and confusion, both domestically in Britain and in the US, and also on the wider international stage. This period represented a nadir in relations between the two countries and resulted in the Pilgrims coming under even greater public scrutiny and criticism in the US than ever before. This chapter will look at some of the other ways in which the Pilgrims related to the popular American anti-Britishness mentioned earlier. Chicago's so-called 'McAndrew Trial' of 1927 – when the city's mayor launched an enquiry into the use of allegedly harmful pro-British school-books – is a particularly instructive example, and demonstrates that the Society was understood by many Americans to wield a perceptible influence on Anglo-American relations. This chapter will show that that influence was not always imagined.

As before, difficult Anglo-American relations only served to give new impetus to the Society's semi-official public diplomacy role. In a speech to the New York Pilgrims to mark their twenty-fifth anniversary in 1928, Harry Brittain noted that the Society's events had 'almost assumed the status of State functions' and that it was the group's 'duty in every way to develop a personal contact between our respective peoples, and with untiring patience on either side, tackle the difficulties as they arise'.[2] As this chapter will argue, the Society's efforts to use public diplomacy solutions was evidenced by its involvement in the naval disarmament issue, and also by its use as a semi-official vehicle for public diplomacy in support of US foreign policy announcements in relation to European interwar tensions. This much was demonstrated by the publicity surrounding the speeches made by US Ambassadors Alanson Houghton and Charles Dawes at their welcome banquets in London in 1925 and 1929 respectively. Through its high profile and prestige, the Society was a facilitator of much of the publicity surrounding these events. Together with George Harvey's League of Nations speech, Houghton's and Dawes' speeches meant that the 1920s witnessed the Pilgrims Society more than ever before become a semi-official venue for official policy announcements.

The ambassadors' speeches in the 1920s spoke to a greater official understanding of the potential benefits of using the Pilgrims Society network. This understanding developed further as the 1920s gave way to the 1930s and 1940s, by which point there was a growth in more official publicity organisations in Britain and the US, such as the British Council and the Division of Cultural Relations. The Pilgrims contributed to this growth through its long-term legitimisation of public diplomacy. Ultimately the presence of new vehicles of public diplomacy meant that the Society became decreasingly relevant as a semi-official international actor in the second half of the twentieth century, but this was not before the Society's activities intersected with noteworthy developments before and during the Second World War. Despite the problems experienced by the Radio Corporation of America in 1926, the benefits of the Pilgrims network had been enhanced by technological improvements. The British Broadcasting Corporation (BBC) had occasionally aired Pilgrims speeches since 1924, while Paramount Sound News filmed an important banquet in London in 1930.[3] Then, in March 1941, significant speeches delivered by Prime Minister Winston Churchill and US Ambassador John G.

Winant at a Pilgrims event in London, and by British Ambassador
Lord Halifax at a Pilgrims banquet in New York, were broadcast
over the airwaves to audiences in Britain and the US. As this chapter will show, these speeches placed the Pilgrims at the centre of
Anglo-American diplomacy in the critical final year of official US
neutrality during the war against the Axis powers.

This chapter traces the Pilgrims' contribution to the history
of public diplomacy across the 1920s, 1930s, and early 1940s. It
does so across three sections. The first section argues that Alanson
Houghton's speech at his welcome banquet in London in 1925
represented an instance when an American ambassador coordinated with figures in the British government to deliver an important foreign policy announcement before an audience of European
diplomats. Importantly, Houghton deliberately chose a Pilgrims
function for this purpose. The second section of the chapter analyses another example of this: Charles Dawes' speech at his welcome banquet in 1929. This took place against the backdrop of
the continued question of naval disarmament, something that had
partly motivated American nativist fears about the dangers of British propaganda during the 1920s. This section, therefore, examines how these fears were manifest, in particular by looking at the
McAndrew Trial of 1927. The final section of the chapter, meanwhile, discusses how the Society responded to the Great Depression and then the Second World War. It will focus in particular
on the Pilgrims Society events held in London and New York in
March 1941.

The Houghton speech, 1925

The 1921 Washington Conference discussed in the previous chapter did not end the Anglo-American naval rivalry and it was this
issue that did particular damage to Anglo-American relations
towards the end of the 1920s. The naval question was raised during the 1924 presidential election, when Democrats had attacked
the Washington Conference's Five-Power Treaty on the basis of
their belief that the US had been tricked into accepting the false
promise of parity between the Royal and US navies. This fed calls
from the naval interest for a programme of shipbuilding, which
ultimately resulted in the convening of a second naval disarmament conference in July 1927, this time in Geneva. This conference

ended in complete failure as neither side agreed on the criteria with which to control the subsequent building of cruisers. The US public ultimately blamed Britain for the unsuccessful outcome, while there was a concurrent strengthening of anti-American feeling in Britain. The damage done to Anglo-American relations was considerable and a perception arose in the UK and the US that war between the two countries had become more likely, so much so that the US Navy Department considered the 'development and refinement' of their war plans for dealing with a conflict with the British Empire.[4] While a war between Britain and the US was unlikely – not least because of an aversion to conflict manifest in the popularity of 1928's Kellogg–Briand Pact for the Outlawry of War – it was something that had been occasionally discussed in the years following the end of the First World War. As early as 1919, the Scottish socialist John Maclean had predicted that such a war would come about because of economic competition between the two countries, especially in light of the US's growing commercial strength and Britain's level of debt. This was set out in his pamphlet 'The Coming War with America'.[5] Maclean's views preempted those of the socialist Representative for Wisconsin, Victor Berger, who wrote in 1929 that American commercial expansion would result in war with Britain. These views were not restricted to the left. At the beginning of 1928, for example, the commander of the Brooklyn Navy Yard, Rear Admiral Charles Plunkett, predicted that a British–American war was unavoidable.[6]

There were two additional diplomatic issues between Britain and the US later in the 1920s: the smuggling of alcohol into the US via British territories in contravention of Prohibition laws and, particularly after 1925, a dispute between the two countries regarding the price of rubber.[7] The Pilgrims, however, had a more direct involvement in another of the primary diplomatic developments of the mid-1920s. Just as Harvey had done in 1921, US Ambassador Alanson B. Houghton used his Pilgrims welcome banquet in London in May 1925 to make a public announcement of major international significance. Unlike Harvey, however, Houghton's speech was largely well received. Amidst ongoing concerns about the economic and political stability of Europe, Ambassador Houghton used his Pilgrims speech to deliver what became known as a 'peace ultimatum' to the effect that the US would cease providing loans to the European countries unless solid commitments to peace were made. It was this intervention by Houghton that helped clear the path for the Locarno Conference in October, at which agreements were made between France, Germany, and Belgium solidifying aspects of the Paris Peace Conference – including the demilitarised zone in the Rhineland – and which resulted in commitments by those countries to avoid future hostilities.[8] Houghton's speech appears to have been made without the knowledge of President Coolidge (though he immediately endorsed what the ambassador had said), but had been pre-approved by the British Foreign Secretary, Austen Chamberlain, who played a principal role in securing the Locarno agreements and who had for some months been examining ways of addressing the hostility between the countries. Through Houghton, the US acted in support of the creation of a nonaggression pact, not least out of a desire to safeguard American investments.[9] During his speech, Houghton acknowledged that the Pilgrims' welcome banquet had become 'a significant, if unofficial step in the routine by which an American Ambassador takes office'. While he noted that he would be 'within the tradition' by saying 'something about Anglo-American relations', he instead wanted to speak about the 'attitude of the plain people of America towards the reconstruction of Europe'. Reading carefully from a script, Houghton explained that the people of America were questioning whether Europe was truly committed to peace, and that if it was not, then 'those helpful processes which are now in motion must inevitably cease'.[10] With the Belgian and German ambassadors in attendance at the dinner, along with the Duke of York and Prime Minister Baldwin, this was indeed an assertive statement delivered to an influential and interested audience. Houghton clearly regarded the Pilgrims as a useful forum for communicating his message. Again, this is indicative of the 'advocacy' stage of public diplomacy. The ambassador's speech was heard by the diplomats present at the event, but also by a wider, public audience that read about it in newspaper reports.

The Belgian ambassador later – and somewhat melodramatically – described his fellow guests as having been 'awed as if God almighty had descended and was talking to them', but there is no doubting the wider impact of Houghton's remarks. Through the press reaction to Houghton's important speech, the Pilgrims were once again at the centre of international attention. The French press was concerned that Houghton was suggesting a revision of the Treaty of Versailles in exchange for the US's continued aid. This was a price too high for *Le Temps*, but was something that the German press were hopeful of. Indeed, it was in Germany that Houghton's speech was best received. Whereas the French detected in Houghton's words an implied criticism of their attitude towards Germany, the Germans felt that the speech was directed at all European nations. Indeed, the German foreign office was reported to have been 'in complete sympathy' with what Houghton had said, not least because they had long been concerned about any future alliance between Britain and France and the continued Allied occupation of the Rhineland, especially in light of the recent invasion of the Ruhr by France and Belgium. For the Germans, Houghton's Pilgrims speech offered a potential solution to their fears about French aggression. On the other hand, the speech was interpreted in some quarters as having been directed at the newly elected German president, Paul von Hindenburg.[11] Meanwhile, in Britain, the *Times* editorialised that Houghton's 'significant speech is of far greater direct political value than a torrent of rhetoric on the old theme of Anglo-American relations', while the *Daily Telegraph* believed that '[e]very word of the Ambassador's plain statement should be marked by those responsible for the conduct of affairs and guidance of public opinion throughout Europe'. Indeed, the paper wrote that there was 'no doubt that the Pilgrims' banquet was chosen for a declaration of first order and importance'.[12] American newspapers also welcomed Houghton's speech. With the exception of an article in the *Atlanta Constitution* which criticised the ambassador for speaking with the 'air of a new teacher who is just taking charge of the schoolroom', Houghton was praised for his 'businesslike diplomacy' and 'plain speaking'. This was contrasted with Harvey's 1921 speech, 'which went round the world on the wings of a blazing indiscretion. Nothing of that sort marred the noteworthy address made by Houghton . . . Its sobriety and power of statement have been everywhere commented upon.'[13]

Whatever the differences between the Harvey and Houghton speeches, the important point is that on both occasions a Pilgrims Society banquet had been chosen as a venue for an important policy announcement by agents of the US government. This demonstrates a desire to use the Society's profile to ensure that these announcements reached as large an audience as possible. The Society's prestige – built up over the previous twenty years by means of the various functions that had been held for prominent statesmen – also lent legitimacy and weight to the ambassadors' words. This was the case more with the Houghton speech; as has been seen, in 1921 the *New York Times* had questioned the propriety of Harvey having made an official and controversial announcement at a Pilgrims event. Yet, the experience of Harvey's 1921 speech meant that the idea of using the Pilgrims as a venue for such an announcement was less noteworthy than it had been previously. Whereas the content of public statements made at Pilgrims functions by statesmen like Earl Grey and Elihu Root in 1906 were more mawkish evocations of Anglo-American friendship within which firmer diplomatic objectives were couched, statements by diplomats like Harvey and Houghton dealt more specifically with items of policy. This is indicative of a greater official understanding on the part of the US of the potential benefits of using the Pilgrims Society network and demonstrated that the Society was regarded as an effective semi-official conduit for influencing official international relations. Such developments are indicative of Gorman's notion of the 'emergence' of an international society based upon non-state actors at a time of difficult state–state relations and are evidence of the Pilgrims' contribution to the evolution of public diplomacy.[14] The Pilgrims Society helped normalise the notion of governments speaking to foreign publics, thus clearing the way for greater official involvement in public diplomacy as it developed into the 1930s and 1940s. Whereas officialdom was hitherto content to let groups like the Pilgrims undertake their own public diplomacy, Society events in the 1920s show that governments were increasingly eager to take on greater responsibilities in this field.[15] In the case of the 1925 Houghton speech, the Pilgrims provided an opportunity for the ambassador to direct his remarks at specific representatives of two principal European actors; namely, the German and Belgian ambassadors. Crucially, Houghton's speech appears to have been coordinated with Austen Chamberlain, suggesting a joint understanding of the utility of the Pilgrims Society amidst ongoing discussions regarding European stability.

The McAndrew Trial and the naval rivalry revisited, 1927–30

While the Houghton speech was an example of cooperation between the Pilgrims and British and US statesmen, the second half of the 1920s represented a low point in relations between the two countries. This was most obviously manifest in the disastrous

naval disarmament conference in Geneva in 1927 and in the realisation that a British–American war was a distinct possibility.[16] In
turn, this resulted in the Pilgrims coming under a greater amount
of public scrutiny and criticism in the US than ever before. There
had always been those who did not share the Society's belief in
the importance of Anglo-American relations, but at no time since
its founding in 1902 had the Pilgrims Society and its aims experienced the level of hostility that they did in the decade or so after
the First World War. That this was indeed the case is demonstrated
by the 'McAndrew Trial' in Chicago in 1927. As has been shown,
George Harvey's interpretation of US war motives was contemporaneous with the development of historical revisionism in relation to the First World War. Yet, and even though they were not
intrinsically anti-British, such histories fed a wider suspicion that
British propaganda had duped the US into becoming a belligerent. There was also a belief that Britain continued into the 1920s
to surreptitiously influence American opinion. A poll found that
by 1939, 40 per cent of Americans thought that 'propaganda and
selfish interests' had tricked the US into entering the First World
War. In the 1920s, such concerns were centred on the content of
school textbooks, which some full-blooded Americans believed
were overly pro-British.[17] The McAndrew Trial implicated the
Pilgrims Society and other elite British–American associations in
this allegedly continuing British propaganda. The McAndrew Trial
was, in fact, a tribunal set up by Chicago's Board of Education in
order to investigate the performance of the city's superintendent
of schools, William McAndrew. It was soon transformed, however, into a high-profile campaign by the city's Al Capone-backed
mayor and Republican presidential hopeful, William Hale Thompson, to sack McAndrew and to expose a massive British con-
spiracy. This focused on allegedly pro-British and anti-American
school textbooks and was always something of a political scheme
by Thompson to court the Irish and German vote.[18] Witnesses
at the tribunal alleged that groups including the Pilgrims Society,
the International Magna Charta Day Association (IMCDA), the
Sulgrave Institute, the Rhodes Scholarship Foundation, and the
ESU were working to propagandise in American schools (including
in support of British naval supremacy), were trying to annexe the
US for the British Empire, and were seeking to have Britain's war
debt written off.[19] One witness, a socialist called Charles Edward
Russell, recalled that when he had visited London during the war as

part of his work for the Committee on Public Information he had been approached by a 'suave, polished gentleman by the name of Harry Britton [sic]' who told him that 'he had founded and created a society called the Pilgrims' with the 'purpose of an amalgamation or affiliation between the United States and Great Britain'.[20] Such lurid and hyperbolic statements made in the course of the tribunal were reported upon nationally and internationally and served to raise the profile of the Pilgrims Society in the public imagination.

The McAndrew Trial was indicative of the American isolationist reaction to the fears and uncertainties of the post-war years. The Pilgrims Society and the other British–American associations were regarded as symbols of the dangerous internationalism from which the US was in retreat during the 1920s.[21] There is unfortunately little evidence as to what the Pilgrims themselves thought of what was happening in Chicago across 1927 and 1928. A meeting of the New York branch in December 1927 did note 'clippings from American and British newspapers commenting on speeches of one Thompson, Mayor of Chicago', but the Society's minutes provide no further comment.[22] Harry Brittain, meanwhile, made a small comment at an ESU function in New York in 1928, when he insisted that Thompson's attitudes were not typical of wider opinion in Britain or the US:

> We have our Bill Thompson's over in England . . . and some of them aren't running around loose. But from my experience . . . I can say that the rank and file of the people are most enthusiastic toward America and things American.[23]

Then, in a speech during a banquet to mark the New York Pilgrims' twenty-fifth anniversary, Sir Esmé Howard, British ambassador to the US, made a speech that obliquely addressed some of the accusations arising from the McAndrew Trial, saying that he had 'read not so long ago in a paper that England had lately been flooding this country with a propaganda oratory of gush and slush and mush', and insisting that 'if there has been a flood of that kind, it is not I who turned on the tap'.[24]

Ironically, the McAndrew Trial – for all its sensationalism and ulterior motivations – was not wrong to cast a light on the role of groups like the Pilgrims Society. As has been seen, the Society had adopted a semi-official public diplomacy and propaganda role during the First World War, including by means of cultural diplomacy highlighting what the Pilgrims regarded as Britain and the US's shared values. Some in the Society wished to expand on this role, for example Welsh-Lee and her 1919 plans for a propaganda sub-committee.[25] Yet the focus on allegedly pro-British textbooks in the 1920s shows that, in fact, the people behind the McAndrew Trial were ignorant of what the Pilgrims had really done during the war; namely, that it served as a semi-official, state–private network. The Society provided a conduit between elites in both countries for messages and ideas in support of the war effort, but it did not directly influence the production of written materials. Even so, many of the other Anglo-American societies did work to influence the education of young people, including the IMCDA and its efforts to promote the celebration of 'Magna Charta Day'.[26] Many in the American press – including the *New York Times'* Garet Garett – understood that the issues raised by the McAndrew Trial were not necessarily trivial. While they criticised Thompson's theatrics, they also expressed what were real, and arguably justified, concerns about British propaganda. It is for that reason – along with the wider tensions between Britain and the US at the end of the 1920s – that Benjamin Rhodes is unwise to argue that the press's criticism of Thompson was evidence 'that the day had passed when politicians could indulge in orgies of anglophobia with a certain guarantee of political acclaim'.[27] The McAndrew Trial had shown that whatever it was that the Pilgrims Society was doing – serving largely as an elite network active in the advocacy, cultural, and exchange elements of public diplomacy, including as a state–private body in support of propaganda during the First World War, as opposed merely to the influencing of school textbooks – was producing a wider effect. Its public and private roles may not have been precisely as described by the witnesses in Chicago, but the fact that there existed an awareness and a distrust of the Pilgrims Society based on some underlying truths gives causality to the organisation's activities.

The following few years witnessed the conclusion of the Anglo-American naval rivalry, something in which the Pilgrims Society also played a part. The two countries came to an amicable compromise on the basis of then US President Herbert Hoover's 'yardstick' idea, through which the age of a navy's vessels was taken into account alongside relative tonnage. The way had been cleared for this outcome by a 'tacit understanding' over belligerent rights at sea, with the British government neither condoning nor condemning Hoover's suggestion that ships carrying food should be exempted from wartime blockades.[28] As it had been by Harvey and Houghton in relation to the League of Nations and Locarno, the Pilgrims Society was used as a platform from which to make an important policy announcement concerning naval disarmament. Shortly after becoming prime minister (for the second time) in June 1929, Ramsay MacDonald had met with the former US vice-president and new ambassador to Britain, Charles Dawes, in Forres to discuss naval disarmament. At the conclusion of the meeting on 16 June, MacDonald confirmed that he was keen to meet with the US president and informed the press that he and Dawes would both make separate speeches on 18 June revealing what they had discussed. MacDonald made his speech at a town council dinner in Lossiemouth, while the new ambassador made his speech – the content of which had been agreed with MacDonald during their meeting in Forres – at the traditional Pilgrims welcome banquet at the Hotel Victoria in London. It was for that reason that the *New York Times*' London correspondent reported ahead of the Pilgrims dinner that '[n]ot in a long time has any speech been so eagerly awaited here'.[29] Likewise, in its report of the banquet the London *Times* explained that the

> discussion between General Dawes and the Prime Minister at Forres last Sunday on naval disarmament, and Mr McDonald's [sic] announcement that both of them would deal with the subject in the public speeches they were to make last night, added interest to the occasion.[30]

In his speech to the Pilgrims, Dawes said that he wanted to focus on 'suggestions as to a change in the method of future negotiations for naval disarmament', before going on to announce Hoover's 'yardstick' idea, 'with which to determine the military value of individual ships'. While 'ships might differ in displacement, size of guns, age, speed, and other characteristics', an 'agreed properly weighted value might be given to each of these differing characteristics as to make it possible to compare, for example, the cruiser fleets or combined fleets of two navies, and establish a parity between them'.[31] As such, the basis for the resolution of the Anglo-American naval rivalry – a rivalry that had plagued relations between the two countries throughout the 1920s – had been announced at a Pilgrims Society function. Following MacDonald's visit to the US to meet with President Hoover in October 1929, the London Naval Conference in 1930 successfully brought the naval rivalry to a close. That same year, the London branch of the Pilgrims Society regarded itself as having maintained 'its high position as the foremost organization in England for goodwill between ourselves and the United States'. The Society had had mixed fortunes in the 1920s, but the importance of the Pilgrims' contribution to the development of public diplomacy meant that this confident statement by the London branch was not necessarily unfounded.[32]

The Pilgrims in the Great Depression and the Second World War

While the London Naval Conference in 1930 meant that Anglo-American relations were in a better state than they had been for much of the previous decade, this did not mean that ill-feeling between the two countries had disappeared. Indeed, Alan Dobson has described the 1930s as a period in which Anglo-American relations 'diminished . . . in terms of active interaction. There was not much to the relationship during this period.'[33] This was a period that had witnessed the collapse of the economic system following the 1929 Wall Street Crash and the subsequent Depression, following which period it became increasingly likely that defaults would occur on Germany's reparation payments and the inter-Allied debt. Indeed, Britain ultimately did default on its debt to the US in 1934. The Depression, meanwhile, had witnessed a renewed anti-British feeling in the US on account of a belief that the British had mismanaged the world economy, combined with suspicions about the allegedly pro-British nature of the American banking industry. While Europeans blamed the Americans for the Wall Street Crash, Americans perceived that the Depression had been caused by the Europeans not paying their debt.[34] The Depression had also resulted in a sad end for one of the Pilgrims' most important members, with George Wilson having died in 1933 allegedly following financial ruin and a drink problem. For Wilson this was perhaps just as well. At least he did not live to see the world descend into another war as many of the fragile agreements and assumptions of the 1920s – in which the Pilgrims Society had shared – collapsed amidst rising bitterness and aggression.[35] The Pilgrims Society also felt the effects of the Depression, albeit not in an especially drastic fashion. Then Chairman of the London Pilgrims, Lord Derby (also of the Travel Association, and who was, during the First World War, responsible for the 'Derby scheme' for conscription before becoming Secretary of State for War), reported at the branch's AGM in 1931 that

> owing to the economic conditions prevailing we have had fewer of our American friends visiting us this year, and that due to the same causes, the Committee have felt that the Pilgrims should not be called upon to assemble unless there were very good grounds.[36]

He also noted that the 'difficult times' had resulted in 'a few more resignations [from the Society] than usual'. The Society had tried in 1931 to secure a number of prominent speakers, including US Secretary of State and future Secretary of War Henry Stimson, and Andrew Mellon, then Secretary of the Treasury and who became ambassador to the UK the following year. Derby noted, however, that the 'men who could say the most interesting things are those most reluctant to say anything'.[37]

The London Pilgrims' difficulties in attracting high-profile guests at the beginning of the 1930s mirrored some of the problems encountered by the New York branch in the 1920s. As before, however, the challenges experienced by the Society did not mean that its contribution to the history of public diplomacy was diminished. Quite the opposite was the case. Indeed, the later 1930s are regarded by Justin Hart as having seen the beginning of the 'first phase' of US public diplomacy, when American policymakers more fully appreciated the importance of international cultural relations. This appreciation was evident in the outcomes and aftermath of the 1936 Buenos Aires Conference, for example small-scale cultural exchanges and the creation of official bodies like the State Department's Division of Cultural Relations and Nelson Rockefeller's Office of the Coordinator of Inter-American Affairs, and was partly intended to underpin Franklin Roosevelt's Good Neighbor Policy in Latin America. The burgeoning official engagement with public diplomacy was also informed by a desire to counter Nazi Germany's use of radio and news publicity in the region.[38] Likewise, the British Council was Britain's first official agency with responsibility for international cultural relations and its foundation in 1934 was also suggestive of a dawning realisation in the Foreign Office that the state had a role to play in addressing the cultural and public aspect of international relations. This occurred concurrently with a growth in the functions of the state more generally, a development characterised by a greater belief in the need to use publicity to support domestic policy too.[39] For Hart, meanwhile, US public diplomacy really came of age in the 1940s with American involvement in the Second World War, when the State Department accepted the inseparability of foreign policy and cultural relations and the utility of public diplomacy as 'a tool of empire to be used to facilitate American hegemony'.[40] Yet the Pilgrims Society, together with those diplomats like Grey, Houghton, and Dawes who had regarded it as a vehicle for engaging with foreign publics, had long demonstrated an awareness of the ways in which public diplomacy could serve foreign policy objectives. In Grey's case in the 1900s, this had also been about promoting concepts of Anglo-American imperialism. As a result of these earlier precedents, Hart's 'first phase' of public diplomacy is a needlessly restrictive concept. There is, rather, a direct line of descent from groups like the Pilgrims Society to the more official organs of public diplomacy in the 1930s and 1940s, which themselves were 'forerunners' to Cold War cultural relations organisations like the United States Information Agency.[41]

Even so, the more institutionalised nature of official involvement in public diplomacy meant that the Pilgrims Society itself became less important as a semi-official publicity organisation during the second half of the twentieth century. That is not to say, however, that the Pilgrims Society was entirely overtaken by events in the 1930s and 1940s. The international crises in Europe in these decades meant that the US once again entered into a debate about its place in the world. The Pilgrims Society had a role to play in this debate. The Neutrality Acts of the later 1930s represented an uneasy compromise between isolationist and interventionist sentiments in an American body politic faced with the challenge of responding to the Spanish Civil War, the Abyssinian Crisis, Germany's invasion of Czechoslovakia and the eventual outbreak of the Second World War in 1939.[42] In this context, and as with George Harvey in 1919, the Pilgrims Society provided the locus for another pronouncement on US foreign policy by a new ambassador in London. Making the traditional maiden speech to the Pilgrims

Society at a banquet in March 1938, Joseph P. Kennedy sought to outline the US's position on the events unfolding in Europe. J. Simon Rofe has noted that Kennedy initially endeared himself to London's elites by means of 'what might today be described as public diplomacy', and his speech to the Pilgrims was an example of this. The content of the speech was agreed beforehand with the State Department – which had advised Kennedy to adopt a more diplomatic tone than he had originally intended – and was later released to the newspapers.[43] The *New York Times* reprinted the full text of Kennedy's speech (indicating that his intended audience was in the US as well as in Britain) and reported that it was 'heard with strained attention by Ambassadors, Cabinet Ministers and almost 400 leaders of British official, diplomatic and business life', including Viscount Halifax, the Foreign Secretary. Kennedy told the Pilgrims that some people were under the impression that the US 'could never remain neutral in the event a general war should unhappily break out', but argued that that was 'just as danger-ously conceived a misapprehension' as the idea that the US would never fight. In sum, the ambassador was attempting to dampen expectations of US intervention in the event of war. He urged his influential audience to realise that there was 'no way of knowing what position the United States would take under circumstances which cannot now be foreseen' and argued that, ultimately, US policy would be guided by self-interest.[44] The speech reflected many of Kennedy's own feelings on the matter and his tenure as ambassador was later characterised by a worsening relationship with Franklin Roosevelt, as Kennedy maintained his opposition to war even while the president was himself examining ways of assisting the Allies once conflict was under way. In 1938, how-ever, Kennedy's speech to the Pilgrims was another example of a senior diplomat using the Society as a vehicle for communicating US policy to foreign and domestic publics.

Once the war had begun, the Pilgrims Society in New York was placed in a similar position to that in which it had found itself at the beginning of the First World War: namely, it was an Anglo-American organisation operating in the US at a time when that country remained officially neutral during an armed struggle involving the British. As in 1914, the American Pilgrims sought ways to articulate their support for Britain. In July 1940, Nicholas Murray Butler, the president of the New York branch, suggested cabling Lord Derby the message that the British people 'have not only our sympathy but every form of support which is permissible to give'. Butler said that the Pilgrims 'hope and pray that the outcome of the struggle against the despots of 1940 will be as successful as was the struggle against Napoleon Bonaparte more than a century ago'.[45] Butler was the long-standing president of Columbia University and had become president of the New York Pilgrims after the death of Chauncey Depew in April 1928.[46] He was a high-profile figure in elite Anglo-American internationalist circles, especially through his role as president of the Carnegie Endowment for International Peace. He won the Nobel Prize in 1931 and had unsuccessfully attempted to become the Republican candidate for US president in 1920. Butler was also an anti-Semite who was remembered in a *New York Times* article in 2006 as a 'natural-born blowhard' and an 'Anglophile philosopher with a phony posh accent'.[47] Butler frequently corresponded in the 1930s and 1940s with the New York lawyer Frederic R. Coudert Senior, who was also involved with the Pilgrims. Both men were keen that the New York Pilgrims were seen to support their British brethren, with Coudert writing that he did not believe that the Pilgrims Society was 'only meant to articulate fine sentiments on sunshiny days and that it retires underground when the skies are darkened and the tempest is on'. For that reason, he had 'somewhat emphatically' informed his fellow Pilgrims that the Society should 'say something in this hour of England's supreme trial and awe-inspiring struggle to save civilization'. In Coudert's view, the war was in 'defense of our common heritage and civilization'.[48] Later, following German air raids, the US Pilgrims provided a more material form of assistance to the British by donating funds to pay for two portable canteens.[49]

Messages of support to the Pilgrims in London and two mobile tea vans were not, however, the only means by which people such as Butler and Coudert demonstrated their support for what was increasingly seen by some in America as a shared war effort. Franklin Roosevelt's version of neutrality was not the same as Woodrow Wilson's. While making commitments to keep the US out of the war, Roosevelt also understood that the conflict posed a threat to American security. As a result, he found ways of offering limited assistance to the Allies, including by successfully arguing for amendments to the neutrality legislation to allow the sale of weapons to Britain and France.[50] This was followed by the destroyers-for-bases agreement in September 1940, which saw the

US provide Britain with a number of First World War-era warships in exchange for access to land for bases on some British imperial territories, and the so-called 'Lend-Lease' Act in March 1941.[51] Importantly, the president made efforts to mould public opinion in favour of his pro-Ally policies. He did this via the Committee to Defend America by Aiding the Allies (CDA), led by the Republican newspaperman William Allen White, and co-founded by Frederic Coudert and by J. P. Morgan chairman and then New York Pilgrims' chairman Thomas Lamont.[52] The CDA worked closely with the White House to argue the case for assisting the Allies, doing so by means of newspaper articles, public meetings, and radio broadcasts. It had up to 20,000 members, including Butler and other Pilgrims such as John W. Davis and Frank Polk. Polk – a legal partner of John Davis' who had previously been Undersecretary of State, and who was chairman of the US Pilgrims between 1924 and 1931 – was also a member of the Century Group, a more stridently interventionist offshoot of the CDA based in Manhattan's Century Club.[53] One example of the CDA's work was its effort to generate public support for the destroyers-for-bases agreement, an endeavour that Coudert hoped Butler would assist with. In a July 1940 letter, Coudert wrote Butler that '[y]ou doubtless saw in the morning papers the White Committee's advertisement on the destroyer question'. Expressing his belief in the 'essential necessity' of the deal, Coudert said that his colleagues on the CDA were meeting with Roosevelt to discuss the matter further and suggested that Butler might also speak with the president on the telephone.[54] The overlap between the CDA, the Century Group, and the Pilgrims serves to underline the long-standing and continuing connection between Anglo-American associationalism and organs of semi-official publicity. This connection was used not only to serve an American agenda; for example, the British government had urged the English-Speaking Union to continue its work in promoting ideas of Anglo-American friendship across 1938 and 1939.[55] The Pilgrims Society itself did not play the same role as the CDA or the ESU. It was never an organisation suited to the delivery of mass propaganda or publicity. Nevertheless, the crossover between the Society and these other organisations is noteworthy: its leaders were the CDA's leaders. This demonstrates the significance of the Pilgrims Society's network to the history of semi-official propaganda, publicity, and public diplomacy.

Rather than undertake the same type of publicity work as the CDA, the Pilgrims Society contributed to the cause of wartime Anglo-American cooperation by its traditional means of hosting high-profile banquets. There are two stand-out examples of this during the Second World War, both of which occurred in the days following Franklin Roosevelt's signing of the Lend-Lease Act on 11 March 1941: the London Pilgrims' welcome for Ambassador John G. Winant, and the US Pilgrims' welcome for Lord Halifax. The lend-lease legislation provided for the loaning of 'war materials' to Britain and was described by then Prime Minister Winston Churchill as a 'most unsordid act'. Such a description did not reflect the motives of self-interest on the part of the US. For one, lend-lease was an example of Roosevelt seeking to secure American national security by undertaking to prop up the defences of another power. In addition, the provisions of the lend-lease legislation – which did not provide immediate aid to Britain in March 1941 – were not meant by the Americans to result simply in the gifting of supplies. While the US did not seek monetary payment, Roosevelt's administration hoped to use the lend-lease agreement to further undermine British economic dominance, including by challenging the concept of imperial preference. These elements of competition and wariness serve to complicate overly simplistic notions of the Anglo-American special relationship, notwithstanding the evident significance of American wartime aid to Britain. For its own part, the British government had initially preferred that the US not enter the war as a belligerent, fearing that this would give America too much influence in the post-war world. This view changed in the wake of the Tripartite Pact between Germany, Japan, and Italy in September 1940, after which British policy-makers became more convinced that US entry into the war was needed if the Axis powers were to be defeated. Against this backdrop, and with lend-lease falling short of the more fulsome action that Britain wanted from the US, Reynolds is correct to describe Churchill's positive interpretation as 'rhetoric, used for the purposes of wartime diplomacy and propaganda'.[56] The speeches at the two Pilgrims dinners in March 1941 served similar purposes. Indeed, Churchill was one of the speakers at the first of these events, which was held on 18 March in the Savoy Hotel in London to officially welcome John G. Winant, Joseph Kennedy's replacement as US ambassador in Britain.[57] In his toast to the new ambassador, Churchill told the Pilgrims that news of lend-lease had come to Britain 'like a draught of life' and that the 'words and acts of the President and people of the United States . . . tell us by an ocean-borne trumpet call that we are no longer alone'. Churchill also took care to highlight the danger posed to the US by the Axis powers. He referenced the ongoing naval Battle of the Atlantic, noting that German warships and submarines had 'crossed to the American side of the Atlantic'. The prime minister then ended his speech by emphasising his hopes for greater Anglo-American cooperation in the future.[58] In this vein, he told Winant that

> you share our purpose, you will share our dangers, you will share our anxieties, you shall share our secrets, and the day will come when the British Empire and the United States will share together the solemn but splendid duties which are the crown of victory.[59]

While his words describe some aspects of what became the special relationship, in early 1941 Churchill was showing more in the way of hope than foresight. Nevertheless, the prime minister now believed that the US was moving ever closer to entering the war as a belligerent and his speech to the Pilgrims Society was designed to engender a sense of inevitability about such an outcome.[60] More than in previous years, Anglo-American diplomacy was conducted not through the ambassadors of the two countries but by the heads of the respective governments. This means that Churchill's decision to speak at the Pilgrims event is all the more significant: the decision underlines the perceived usefulness of the Society as a public diplomacy actor.

Winant's own speech at the event, meanwhile, was in marked contrast to the one Joseph Kennedy had given to the Society a few years previously. Winant's support for the British was less ambiguous and he had been a long-term critic of Nazi Germany. He described to the Pilgrims the 'policies which draw your country and mine more closely together in [the] face of a common peril' and said that the US was in the process of 'mobilizing with ever-growing speed its tremendous resources to make available to you the sinews of war'. Remarks such as these ensured that Winant was a popular figure during his time in Britain; he was well liked by Churchill, senior officials, and the wider public.[61] Importantly, both Churchill's and Winant's speeches to the Pilgrims were broadcast to the British and American publics. They were covered even in Germany, where the Nazi Foreign Office publication the

Deutsche Diplomatische-Politische Korrespondenz reported that Churchill's words were evidence of 'Anglo-Saxons on both sides of the Atlantic' having 'worked each other up into a state of intoxication, marked by overweening arrogance'. Indeed, the Germans believed that while such arrogance was 'congenital' in the case of the British, it was 'created' in America by 'unscrupulous hate and fear propaganda'.[62] For the Nazis, Churchill's speech to the Pilgrims was an example of this sort of propaganda and their identification of it as such provides further evidence of the Society's public diplomacy role. The speech was, meanwhile, covered favourably by the press in Greece, where the British would soon intervene in an ultimately unsuccessful attempt to halt a German advance undertaken in support of Mussolini's Italy.[63]

Whatever the extent of the news coverage of Churchill's speech to the Pilgrims, the British were wary of undertaking sustained and obvious propaganda in the US (even though the official Ministry of Information did coordinate British publicity there), not least for fear of inflaming the sorts of attitudes that had been evident during the McAndrew affair and which still held sway with some Americans.[64] Indeed, this fear had motivated the US Pilgrims' decision to postpone its welcome dinner for Lord Halifax, who arrived in the US as the new British ambassador in early 1941. Concerned that speeches at the event could be misreported or misrepresented and thus undermine public support for aid to Britain, the Pilgrims decided to wait until after lend-lease had been signed into law before hosting the traditional welcome banquet for the new ambassador. The dinner was eventually held on 25 March at the Waldorf-Astoria, with Halifax's speech broadcast 'on the three major radio networks on short-wave to the world'.[65] Halifax, hitherto Foreign Secretary, had not wanted to become ambassador and his formal manners meant that he was ill-suited to American political and cultural styles. In truth, Churchill's decision to appoint Halifax ambassador was partly a political one in an effort to remove from the Cabinet a man who had a reputation as a supporter of appeasement and who may in future have argued for a compromise peace with Germany.[66] Halifax's reticence about his new posting was evident in his maiden speech to the Pilgrims, for example when he spoke of his 'sadness' upon leaving Britain. The rest of his remarks to the Society, however, dealt with the importance of UK–US cooperation both during the war and afterwards. The *New York Times* reprinted his speech in full and described it as 'a more advanced official expression than heretofore' of 'British intentions in a post-war world'. Indeed, the newspaper had reported back in February that it expected Halifax's first public speech to 'rank as one of the important declarations of British policy on the war and ultimate peace'.[67] In the end, Halifax delivered the usual platitudes about Anglo-American friendship – for example repeating Churchill's overwhelmingly positive public interpretation of lend-lease – and only very vaguely addressed British war aims. He said that Britain was fighting for 'democracy and freedom' and argued that international economic cooperation would be key to securing a peaceful post-war world. Nevertheless, the speech served an important public diplomacy function and Halifax attempted to contrast what he regarded as Britain and America's shared liberal principles against the tenets of Nazism.[68] This was an attempt both to legitimise lend-lease to those Americans still sceptical of US aid to Britain and to contextualise the need for additional support in the future. In the opinion of the writer of one letter to the editor of the *New York Times*, this attempt worked. Writing from Wood, Wisconsin, Guy D'Aulby said that '[h]ere in the Middle West doubts have existed in the minds of a large number of sincere persons about the wisdom of our all-out effort to help Great Britain'. D'Aulby believed that such people 'should be comforted by the assurances of Lord Halifax'. In his view, 'this section of the country ought to see very plainly how important must be America's contribution whereby the restoration of religious tolerance, individual worth, justice under law and the moral order is its own reward'. For D'Aulby, Lord Halifax's 'confidence in the ultimate victorious outcome' was 'undoubtedly shared by the majority of Americans, as proved by the Gallup polls of public opinion'.[69] The extent to which statements from British ambassadors like Halifax, and his predecessor Lord Lothian, encouraged Americans to support an aid programme is difficult to gauge. Indeed, Roosevelt himself – partly through the publicity work of the CDA – had taken care to ensure public backing before presenting the lend-lease legislation to Congress in the first place.[70] That very fact, however, only serves to underline the importance of public diplomacy and publicity in arguing for a policy position. This was as true for Roosevelt as it was for Churchill, though in March 1941 the two leaders were not yet of the same opinion regarding what role the US should play in the ongoing conflict. The Pilgrims dinner in London on 18 March, together with the event in New

York a few days later, enabled the British government to push its agenda of seeking US entry into the war but to do so in gentle tones and before an audience of sympathetic elite Anglo-Americans. Halifax's speech to the New York Pilgrims and Winant's speech to the London Pilgrims provide evidence of the continued importance attached to the Society's heritage of providing a venue for significant ambassadorial maiden speeches. Churchill's speech, meanwhile, is an example of the British prime minister conducting his own public diplomacy and doing so via the Pilgrims Society.

In March 1946, after the war – and after his time as prime minister had ended – Churchill would deliver his much-quoted 'Iron Curtain' speech at Fulton in Missouri. This speech also included perhaps the best-known, if not the first, use of the term 'the special relationship' to describe the Anglo-American connection. For Churchill in 1946, the special relationship meant an Anglo-Saxon military alliance against the threat of Soviet Russia.[71] This differed in context though not in sentiment to his wish for American assistance against Nazi Germany as expressed in his Pilgrims speech in March 1941. The US did, of course, enter the Second World War following the Japanese bombing of Pearl Harbor in December 1941, though by that point the US's support for Britain had gone beyond even the scope of lend-lease. August had seen Churchill and Roosevelt's creation of the Atlantic Charter, which outlined the war aims of the non-Axis powers. September witnessed the expansion of American escorts of Allied shipping in the Atlantic, meaning that the US Navy could engage with Axis ships across a much wider geographical area than before. Then in November, Congress repealed important aspects of the neutrality legislation. It is for some of these reasons that 1941 could be regarded as the beginning of the special relationship.[72] Such a periodisation might be debated, as indeed might the 'special' nature of that relationship. There is much truth, for example, in J. Simon Rofe's comment that the Second World War was ultimately characterised by the 'waning of British power and prerogative and surging American might, realities that fit awkwardly in Churchill's consoling mythology rooted in a "special relationship"'.[73] Indeed, 1941 was less the beginning of the special relationship than the end of American isolationism. This was true even before Pearl Harbor and was evidenced by the growing support amongst Americans for US membership in any future League of Nations-type organisation. The move away from isolationism was also manifest in an article written by publisher Henry Luce (member of the Century Group and father of the later Pilgrims president and heir to the *Time* empire Henry Luce III), which was published in February and called for an 'American Century'. In the context of the US's demonstrable potential as a global super-power, the old nationalist fears about British 'imperial' propaganda seemed decreasingly relevant. Instead, Luce outlined that American ascendancy could be achieved by means of soft power, including the spread of American movies and music.[74] This was a manifesto for cultural diplomacy, as Justin Hart has argued; but with the history of the Pilgrims' contribution to public diplomacy in mind, it was neither a surprising nor a new development, even though the Anglo-American relationship had been fundamentally altered in the years since the founding of the Society in the 1900s.

Conclusion

Just as the Pilgrims was one of the preoccupations of some 1920s American nationalists, including those involved in Chicago's 'McAndrew Trial', the Society was, in 1941, at the centre of the evolving Anglo-American connection. The nature of the relationship between the two countries had changed utterly since the founding of the Pilgrims in the era of the 'great rapprochement', but if in the 1940s it was becoming more special – and more unequal – than could have been foreseen by the Pilgrims in the 1900s then the Society could at least claim a continuing role in smoothing its frequently rough contours. The Pilgrims events examined in this chapter – the Houghton dinner in 1925, the Dawes banquet in 1929, and the two gatherings in March 1941 – signified an evolution in the Society's public diplomacy role from the largely private initiative that lay behind its activities hitherto, to a greater degree of government involvement in cultural and public international relations. The Pilgrims' activities were perhaps not as extensive as the American nationalists in Chicago had feared, but the 1920s, 1930s, and the Second World War nevertheless demonstrated that the Society had a role to play in support of international relations and public diplomacy.

The previous chapter showed that George Harvey used his 1921 speech to explicitly rule out American membership of the League of Nations. As this chapter has argued, meanwhile, Houghton used his 1925 speech to make his famous 'peace ultimatum', while

Dawes used his 1929 speech to outline Herbert Hoover's 'yard-stick' idea for naval disarmament. These events solidified the tradition of British–American ambassadors making their first public speeches at Pilgrims events and demonstrated a belief that such functions lent legitimacy and weight to official statements. With officials using the events for the 'creation and dissemination of information materials to build understanding of a policy', they were also examples of advocacy diplomacy.[75] This represented an expansion both of the role of the Pilgrims Society and of the concept of public diplomacy.

The Houghton and Dawes speeches demonstrated a greater official understanding of the benefits of utilising the network and profile of the Pilgrims Society as a public diplomacy means of advocating specific policy positions on issues of international importance. This was even more the case with the Churchill, Winant, and Halifax speeches in 1941, all of which were delivered in the complex context of America's increasingly strained neutrality during the Second World War. These three speeches were broadcast widely and received generous press attention. This was particularly true of Prime Minister Churchill's speech, which was reported by the German press. By this point, the Pilgrims Society was by no means the main player in Anglo-American public diplomacy. Britain had the British Council while the US had the Division of Cultural Relations. These served slightly different functions to the Pilgrims, as did those British covert intelligence bodies that operated to try to encourage American entry into the Second World War. Nevertheless, the Pilgrims had legitimised and encouraged official involvement in international publicity and public diplomacy across the preceding years. It had, moreover, long conducted its public diplomacy in the same Anglo-Saxonist terms that were central to Churchill's conception of the unfolding history of the so-called 'English-speaking peoples'.[76] This meant that the Society still provided a relevant and high-profile Anglo-American connection at the beginning of the 'special relationship'.

Notes

1. *New York Times*, 1 May 1926.
2. 'Speeches at Dinner to celebrate the Twenty-Fifth Anniversary of the Founding of the Pilgrims of the United States', 9 February 1928, Pilgrims Mss, NYC.

3. Baker, *Pilgrims of Britain*, p. 22.
4. Moser, *Twisting the Lion's Tail*, pp. 52–9; Dobson, *Anglo-American Relations*, pp. 60–1; McKercher, "'The Deep and Latent Distrust'", pp. 227–9.
5. John Maclean, 'The Coming War with America', in Nan Milton (ed.), *John Maclean: In the Rapids of Revolution: Essays, Articles and Letters, 1902–1923* (Glasgow, 1978), pp. 182–90.
6. Moser, *Twisting the Lion's Tail*, pp. 59–60.
7. Phillips Payson O'Brien, 'Herbert Hoover, Anglo-American Relations and Republican Party Politics in the 1920s', *Diplomacy and Statecraft*, Vol. 22, Issue 2 (2011), pp. 200–18; Moser, *Twisting the Lion's Tail*, p. 33 and pp. 45–6; Rhodes, 'Image of Britain', p. 202; Lawrence Spinelli, *Dry Diplomacy: The United States, Great Britain, and Prohibition* (Lanham, 2008).
8. Herring, *From Colony to Superpower*, p. 460; in his analysis of the Houghton intervention, Herring does not mention that the 'peace ultimatum' was delivered in front of the Pilgrims, simply stating that Houghton's statement was made as part of 'a speech in London'. Herring does, however, reference Jeffrey Matthews (see below), who does mention the Pilgrims Society. It is clear, therefore, that Herring's analysis – which forms the basis of this presentation of the 'peace ultimatum' – is referring to the Pilgrims speech.
9. Throughout the summer of 1925 Houghton worked 'unofficially as a mediator among the parties'. See Jeffrey J. Matthews, *Alanson B. Houghton: Ambassador of the New Era* (Lanham, 2004), p. 123; *New York Times*, 6 May 1925; McKercher, *Second Baldwin Government*, p. 9; William N. Medlicott, *British Foreign Policy Since Versailles, 1919–1963* (London, 1968), p. 59; McKercher, "'The Deep and Latent Distrust'", p. 225; Cohrs, *Unfinished Peace*, pp. 222–3; unfortunately, it has not been possible to uncover official primary source information on this event, neither in FRUS nor in the Foreign Office series FO800/257 and FO800/258.
10. *New York Times*, 5 May 1925; *The Times*, 5 May 1925.
11. *Le Temps* quoted in the *Boston Daily Globe*, 6 May 1925; *Washington Post*, 6 May 1925; Matthews, *Houghton*, pp. 120–2.
12. *The Times*, 5 May 1925; *Daily Telegraph* quoted in *Washington Post*, 6 May 1925.
13. *New York Times*, 5 and 6 May 1925; there appears to be no information in FRUS or in the Foreign Office series FO800/257 and FO800/258.
14. Gorman, *International Society*, pp. 15–16 and p. 211.
15. Taylor, *Projection of Britain*, p. 112.
16. Moser, *Twisting the Lion's Tail*, pp. 52–9; Dobson, *Anglo-American Relations*, pp. 60–1; McKercher, "'The Deep and Latent Distrust'", pp. 227–9.

17. Moser, *Twisting the Lion's Tail*, pp. 38–41; for information on the 1939 poll, see Fred M. Leventhal, 'Public Face and Public Space: The Projection of Britain in America Before the Second World War', in Fred M. Leventhal and Roland Quinault (eds), *Anglo-American Attitudes: From Revolution to Partnership* (Aldershot, 2000), p. 213.

18. *Chicago Daily Tribune*, 1 April 1927; Moser, *Twisting the Lion's Tail*, pp. 63–6; MacRaild et al., 'Interdependence Day and Magna Charta', p. 151; Rhodes, 'Anglophobia in Chicago; Mayor William Hale Thompson's 1927 Campaign Against King George V', *Illinois Quarterly*, Vol. 39 (Summer 1977), pp. 5–14; Dominic A. Pacyga, *Chicago: A Biography* (Chicago, 2009), pp. 242–6.

19. *The Times*, 16 and 18 November 1927 and 23 March 1928; *Chicago Daily Tribune*, 3 November 1927; the IMCDA was described by one witness as the 'Magna Charta Association for annihilating the Fourth of July'. See *The Times*, 18 November 1927; McAndrew was allegedly a member of the ESU. See *Chicago Daily Tribune*, 20 October 1927. See also *Chicago Daily Tribune*, 17 October 1927.

20. *New York Times*, 17 November 1927.

21. Gorman, *International Society*, p. 210.

22. Minute Book 3, 7 December 1927, Pilgrims Mss, NYC.

23. *New York Times*, 11 February 1928; Brittain's comments about British versions of William Hale Thompson will have been referring to those people in Britain who were unhappy about perceived cultural Americanisation. It is striking that some sections of British society were as repulsed by foreign influences as were some Americans. See Chris Waters, '"Beyond Americanization": Re-thinking Anglo-American Cultural Exchange Between the Wars', *Cultural and Social History*, Vol. 4, Issue 4 (2007), pp. 451–9.

24. 'Speeches at Dinner to celebrate the Twenty-Fifth Anniversary of the Founding of the Pilgrims of the United States', 9 February 1928, Pilgrims Mss, NYC.

25. 'Suggestions for the immediate re-organisation and for the future of the Pilgrims' Society', July 1919, Pilgrims Mss, LMA/4632/A/05/004.

26. MacRaild et al., 'Interdependence Day and Magna Charta', p. 152.

27. Moser, *Twisting the Lion's Tail*, p. 65; Rhodes, 'Anglophobia in Chicago', p. 13.

28. Burk, *Old World, New World*, pp. 472–3; McKercher, *Second Baldwin Government*, p. 197.

29. *New York Times*, 18 June 1929; 'The Ambassador in Great Britain (Dawes) to the Secretary of State', 17 June 1929, FRUS, <http://uwdc.library.wisc.edu/collections/FRUS> (last accessed 26 May 2014); 'The Ambassador in Great Britain (Dawes) to the Secretary of State', 18 June 1929, FRUS, <http://uwdc.library.wisc.edu/collections/FRUS> (last accessed 24 January 2017).

30. *The Times*, 19 June 1929.
31. Ibid.
32. Minutes, 9 July 1930, Pilgrims Mss, LMA/4632/A/01/001.
33. Dobson, *Anglo-American Relations*, pp. 65–7.
34. Ibid. pp. 65–7; Moser, *Twisting the Lion's Tail*, pp. 77–80; Temperley, *Britain and America*, pp. 129–31.
35. For Wilson's obituary, see *New York Times*, 30 September 1933. The obituary explains that Wilson had been ill following a stroke in 1932, but Lindsay Russell recalled in 1939 that he had 'dropped out of sight about ten years ago, as a result of financial troubles and drank and passed away from dissipation'. See Russell to Barratt, 26 January 1939, Pilgrims Mss, LMA4632/C/05/001; Temperley, *Britain and America*, p. 131.
36. Minutes, 9 July 1931, Pilgrims Mss, LMA/4632/A/01/001
37. Ibid.
38. Hart, *Empire of Ideas*, pp. 15–40.
39. Taylor, *British Propaganda*, pp. 76–7; Ninkovich, *Diplomacy of Ideas*, pp. 8–34; as it happened, due to a concern that it would be perceived as an underhand British propaganda agency, the British Council did not operate in the US. In light of this, groups like the Pilgrims would have remained of use. See Leventhal, 'The Projection of Britain in America Before the Second World War', p. 212; Gienow-Hecht, 'Cultural Diplomacy and Civil Society Since 1850', p. 46; Cull, *American Propaganda and Public Diplomacy*, p. 11; Muriel Grant, *Propaganda and the Role of the State in Inter-War Britain* (Oxford, 1994).
40. Hart, *Empire of Ideas*, pp. 41–70.
41. Gienow-Hecht, 'Cultural Diplomacy and Civil Society Since 1850', p. 47.
42. Hart, *Empire of Ideas*, p. 19; David Reynolds, *The Creation of the Anglo-American Alliance, 1937–41: A Study in Competitive Co-operation* (London, 1981), pp. 30–1.
43. J. Simon Rofe, 'Joseph P. Kennedy, 1938–40', in Alison R. Holmes and J. Simon Rofe (eds), *The Embassy in Grosvenor Square: American Ambassadors to the United Kingdom, 1938–2008* (Basingstoke, 2012), pp. 27–8.
44. *New York Times*, 19 March 1938.
45. Butler to Frederic R. Coudert, 31 July 1940, Butler Papers, CUBL, Box 95.
46. Baker, *Pilgrims of the US*, p. 152; Minute Book 1, 26 December 1909, Pilgrims Mss, NYC.
47. See Butler's obituary in *The Times*, 8 December 1947; *New York Times*, 22 January 2006; Michael Rosenthal, *Nicholas Miraculous:*

The Amazing Career of the Redoubtable Dr. Nicholas Murray Butler (New York, 2006).

48. Coudert to Butler, 25 July and 30 July 1940, Butler Papers, CUBL, Box 95.
49. Baker, *Pilgrims of Britain*, p. 28; Baker, *Pilgrims of the US*, p. 113.
50. Herring, *From Colony to Superpower*, p. 518.
51. Reynolds, *Anglo-American Alliance*, p. 121; Herring, *From Colony to Superpower*, p. 525.
52. Lise Namikas, 'The Committee to Defend America and the Debate Between Internationalists and Interventionists, 1939–1941', *Historian*, 61 (1999), p. 844; Baker, *Pilgrims of the US*, p. 55; for Lamont's obituary, see *New York Times*, 3 February 1948.
53. Namikas, 'The Committee to Defend America', p. 848; Baker, *Pilgrims of the US*, p. 38; for Polk's obituary, see *New York Times*, 8 February 1943.
54. Coudert to Butler, 30 July 1940, Butler Papers, CUBL, Box 95.
55. Cull, *Selling War: The British Propaganda Campaign Against American 'Neutrality' in World War II* (Oxford, 1995), pp. 22–9.
56. Reynolds, *Anglo-American Alliance*, pp. 161–6; Burk, *Old World, New World*, p. 495; Herring, *From Colony to Superpower*, pp. 524–6; Christopher Hitchens, *Blood, Class and Empire: The Enduring Anglo-American Relationship* (London, 2006), p. 212.
57. Reynolds, *Anglo-American Alliance*, pp. 79–80 and pp. 140–3.
58. *The Times*, 19 March 1941
59. Ibid.
60. Reynolds, *Anglo-American Alliance*, p. 168.
61. *The Times*, 19 March 1941; David Mayers, 'John Gilbert Winant, 1941–46', in Holmes and Rofe (eds), *The Embassy in Grosvenor Square*, p. 51.
62. *Deutsche Diplomatische-Politische Korrespondenz* quoted in *The Scotsman*, 20 March 1941; Baker, *Pilgrims of Britain*, p. 28.
63. *The Scotsman*, 20 March 1941; Reynolds, *Anglo-American Alliance*, p. 189; A. J. P. Taylor, *The Second World War: An Illustrated History* (Harmondsworth, 1975), pp. 87–91.
64. Reynolds, *Anglo-American Alliance*, p. 200; Cull, *Selling War*, passim; Temperley, *Britain and America*, p. 148.
65. *New York Times*, 26 March 1941; Baker, *Pilgrims of the US*, pp. 17–18.
66. Reynolds, *Anglo-American Alliance*, pp. 177–8.
67. *New York Times*, 26 March and 3 February 1941.
68. *New York Times*, 26 March 1941.
69. *New York Times*, 31 March 1941.
70. Herring, *From Colony to Superpower*, p. 525.

71. Burk, *Old World, New World*, p. 476; Vucetic, 'The Fulton Address as Racial Discourse', pp. 96–115.
72. Reynolds, *Anglo-American Alliance*, pp. 213–16 and p. 283; Temperley, *Britain and America*, pp. 144–5.
73. Rofe, 'Joseph P. Kennedy', pp. 57–8.
74. Hart, *Empire of Ideas*, pp. 44–5; Baker, *Pilgrims of the US*, p. 38.
75. Cull, *American Propaganda and Public Diplomacy*, p. xv.
76. Vucetic, 'The Fulton Address as Racial Discourse', p. 109.

Conclusion

... innumerable friendships have been made between men 'who count', which have, I know, in many cases, been of real practical service to the two countries
(Harry Brittain)

The Pilgrims Society was a semi-official public diplomacy actor in the field of foreign relations and a trailblazer for organisations like the British Council and the Division of Cultural Relations, which themselves were precursors to Cold War organisations like the United States Information Agency. The history of the Pilgrims Society tells of a gradual shift from unofficial actors providing the main impetus in public diplomacy to official actors providing the main impetus. The Society contributed to this shift by its support and facilitation of Earl Grey's cultural diplomacy in 1906; through its propaganda, advocacy, and exchange diplomacy during the First World War; and by means of the increasing use of the Society as a venue for policy announcements and advocacy diplomacy by US ambassadors in the 1920s and 1930s, and again in the critical year of 1941.

The Society's decreased relevance in more recent years was to a degree caused by the increased part played by the state in public diplomacy and propaganda roles. This was a development that the Pilgrims contributed to in the first half of the twentieth century. As such, the Pilgrims Society confounded early twentieth-century definitions of 'public diplomacy' as 'open diplomacy'. Firstly, the Pilgrims' involvement in foreign and international relations was by no means 'open'. The Pilgrims represented an exclusive network of elites, closed to democratic accountability or popular involvement. For the entirety of the period covered by this book, the Society excluded people on the basis of class, gender, and race.

At the same time, it sought to influence official and unofficial relations between the two polities in which it operated. Secondly, and more importantly, the Pilgrims acted primarily in the realms of advocacy and cultural diplomacy in an attempt to influence foreign and international relations by engaging with foreign publics. These actions characterise public diplomacy as it is understood today and, indeed, helped formulate that characterisation. The Society was able to do this via its status as an elite club rooted in the associational culture of London and New York. It couched its appeals for Anglo-American rapprochement in the language of Anglo-Saxonism and adopted a public diplomacy programme that highlighted the perceived shared cultural heritage of Britain and the US, and when necessary, Canada.

The Pilgrims Society has a history that extends beyond the scope of this book. It is still in existence today and has been a keen observer of Anglo-American relations across the second half of the twentieth century and the beginning of the twenty-first. In that time, it has seen the idea of the UK–US special relationship enter the common lexicon. The strength of that official relationship has waxed and waned, from the low of the 1956 Suez crisis to the dubious high of 2003, when President George W. Bush and Prime Minister Tony Blair oversaw the coming together of the two countries' military and intelligence forces to such damaging effect in Iraq. By this later period, the Pilgrims Society had all the hallmarks of a rarefied dining club for self-congratulatory elites, far removed from the ken of the wider public and from the conduct of hard diplomacy. This much had always been true of the Society – but only up to a point. Whereas today news of, or comment by, the Pilgrims rarely, if ever, appears in newspaper reports, the history of the Society in the early years of the twentieth century tells of a well-connected organisation with a high public profile working hard to secure Anglo-American friendship. It did this sometimes in cooperation with the state and almost always with a view to changing public and elite opinion. That is the why the Society is important to the history of public diplomacy.

The Pilgrims was an internationalist organisation, though the limits of that internationalism did not necessarily extend beyond the English-speaking, or 'Anglo-Saxon', world. To the early twenty-first-century reader conscious of debates regarding an apparently inward-looking and isolationist Anglo-American challenge to the liberal order, this may seem a strange form of internationalism.

Yet in the period covered by this book the Pilgrims often found themselves the brunt of American nationalist suspicion and not all of its members would entirely agree with the world-view of the most narrow-minded Brexiteers or Donald Trump supporters. The Pilgrims' members were attracted to the Society and to the cause of Anglo-American relations for a variety of reasons. Some, like Henry Codman Potter and Richard Watson Gilder, were genuinely internationalist in outlook. Others, like Charles Beresford and Lord Roberts, sought in Anglo-American friendship a means for commercial success and imperial prestige. This was often articulated in terms of idealised notions of civilisation, the rule of law, and democracy. In that respect, the Pilgrims Society's conception of Anglo-American relations was perhaps more Blair–Bush than May–Trump. As such, the Pilgrims Society can justifiably stand accused as an elitist mouthpiece for an interventionist and imperialist Anglo-American world order. It sought for itself an active public diplomacy role in Anglo-American relations and sought an active role in the world for Britain and the US. Unknown by most today, the Pilgrims Society nevertheless influenced in important ways both the development of public diplomacy and how people have come to think about the Anglo-American relationship.

Bibliography

Manuscript sources

Official records
Library and Archives Canada

Office of the Governor General of Canada Mss.

National Archives, Kew, Richmond, Surrey
CAB24 Cabinet Papers.
FO 5 Foreign Office, United States of America.
FO 96 Foreign Office, Political and Other Departments, Miscellanea.
FO 368 Foreign Office, Commercial and Sanitary Department.
FO 371 Foreign Office, Political Departments, US Files.
FO 395 Foreign Office, News Department.
FO 800 Foreign Office, Private Offices.
FO 881 Foreign Office, Confidential Prints.
INF 4 Ministry of Information and Predecessors.
PRO 30/60 Arthur Balfour Papers.
T102 Treasury, National War Aims Committee.

National Archives, College Park, Maryland
RG59 Department of State.

Miscellaneous
Hansard.
United States Congressional Record.

Personal and institutional collections
Arthur Balfour Papers, British Library, London.
Harry Brittain Papers, British Library of Political and Economic Science, London.

Nicholas Murray Butler Papers, Butler Library, Columbia University.

Joseph Choate Papers, Library of Congress, Washington DC.

Frederic Coudert Senior Papers, Butler Library, Columbia University.

Chauncey Depew Papers, Gelman Library, George Washington University.

Chauncey Depew Papers, New York Public Library.

Richard Watson Gilder Papers, New York Public Library.

Grey Papers, Durham University Special Collections.

Lord Northcliffe Papers, British Library, London.

Walter Hines Page Papers, Houghton Library, Harvard University.

Pilgrims Society of Great Britain Mss, London Metropolitan Archives.

Pilgrims Society of the United States Mss, Pilgrims of the United States Head Office, New York City.

Whitelaw Reid Papers, Library of Congress, Washington DC.

John A. Stewart Papers, New York Public Library.

Sulgrave Mss, Sulgrave Manor Trust Archives.

Published primary sources

Books, articles, and pamphlets

Anon., *A History of the St. George's Society of New York from 1770–1913* (New York: St. George's Society, 1913).

Besant, Walter, *Autobiography of Sir Walter Besant: With a Prefatory Note by S. Squire Sprigge* (London: Hutchinson, 1902).

Brittain, Harry, *Pilgrim Partners* (London: Hutchinson, 1942).

Brittain, Harry, *Pilgrims and Pioneers* (London: Hutchinson, 1946).

Bryce, James, *The American Commonwealth* (London: Macmillan, 1888).

Crosby, F. V. S., *Anglo-American Relations: Concerning the Origin of the Pilgrims Society* (New York: self-published, 1920).

DeWolfe Howe, Mark (ed.), *Holmes–Pollock Letters: The Correspondence of Mr Justice Holmes and Sir Frederick Pollock, 1874–1932* (Cambridge, MA: Belknap Press, 1961).

Dilke, Charles, *Greater Britain: A Record of Travel in English-Speaking Countries During 1866–7* (London: Macmillan, 1869).

Doyle, Arthur Conan, 'The Adventure of the Noble Bachelor', in *The Adventures of Sherlock Holmes* (London: Penguin Red Classics, 2007).

Doyle, Arthur Conan, *The Adventures of Sherlock Homes* (New York: Harpers and Brothers, 1902).

Hart, Charles Henry, 'The Wilson Portrait of Franklin: Earl Grey's Gift to the Nation', *The Pennsylvania Magazine of History and Biography*, Vol. 30, No. 4 (1906), pp. 409–16.

Maclean, John, 'The Coming War with America', in Milton, Nan (ed.), *John Maclean: In the Rapids of Revolution: Essays, Articles and Letters, 1902–1923* (Glasgow: The Tramp Trust Unlimited, 1978), pp. 182–90.

Morison, Elting E. (ed.), *The Letters of Theodore Roosevelt, Vol. 5: The Big Stick, 1905–1907* (Cambridge, MA: Harvard University Press, 1952).

Morison, Elting E. (ed.), *The Letters of Theodore Roosevelt, Vol. 6: The Big Stick, 1907–1909* (Cambridge, MA: Harvard University Press, 1952).

Stead, William T., *The Americanization of the World or The Trend of the Twentieth Century* (New York: Horace Markley, 1902).

Strong, Frank, *Benjamin Franklin: A Character Sketch* (New York: Instructor Publishing, 1898).

Newspapers and magazines

Atlanta Constitution.
Belfast News-Letter.
Birmingham Gazette.
Boston Daily Globe.
Boston Evening Transcript.
Buffalo Commercial.
Chicago Daily Tribune.
Christian Science Monitor.
Daily Herald (Calgary).
Daily News.
Evening Public Ledger.
Gaelic American.
Knoxville Sentinel.
Los Angeles Herald.
Mail and Empire.
New York Times.
New-York Tribune.
Oil City Derrick (Pennsylvania).
Pall Mall Gazette.
Philadelphia Inquirer.
Review of Reviews.
Telegraph (Macon, GA).
The English Race.
The Evening Statesman (Walla Walla, Washington).
The Globe (Toronto).
The Scotsman.
The Snyder Signal.
The Sun (New York).

The Times.
The Western Australian.
Washington Post.

Secondary sources

Monographs

Adams, Iestyn, *Brothers Across the Ocean: British Foreign Policy and the Origins of the Anglo-American 'Special Relationship' 1900–1905* (London: I. B. Tauris, 2005).

Allen, H. C., *Great Britain and the United States: A History of Anglo-American Relations (1783–1952)* (London: St Martin's Press, 1954).

Anderson, Stuart, *Race and Rapprochement: Anglo-Saxonism and Anglo-American Relations, 1895–1904* (London: Fairleigh Dickinson University Press, 1981).

Arndt, Richard T., *The First Resort of Kings: American Cultural Diplomacy in the Twentieth Century* (Washington DC: Potomac Books, 2005).

Axelrod, Alan, *Selling the Great War: The Making of American Propaganda* (New York: Palgrave Macmillan, 2009).

Baker, Anne P., *The Pilgrims of Great Britain: A Centennial History* (London: Profile Books, 2002).

Baker, Anne P., *The Pilgrims of the United States: A Centennial History* (London: Profile Books, 2003).

Beckert, Sven, *The Monied Metropolis: New York City and the Consolidation of the American Bourgeoisie, 1850–1896* (Cambridge: Cambridge University Press, 2001).

Belich, James, *Replenishing the Earth: The Settler Revolution and the Rise of the Anglo-World, 1783–1939* (Oxford: Oxford University Press, 2009).

Bell, Duncan, *The Idea of Greater Britain: Empire and the Future of World Order, 1860–1900* (Princeton: Princeton University Press, 2007).

Berghan, Volker R., *America and the Intellectual Cold Wars in Europe* (Princeton: Princeton University Press, 2001).

Brebner, John Bartlet, *North Atlantic Triangle: The Interplay of Canada, the United States and Great Britain* (New Haven: Yale University Press, 1945).

Brundage, Anthony and Richard A. Cosgrove, *The Great Tradition: Constitutional History and National Identity in Britain and the United States, 1870–1960* (Stanford: Stanford University Press, 2007).

Bueltmann, Tanja, *Scottish Ethnicity and the Making of New Zealand Society, 1850–1930* (Edinburgh: Edinburgh University Press, 2011).

Buitenhuis, Peter, *The Great War of Words: British, American and Canadian Propaganda and Fiction, 1914–33* (Vancouver: University of British Columbia Press, 1987).

Bukowski, Douglas, *Big Bill Thompson, Chicago, and the Politics of Image* (Urbana: University of Illinois Press, 1998).

Burk, Kathleen, *Britain, America and the Sinews of War, 1914–1918* (London: George Allen & Unwin, 1985).

Burk, Kathleen, *Old World, New World* (New York: Grove Press, 2007).

Burns, Edward McNall, *The American Idea of Mission: Concepts of National Purpose and Destiny* (New Brunswick: Rutgers University Press, 1957).

Burton, David H., *British–American Diplomacy 1895–1917: Early Years of the Special Relationship* (Malabar: Krieger Publishing, 1999).

Butler, Leslie, *Critical Americans: Victorian Intellectuals and Transatlantic Liberal Reform* (Chapel Hill: University of North Carolina Press, 2007).

Campbell, Charles S., *From Revolution to Rapprochement: The United States and Great Britain, 1783–1900* (New York: John Wiley and Sons, 1974).

Cervetti, Nancy, *S. Weir Mitchell, 1829–1914: Philadelphia's Literary Physician* (University Park: Pennsylvania State University Press, 2012).

Chernow, Ron, *The House of Morgan: An American Banking Dynasty and the Rise of Modern Finance* (New York: Simon & Schuster, 1990).

Clark, Peter, *British Clubs and Societies 1580–1800: The Origins of an Associational World* (Oxford: Oxford University Press, 2000).

Cohen, Naomi W., *Jacob H. Schiff: A Study in American Jewish Leadership* (Hanover: Brandeis University Press, 1999).

Cohrs, Patrick O., *The Unfinished Peace After World War 1: America, Britain and the Stabilisation of Europe, 1919–1932* (Cambridge: Cambridge University Press, 2006).

Conforti, Joseph A., *Imagining New England: Explorations of Regional Identity from the Pilgrims to the Mid-Twentieth Century* (Chapel Hill: University of North Carolina Press, 2000).

Cooper, Dana, Informal Ambassadors: American Women, Transatlantic Marriages, and Anglo-American Relations, 1865-1945 (Ashland, OH: Kent State University Press, 2014).

Cooper, Jr., John Milton, *The Warrior and the Priest: Woodrow Wilson and Theodore Roosevelt* (Cambridge, MA: Belknap Press, 1983).

Costigliola, Frank, *Awkward Dominion: American Political, Economic, and Cultural Relations with Europe, 1919–1933* (Ithaca: Cornell University Press, 1984).

Costigliola, Frank, *Roosevelt's Lost Alliances: How Personal Politics Helped Start the Cold War* (Princeton: Princeton University Press, 2012).

Crapol, Edward P., *America for Americans: Economic Nationalism and Anglophobia in the Late Nineteenth Century* (Westport: Greenwood Press, 1973).

Cull, Nicholas J., *The Cold War and the United States Information Agency: American Propaganda and Public Diplomacy, 1945–1989* (Cambridge: Cambridge University Press, 2008).

Cull, Nicholas J., *Selling War: The British Propaganda Campaign Against American 'Neutrality' in World War II* (Oxford: Oxford University Press, 1995).

Cullinane, Michael Patrick, *Liberty and American Anti-Imperialism, 1898–1909* (London: Palgrave Macmillan, 2012).

Danchev, Alex, *On Specialness: Essays in Anglo-American Relations* (London: Macmillan Press, 1998).

DeConde, Alexander, *Ethnicity, Race and American Foreign Policy: A History* (Boston: Northeastern University Press, 1992).

Dilks, David, *Neville Chamberlain, Vol. 1, 1869–1929* (Cambridge: Cambridge University Press, 1984).

Dimbleby, David and David Reynolds, *An Ocean Apart: The Relationship Between Britain and America in the Twentieth Century* (London: Hodder & Stoughton, 1988).

Dobson, Alan P., *Anglo-American Relations in the Twentieth Century: Of Friendship, Conflict and the Rise and Decline of Superpowers* (London: Routledge, 1995).

Dumbrell, John, *A Special Relationship: Anglo-American Relations in the Cold War and After* (Basingstoke: Palgrave Macmillan, 2001).

Dyer, John P., *From Shiloh to San Juan: The Life of 'Fightin' Joe' Wheeler* (Baton Rouge: Louisiana State University Press, 1961).

Edwards, John Carver, *Patriots in Pinstripe: Men of the National Security League* (Washington DC: University Press of America, 1982).

Friedberg, Aaron L., *The Weary Titan: Britain and the Experience of Relative Decline, 1895–1905* (Princeton: Princeton University Press, 1988).

Gelber, Lionel M., *The Rise of Anglo-American Friendship: A Study in World Politics, 1898–1906* (London: Oxford University Press, 1938).

Glad, Betty, *Charles Evans Hughes and the Illusions of Innocence: A Study in American Diplomacy* (Urbana: University of Illinois Press, 1966).

Gorman, Daniel, *The Emergence of International Society in the 1920s* (Cambridge: Cambridge University Press, 2012).

Gosden, P. H. J. H., *Self-Help: Voluntary Associations in Nineteenth-Century Britain* (London: Batsford, 1974).

Granatstein, J. L. and Norman Hillmer, *For Better or for Worse: Canada and the United States to the 1990s* (Toronto: Copp Clark Pitman, 1991).

Grose, Peter, *Continuing the Inquiry: The Council on Foreign Relations from 1921 to 1996* (New York: Council on Foreign Relations, 1996).

Groth, Paul, *The History of Residential Hotels in the United States* (Berkeley: University of California Press, 1994).

Hackett Fischer, David, *Albion's Seed: Four British Folkways in America* (New York: Oxford University Press, 1992).

Hart, Justin, *Empire of Ideas: The Origins of Public Diplomacy and the Transformation of US Foreign Policy* (Oxford: Oxford University Press, 2013).

Harvie, Alida, *Those Glittering Years* (London: Regency Press, 1980).

Haste, Cate, *Keep the Home Fires Burning: Propaganda in the First World War* (London: Allen Lane, 1977).

Herring, George C., *From Colony to Superpower: US Foreign Relations Since 1776* (New York: Oxford University Press, 2008).

Hicks, John D., *Republican Ascendancy, 1921–1933* (London: Hamish Hamilton, 1960).

Hinton, James, *The First Shop Stewards' Movement* (London: George Allen & Unwin, 1973).

Hitchens, Christopher, *Blood, Class and Empire: The Enduring Anglo-American Relationship* (London: Atlantic Books, 2006).

Hobsbawm, Eric, *The Age of Empire, 1875–1914* (London: Abacus, 1987).

Hobsbawm, Eric, *The Age of Extremes: The Short Twentieth Century 1914–1991* (London: Abacus, 1994).

Hogan, Michael J., *Informal Entente: The Private Structure of Anglo-American Economic Diplomacy, 1918–1928* (Columbia: University of Missouri Press, 1977).

Homberger, Eric, *Mrs. Astor's New York: Money and Social Power in a Gilded Age* (New Haven: Yale University Press, 2002).

Horsman, Reginald, *Race and Manifest Destiny: The Origins of American Racial Anglo-Saxonism* (Cambridge, MA: Harvard University Press, 1981).

Hunt, Michael H., *Ideology and US Foreign Policy* (New Haven: Yale University Press, 1987).

Johnson, Kathleen Eagen, *The Hudson–Fulton Celebration: New York's River Festival of 1909 and the Making of a Metropolis* (New York: Fordham University Press, 2009).

Johnson, Wills Fletcher, *George Harvey: 'A Passionate Patriot'* (Cambridge, MA: Riverside Press, 1929).

Judd, Denis, *Empire: The British Imperial Experience, from 1765 to the Present* (London: Fontana Press, 1997).

Keller, Morton, *In Defense of Yesterday: James M. Beck and the Politics of Conservatism 1861–1936* (New York: Coward-McCann, 1958).

Kelley, R., *The Transatlantic Persuasion: The Liberal-Democratic Mind in the Age of Gladstone* (New Brunswick: Transaction Publishers, 1990).

Kennedy, David M., *Over Here: The First World War and American Society* (Oxford: Oxford University Press, 2004).

Kennedy, Paul, *The Realities Behind Diplomacy: Background Influences on British External Policy, 1865–1980* (London Fontana, 1981).

Kennedy, Paul, *The Rise and Fall of the Great Powers: Economic Change and Military Conflict from 1500 to 2000* (London: Fontana, 1989).

Kent, Marian, *Oil and Empire: British Policy and Mesopotamian Oil, 1900–1920* (London: Macmillan, 1976).

Kessner, Thomas, *Capital City: New York City and the Men Behind America's Rise to Economic Dominance, 1860–1900* (New York: Simon & Schuster, 2003).

Kidd, Colin, *Subverting Scotland's Past: Scottish Whig Historians and the Creation of an Anglo-British Identity, c. 1689–1830* (Cambridge: Cambridge University Press, 2003).

Kohn, Edward P., *This Kindred People: Canadian–American Relations and the Anglo-Saxon Idea, 1895–1903* (Montreal: McGill-Queen's University Press, 2005).

Longacre, Edward G., *A Soldier to the Last: Maj. Gen. Joseph Wheeler in Blue and Gray* (Washington DC: Potomac Books, 2007).

MacKenzie, John M., *Propaganda and Empire: The Manipulation of British Public Opinion, 1880–1960* (Manchester: Manchester University Press, 1984).

McKercher, B. J. C., *The Second Baldwin Government and the United States, 1924–1929: Attitudes and Diplomacy* (Cambridge: Cambridge University Press, 1984).

Martin, Lawrence, *The Presidents and the Prime Ministers: Washington and Ottawa Face to Face – The Myth of Bilateral Bliss, 1867–1982* (Toronto: Doubleday, 1982).

Matthews, Jeffrey J., *Alanson B. Houghton: Ambassador of the New Era* (Lanham: SR Books, 2004).

Mead, Walter R., *God and Gold: Britain, America, and the Making of the Modern World* (New York: Alfred A. Knopf, 2008).

Medlicott, William N., *British Foreign Policy Since Versailles, 1919–1963* (London: Methuen, 1968).

Miller, Russell, *The Adventures of Arthur Conan Doyle* (London: Random House, 2008).

Millman, Brock, *Managing Domestic Dissent in First World War Britain* (London: Frank Cass, 2000).

Mills, Charles Wright, *The Power Elite* (New York: Oxford University Press, 1959).

Mock, James R. and Cedric Larson, *Words that Won the War: The Story of the Committee on Public Information* (Princeton: Princeton University Press, 1939).

Monger, David, *Patriotism and Propaganda in First World War Britain: The National War Aims Committee and Civilian Morale* (Liverpool: Liverpool University Press, 2012).

Montgomery, Maureen E., 'Gilded Prostitution': Status, Money, and Transatlantic Marriages, 1870–1914 *(London: Routledge, 1989).*

Moser, John E., *Twisting the Lion's Tail: Anglophobia in the United States, 1921–48* (London: Macmillan Press, 1999).

Mowat, Charles Loch, *Britain Between the Wars, 1918–1940* (London: Methuen, 1955).

Murray, Robert K., *The Harding Era: Warren G. Harding and His Administration* (Minneapolis: University of Minnesota Press, 1969).

Nicholas, H. G., *The United States and Britain* (Chicago: Chicago University Press, 1975).

Ninkovich, Frank, *The Diplomacy of Ideas: US Foreign Policy and Cultural Relations, 1938–1950* (Cambridge: Cambridge University Press, 1981).

Ninkovich, Frank, *Global Dawn: The Cultural Foundation of American Internationalism, 1865–1890* (Cambridge, MA: Harvard University Press, 2009).

Nye, Joseph S., *Soft Power: The Means to Success in World Politics* (New York: Public Affairs, 2004).

Otte, T. G., *The Foreign Office Mind: The Making of British Foreign Policy, 1865–1914* (Cambridge: Cambridge University Press, 2011).

Pacyga, Dominic A., *Chicago: A Biography* (Chicago: University of Chicago Press, 2009).

Palmer, Niall, *The Twenties in America: Politics and History* (Edinburgh: Edinburgh University Press, 2006).

Parmar, Inderjeet, *Foundations of the American Century: The Ford, Carnegie, and Rockefeller Foundations in the Rise of American Power* (New York: Columbia University Press, 2012).

Parrish, Michael E., *Anxious Decades: America in Prosperity and Depression, 1920–1941* (New York: W. W. Norton, 1992).

Perkins, Bradford, *The Great Rapprochement: England and the United States, 1895–1914* (London: Victor Gollancz, 1969).

Peterson, Merrill D., *The Jefferson Image in the American Mind* (Charlottesville: University of Virginia Press, 1998).

Pfannestiel, Todd J., *Rethinking the Red Scare: The Lusk Committee and New York's Crusade Against Radicalism, 1919–1923* (New York: Routledge, 2003).

Potter, Simon J., *News and the British World: The Emergence of an Imperial Press System, 1876–1922* (Oxford: Clarendon Press, 2003).

Prochaska, Frank, *Eminent Victorians on American Democracy: The View from Albion* (Oxford: Oxford University Press, 2012).

Rachlin, Harvey, *Scandals, Vandals and da Vincis: A Gallery of Remarkable Art Tales* (London: Robson Books, 2007).

Reitano, Joanne R., *The Restless City: A Short History of New York from Colonial Times to the Present* (New York: Routledge, 2010).

Reynolds, David, *The Creation of the Anglo-American Alliance, 1937–41: A Study in Competitive Co-operation* (London: Europa, 1981).

Rich, Paul B., *Race and Empire in British Politics* (Cambridge: Cambridge University Press, 1986).

Rodgers, Daniel T., *Atlantic Crossings: Social Politics in a Progressive Age* (Cambridge, MA: Harvard University Press, 1998).

Rosenberg, Emily S., *Financial Missionaries in the World: The Politics and Culture of Dollar Diplomacy, 1900–1930* (Durham, NC: Duke University Press, 2003).

Rosenberg, Emily S., *Spreading the American Dream: American Economic and Cultural Expansion, 1890–1945* (New York: Hill and Wang, 1982).

Rosenthal, Michael, *Nicholas Miraculous: The Amazing Career of the Redoubtable Dr. Nicholas Murray Butler* (New York: Farrar, Straus and Giroux, 2006).

Ryan, Henry Butterfield, *The Vision of Anglo-America: The US–UK Alliance and the Emerging Cold War, 1943–1946* (Cambridge: Cambridge University Press, 1987).

Rydell, Robert W., *All the World's a Fair: Visions of Empire at American International Expositions, 1876–1916* (Chicago: University of Chicago Press, 1984).

Sanders, Michael and Philip M. Taylor, *British Propaganda During the First World War, 1914–1918* (London: Macmillan, 1982).

Self, Robert C., *Britain, America and the War Debt Controversy: The Economic Diplomacy of an Unspecial Relationship* (London: Routledge, 2006).

Semmel, Bernard, *Imperialism and Social Reform: English Social-Imperial Thought, 1895–1914* (London: George Allen & Unwin, 1960).

Spinelli, Lawrence, *Dry Diplomacy: The United States, Great Britain, and Prohibition* (Lanham: Rowman & Littlefield, 2008).

Steiner, Zara, *The Lights that Failed: European International History, 1919–1933* (Oxford: Oxford University Press, 2005).

Taylor, A. J. P., *The Second World War: An Illustrated History* (Harmondsworth: Penguin, 1975).

Taylor, Philip M., *British Propaganda in the Twentieth Century: Selling Democracy* (Edinburgh: Edinburgh University Press, 1999).

Taylor, Philip M., *The Projection of Britain: British Overseas Publicity and Propaganda, 1919–1939* (Cambridge: Cambridge University Press, 1981).

Temperley, Howard, *Britain and America Since Independence* (Basingstoke: Palgrave, 2002).

Thompson, J. Lee, *Politicians, the Press and Propaganda: Lord Northcliffe and the Great War, 1914–1919* (Ashland, OH: Kent State University Press, 1999).

Tilchin, William N., *Theodore Roosevelt and the British Empire: A Study in Presidential Statecraft* (Basingstoke: Macmillan, 1997).

Tucker, Robert W., *Woodrow Wilson and the Great War: Reconsidering America's Neutrality, 1914–1917* (Charlottesville: University of Virginia Press, 2007).

Vucetic, Srdjan, *The Anglosphere: A Genealogy of Racialized Identity in International Relations* (Stanford: Stanford University Press, 2011).

Watt, Donald C., *Personalities and Policies: Studies in the Formulation of British Foreign Policy in the Twentieth Century* (London: Longmans, 1965).

Watt, Donald C., *Succeeding John Bull: America in Britain's Place 1900–1975* (Cambridge: Cambridge University Press, 1984).

Whatley, Harlan D., *Two Hundred Fifty Years: The History of Saint Andrew's Society of the State of New York* (New York: Saint Andrew's Society of the State of New York, 2008).

Wills, Garry, *Inventing America: Jefferson's Declaration of Independence* (London: Athlone, 1980).

Wynne-Parker, Michael, *Bridge Over Troubled Water: Insight into the English-Speaking Union and Its Influence in South Asia* (London: Kingston Books, 1989).

Zieger, Robert H., *America's Great War: World War 1 and the American Experience* (Lanham: Rowman & Littlefield, 2000).

Zimmermann, Warren, *First Great Triumph: How Five Americans Made Their Country a World Power* (New York: Farrar, Straus and Giroux, 2004).

Chapters and articles in books

Bell, Duncan, 'Dreaming the Future: Anglo-America as Utopia, 1880–1914', in Ella Dzelzainis and Ruth Livesey (eds), *The American Experiment and the Idea of Democracy in British Culture, 1776–1914* (Farnham: Ashgate, 2013), pp. 197–210.

Bell, Duncan, 'The Project for a New Anglo Century: Race, Space, and Global Order', in Peter Katzenstein (ed.), *Anglo-America and Its Discontents: Civilizational Identities Beyond West and East* (New York: Routledge, 2012), pp. 33–55.

Beloff, Max, 'The Special Relationship: An Anglo-American Myth', in Martin Gilbert (ed.), *A Century of Conflict: Essays in Honour of A. J. P. Taylor* (London: Hamish Hamilton, 1966), pp. 151–71.

Bennett, Jessica and Mark Hampton, 'World War 1 and the Anglo-American Imagined Community: Civilization vs. Barbarism in British Propaganda and American Newspapers', in Joel Wiener and Mark Hampton (eds), *Anglo-American Media Interactions, 1850–2000* (New York: Palgrave Macmillan, 2007), pp. 155–75.

Buckner, Philip, 'The Creation of the Dominion of Canada, 1860–1901', in Philip Buckner (ed.), *Canada and the British Empire* (Oxford: Oxford University Press, 2010), pp. 67–86.

Bueltmann, Tanja, 'Anglo-Saxonism and the Racialization of the English Diaspora', in Tanja Bueltmann, David Gleeson and Donald M. MacRaild (eds), *Locating the English Diaspora, 1500–2010* (Liverpool: Liverpool University Press, 2012), pp. 118–34.

Bueltmann, Tanja, Andrew Hinson and Graeme Morton, 'Introduction: Diaspora, Associations and Scottish Identity', in Tanja Bueltmann, Andrew Hinson and Graeme Morton (eds), *Ties of Bluid, Kin and Countrie: Scottish Associational Culture in the Diaspora* (Ontario: Stewart Publishing, 2009), pp. 1–18.

Burk, Kathleen, 'Anglo-American Relations Before They Were "Special"', in Antoine Capet (ed.), The Special Relationship: La 'relation spéciale' entre le Royaume-Uni et les États-Unis, 1945–1990 (Rouen: Publications de l'université de Rouen, 2003), pp. 3–17.

Campbell, Charles S., 'Anglo-American Relations, 1897–1901', in Paolo E. Coletta (ed.), *Threshold to American Internationalism: Essays on the Foreign Policies of William McKinley* (New York: Exposition Press, 1970), pp. 221–55.

Comerford, R. V., 'Isaac Butt and the Home Rule Party, 1870–77', in W. E. Vaughan (ed.), *A New History of Ireland VI: Ireland Under the Union, 1870–1921* (Oxford: Oxford University Press, 1989), pp. 1–25.

Crapol, Edward P., 'From Anglophobia to Fragile Rapprochement: Anglo-American Relations in the Early Twentieth Century', in Hans-Jürgen Schroder (ed.), *Confrontation and Cooperation: Germany and the United States in the Era of World War 1, 1900–1924* (Providence: Berg Publishers, 1993), pp. 13–31.

Doyle, Joe, 'Striking for Ireland on the New York Docks', in Ronald H. Bayor and Timothy J. Meagher (eds), *The New York Irish* (Baltimore: Johns Hopkins University Press, 1996), pp. 357–73.

Fisher, John and Antony Best, 'Introduction', in John Fisher and Antony Best (eds), *On the Fringes of Diplomacy: Influences on British Foreign Policy, 1800–1945* (Farnham: Ashgate, 2011), pp. 1–15.

Geppert, Dominik, 'The Public Challenge to Diplomacy: German and British Ways of Dealing with the Press, 1890–1914', in Markus Mösslang and Torsten Riotte (eds), *The Diplomats' World: A Cultural History of Diplomacy, 1815–1914* (Oxford: Oxford University Press, 2008), pp. 133–64.

Gienow-Hecht, Jessica, 'The Anomaly of the Cold War: Cultural Diplomacy and Civil Society Since 1850', in Kenneth Osgood and Brian Etheridge (eds), *The United States and Public Diplomacy: New Directions in Cultural and International History* (Leiden and Boston: Brill, 2010), pp. 29–56.

Girard, Philip, 'British Justice, English Law, and Canadian Legal Culture', in Philip Buckner (ed.), *Canada and the British Empire* (Oxford: Oxford University Press, 2010), pp. 259–77.

Grant, Muriel, *Propaganda and the Role of the State in Inter-War Britain* (Oxford: Clarendon Press, 1994).

Greene, Jack P., 'Introduction: Empire and Liberty', in Jack P. Greene (ed.), *Exclusionary Empire: English Liberty Overseas, 1600–1900* (Cambridge: Cambridge University Press, 2010), pp. 1–24.

Hardwick, Joe, 'An English Institution? The Colonial Church of England in the First Half of the Nineteenth Century', in Tanja Bueltmann, David Gleeson and Donald M. MacRaild (eds), *Locating the English Diaspora, 1500–2010* (Liverpool: Liverpool University Press, 2012), pp. 84–99.

Hendershot, Robert M., '"Affection Is the Cement which Binds Us": Understanding the Cultural Sinews of the Anglo-American Special Relationship', in Alan P. Dobson and Steve Marsh (eds), *Anglo-American Relations: Contemporary Perspectives* (London: Routledge, 2013), pp. 52–81.

Hiller, James K., 'Status Without Stature: Newfoundland, 1869–1949', in Philip Buckner (ed.), *Canada and the British Empire* (Oxford: Oxford University Press, 2010), pp. 127–39.

Iriye, Akira, 'Culture and International History', in Michael J. Hogan and Thomas G. Paterson (eds), *Explaining the History of American Foreign Relations* (Cambridge: Cambridge University Press, 2004), pp. 241–56.

Kelly, Jennifer and R. V. Comerford, 'Introduction', in Jennifer Kelly and R. V. Comerford (eds), *Associational Culture in Ireland and Abroad* (Dublin: Irish Academic Press, 2010), pp. 1–9.

Kramer, Paul A., 'Race, Empire, and Transnational History', in Alfred W. McCoy and Francisco A. Scarano (eds), *Colonial Crucible: Empire in the Making of the Modern American State* (Madison: University of Wisconsin Press, 2009), pp. 199–209.

Leventhal, Fred M., 'Public Face and Public Space: The Projection of Britain in America Before the Second World War', in Fred M. Leventhal and

Roland Quinault (eds), *Anglo-American Attitudes: From Revolution to Partnership* (Aldershot: Ashgate, 2000), pp. 212–26.

Leventhal, Fred M. and Roland Quinault, 'Introduction', in Fred M. Leventhal and Roland Quinault (eds), *Anglo-American Attitudes: From Revolution to Partnership* (Aldershot: Ashgate, 2000), pp. 1–8.

Link, Arthur S., 'Woodrow Wilson's Perspective', in Thomas G. Paterson (ed.), *Major Problems in American Foreign Policy, Volume II: Since 1914* (Lexington: D. C. Heath, 1989), pp. 80–93.

Lyons, F. S. L., 'The Revolution in Train, 1914–1916', in W. E. Vaughan (ed.), *A New History of Ireland VI: Ireland Under the Union, 1870–1921* (Oxford: Oxford University Press, 1989), pp. 189–206.

Lyons, F. S. L., 'The War of Independence, 1919–21', in W. E. Vaughan (ed.), *A New History of Ireland VI: Ireland Under the Union, 1870–1921* (Oxford: Oxford University Press, 1989), pp. 240–59.

McKercher, B. J. C., '"The Deep and Latent Distrust": The British Official Mind and the United States, 1919–1929', in B. J. C. McKercher (ed.), *Anglo-American Relations in the 1920s: The Struggle for Supremacy* (London: Macmillan, 1991), pp. 209–39.

Mayers, David, 'John Gilbert Winant, 1941–46', in Alison R. Holmes and J. Simon Rofe (eds), *The Embassy in Grosvenor Square: American Ambassadors to the United Kingdom, 1938–2008* (Basingstoke: Palgrave Macmillan, 2012), pp. 49–63.

Morgan, David, 'Woman Suffrage in Britain and America in the Early Twentieth Century', in H. C. Allen and R. Thompson (eds), *Contrast and Connection: Bicentennial Essays in Anglo-American History* (London: G. Bell and Sons, 1976), pp. 272–95.

Morris, R. J., 'Clubs, Societies and Associations', in F. M. L. Thompson (ed.), *The Cambridge Social History of Britain 1750–1950, Volume 3: Social Agencies and Institutions* (Cambridge: Cambridge University Press, 1990), pp. 395–443.

Morris, R. J., 'Introduction: Civil Society, Associations and Urban Places: Class, Nation and Culture in Nineteenth-Century Europe', in Graeme Morton, Boudien de Vries and R. J. Morris (eds), *Civil Society, Associations and Urban Places: Class, Nation and Culture in Nineteenth-Century Europe* (Aldershot: Ashgate, 2006), pp. 1–16.

Osgood, Kenneth and Brian Etheridge, 'Introduction: The New International History Meets the New Cultural History: Public Diplomacy and US Foreign Relations', in Kenneth Osgood and Brian Etheridge (eds), *The United States and Public Diplomacy: New Directions in Cultural and International History* (Leiden and Boston: Brill, 2010), pp. 1–25.

Otte, T. G., '"The Shrine at Sulgrave": The Preservation of the Washington Ancestral Home as an "English Mount Vernon" and Transatlantic Relations', in Melanie Hall (ed.), *Towards World Heritage: International*

Origins of the Preservation Movement, 1870–1930 (Farnham: Ashgate, 2011) pp. 109–39.

Parmar, Inderjeet, 'Conceptualising the State–Private Network in American Foreign Policy', in Helen Laville and Hugh Wilford (eds), *The US Government, Citizen Groups and the Cold War: The State–Private Network* (London: Routledge, 2005), pp. 13–27.

Patterson, David S., 'Japanese–American Relations: The 1906 California Crisis, the Gentlemen's Agreement, and the World Cruise', in Serge Ricard (ed.), *A Companion to Theodore Roosevelt* (Chichester: John Wiley and Sons, 2011), pp. 391–416.

Reinhard, Keith, 'American Business and Its Role in Public Diplomacy', in Nancy Snow and Philip Taylor (eds), *The Routledge Handbook to Public Diplomacy* (New York: Routledge, 2009), pp. 195–200.

Rhodes, Benjamin D., 'The Image of Britain in the United States, 1919–1929: A Contentious Relative and Rival', in B. J. C. McKercher (ed.), *Anglo-American Relations in the 1920s: The Struggle for Supremacy* (London: Macmillan, 1991), pp. 187–207.

Roberts, Priscilla, 'Underpinning the Anglo-American Alliance: The Council on Foreign Relations and Britain Between the Wars', in Jonathan Hollowell (ed.), *Twentieth-Century Anglo-American Relations* (New York: Palgrave, 2001), pp. 25–43.

Rofe, J. Simon, 'Joseph P. Kennedy, 1938–40', in Alison R. Holmes and J. Simon Rofe (eds), *The Embassy in Grosvenor Square: American Ambassadors to the United Kingdom, 1938–2008* (Basingstoke: Palgrave Macmillan, 2012), pp. 23–48.

Smith, Adam I. P., '"The Stuff Our Dreams Are Made Of": Lincoln in the English Imagination', in Richard Carwardine and Jay Sexton (eds), *The Global Lincoln* (Oxford: Oxford University Press, 2011), pp. 123–38.

Snow, Nancy, 'Rethinking Public Diplomacy', in Nancy Snow and Philip Taylor (eds), *The Routledge Handbook to Public Diplomacy* (New York: Routledge, 2009), pp. 3–11.

Thompson, John Herd, 'Canada and the "Third British Empire", 1901–1939', in Philip Buckner (ed.), *Canada and the British Empire* (Oxford: Oxford University Press, 2010), pp. 87–106.

Tilchin, William N., 'Setting the Foundation: Theodore Roosevelt and the Construction of an Anglo-American Special Relationship', in William N. Tilchin and Charles E. Neu (eds), *Artists of Power: Theodore Roosevelt, Woodrow Wilson, and Their Enduring Impact on US Foreign Policy* (Westport: Praeger Security International, 2006), pp. 45–65.

Vucetic, Srdjan, 'The Fulton Address as Racial Discourse', in Alan Dobson and Steve Marsh (eds), *Churchill and the Anglo-American Special Relationship* (London: Routledge, 2017), pp. 96–115.

Welch, David, 'Introduction', in Mark Connelly and David Welch (eds), *War and the Media: Reportage and Propaganda, 1900–2003* (London: I. B. Tauris, 2004), pp. xi–xxi.

Widenor, William C., 'Henry Cabot Lodge's Perspective', in Thomas G. Paterson (ed.), *Major Problems in American Foreign Policy, Volume II: Since 1914* (Lexington: D. C. Heath, 1989), pp. 93–108.

Journal articles

Allen, Charles, 'The Myth of Chumik Shenko', *History Today*, Vol. 54, Issue 4 (2004), pp. 10–17.

Andreasen, Bethany, 'Treason or Truth: The New York City Text Book Controversy, 1920–1923', *New York History*, Vol. 66 (1985), pp. 396–419.

Beach, Jim, 'Origins of the Special Intelligence Relationship? Anglo-American Intelligence Co-operation on the Western Front, 1917–18', *Intelligence and National Security*, Vol. 22, No. 2 (April 2007), pp. 229–49.

Bell, Duncan, 'Before the Democratic Peace: Racial Utopianism, Empire, and the Abolition of War', *European Journal of International Relations*, Vol. 20, Issue 3 (2014), pp. 647–70.

Bell, Duncan, 'Beyond the Sovereign State: Isopolitan Citizenship, Race and Anglo-American Union', *Political Studies*, Vol. 62 (2014), pp. 418–34.

Bowman, Stephen, 'An Englishman Abroad and an American Lawyer in Europe: Harry Brittain, James Beck and the Pilgrims Society During the First World War', *Journal of Transatlantic Studies*, Vol. 12, No. 3 (2014), pp. 258–81.

Boyle, T., 'The Venezuela Crisis and the Liberal Opposition, 1895–1896', *Journal of Modern History*, Vol. 50, No. 3 (1979), pp. 1185–212.

Burk, Kathleen, 'Great Britain in the United States, 1917–1918: The Turning Point', *International History Review*, Vol. 1, No. 2 (April 1979), pp. 228–45.

Clarke, Peter, 'The English-Speaking Peoples Before Churchill', *Britain and the World*, Vol. 4, No. 2 (2011), pp. 199–231.

Crapol, Edward P., 'Coming to Terms with Empire: Historiography of Late Nineteenth-Century American Foreign Relations', *Diplomatic History*, Vol. 16, No. 4 (1992), pp. 573–97.

Cull, Nicholas J., 'Overtures to an Alliance: British Propaganda at the New York World's Fair, 1939–1940', *Journal of British Studies*, Vol. 36, Issue 3 (July 1997), pp. 325–54.

Cull, Nicholas J., 'Selling Peace: The Origins, Promotion and Fate of the Anglo-American New Order During the Second World War', *Diplomacy and Statecraft*, Vol. 7, No. 1 (1996), pp. 1–28.

Ewalt, Donald, 'The Fight for Oil: Britain in Persia, 1919', *History Today*, Vol. 31, Issue 9 (1981), pp. 11–16.

Farwell, Byron, 'Taking Sides in the Boer War', *American Heritage*, Vol. 27 (April 1976), pp. 21–5.

Ferris, John R., '"The Greatest Power on Earth": Great Britain in the 1920s', *International History Review*, Vol. 13, No. 4 (November 1991), pp. 726–50.

Gluek, Alvin C., 'The Invisible Revision of the Rush–Bagot Agreement, 1898–1914', *Canadian Historical Review*, Vol. 60, Issue 4 (1979), pp. 466–84.

Gluek, Alvin C., 'Pilgrimages to Ottawa: Canadian–American Diplomacy, 1903–13', Canadian Historical Association, *Historical Papers* (1968), pp. 65–83.

Haglund, David G., 'Brebner's *North Atlantic Triangle* at Sixty: A Retrospective Look at a Retrospective Book', *The London Journal of Canadian Studies*, Vol. 20 (2004–5), pp. 117–40.

Kennedy, Paul, 'The Tradition of Appeasement in British Foreign Policy, 1865–1939', *Review of International Studies*, Vol. 2, Issue 3 (October 1976), pp. 195–215.

Kramer, Paul A., 'Empires, Exceptions and Anglo-Saxons: Race and Rule Between the British and United States Empires, 1880–1910', *Journal of American History*, Vol. 88, No. 4 (March 2002), pp. 1315–53.

McCormick, Thomas, 'Insular Imperialism and the Open Door: The China Market and the Spanish-American War', *Pacific Historical Review*, Vol. 32, No. 2 (May 1963), pp. 155–69.

McCulloch, Tony, 'The North Atlantic Triangle: A Canadian Myth?', *International Journal*, Vol. 66, Issue 1 (Winter 2010–11), pp. 197–207.

McKercher, B. J. C., 'Wealth, Power, and the New International Order: Britain and the American Challenge in the 1920s', *Diplomatic History*, Vol. 12, Issue 4 (1988), pp. 411–41.

McKercher, B. J. C., 'Reaching for the Brass Ring: The Recent Historiography of Interwar American Foreign Relations', *Diplomatic History*, Vol. 15, Issue 4 (1991), pp. 565–98.

MacRaild, Donald M., Sylvia Ellis, and Stephen Bowman, 'Interdependence Day and Magna Charta: James Hamilton's Public Diplomacy in the Anglo-World, 1907–1940s', *Journal of Transatlantic Studies*, Vol. 12, Issue 2 (2014), pp. 140–62.

Milne-Smith, Amy, 'Club Talk: Gossip, Masculinity and Oral Communities in Late Nineteenth-Century London', *Gender and History*, Vol. 21, No. 1 (April 2009), pp. 86–106.

Morris, R. J., 'Voluntary Societies and British Urban Elites', *The Historical Journal*, Vol. 26, No. 1 (1983), pp. 95–118.

Moya, Jose C., 'Immigrants and Associations: A Global and Historical Perspective', *Journal of Ethnic and Migration Studies*, Vol. 31, No. 5 (September 2005), pp. 833–64.

Mulford, Carla, 'Figuring Benjamin Franklin in American Cultural Memory', *The New England Quarterly*, Vol. 72, No. 3 (September 1999), pp. 415–43.

Namikas, Lise, 'The Committee to Defend America and the Debate Between Internationalists and Interventionists, 1939–1941', *Historian*, 61 (1999), p. 843–63.

Neary, Peter, 'Grey, Bryce, and the Settlement of Canadian–American Differences, 1905–1911', *The Canadian Historical Review*, Vol. XLIX, No. 4 (1968), pp. 357–80.

Neilson, Keith, '"Greatly Exaggerated": The Myth of the Decline of Great Britain Before 1914', *International History Review*, Vol. 13, No. 4 (November 1991), pp. 695–725.

O'Brien, Phillips Payson, 'The American Press, Public, and the Reaction to the Outbreak of the First World War', *Diplomatic History*, Vol. 37, No. 3 (2013), pp. 446–75.

O'Brien, Phillips Payson, 'Herbert Hoover, Anglo-American Relations and Republican Party Politics in the 1920s', *Diplomacy and Statecraft*, Vol. 22, Issue 2 (2011), pp. 200–18.

Onuf, Peter S., 'The Scholars' Jefferson', *The William and Mary Quarterly*, Third Series, Vol. 50, No. 4 (October 1993), pp. 671–99.

Parmet, Robert D., 'The Presidential Fever of Chauncey Depew', *New-York Historical Society Quarterly*, Vol. 54 (1970), pp. 269–90.

Pessen, Edward, 'Philip Hone's Set: The Social World of the New York City Elite in the "Age of Egalitarianism"', *New-York Historical Society Quarterly*, Vol. 56 (1972), pp. 285–308.

Reynolds, David, 'Rethinking Anglo-American Relations', *International Affairs*, Vol. 65, No. 1 (Winter 1988–9), pp. 89–111.

Rhodes, Benjamin D., 'Anglophobia in Chicago; Mayor William Hale Thompson's 1927 Campaign Against King George V', *Illinois Quarterly*, Vol. 39 (Summer 1977), pp. 5–14.

Richards, David A., 'America Conquers Britain: Anglo-American Conflict in the Popular Media During the 1920s', *Journal of American Culture*, Vol. 3, Issue 1 (Spring 1980), pp. 95–103.

Rietzler, Katharina, 'Beyond the Cultural Cold Wars: American Philanthropy and Cultural Diplomacy in the Inter-War Years', *Historical Research*, Vol. 84, No. 223 (February 2011), pp. 148–64.

Roberts, Andrew, 'Forging the Special Relationship', *The New Criterion*, Vol. 29, No. 10 (June 2011), pp. 30–3.

Roberts, Priscilla, '"All the Right People": The Historiography of the American Foreign Policy Establishment', *Journal of American Studies*, Vol. 26, Issue 3 (December 1992), pp. 409–34.

Roberts, Priscilla, 'The Anglo-American Theme: American Visions of an Atlantic Alliance, 1914–1933', *Diplomatic History*, Vol. 21, No. 3 (1997), pp. 333–64.

Roberts, Priscilla, 'The First World War and the Emergence of American Atlanticism, 1914–1920', *Diplomacy and Statecraft*, Vol. 5, Issue 3 (1994), pp. 569–619.

Roberts, Priscilla, 'The Transatlantic American Foreign Policy Elite: Its Evolution in Generational Perspective', *Journal of Transatlantic Studies*, Vol. 7 (2009), pp. 163–83.

Sanders, M. L., 'Wellington House and British Propaganda During the First World War', *The Historical Journal*, Vol. 18, Issue 1 (1975), pp. 119–46.

Taddei, Antonia, 'London Clubs in the Late Nineteenth Century', *University of Oxford Discussion Papers in Economic and Social History*, Number 28 (April 1999).

Thompson, J. Lee, '"To Tell the People of America the Truth": Lord Northcliffe in the USA, Unofficial British Propaganda, June–November 1917', *Journal of Contemporary History*, Vol. 34 (1999), pp. 243–62.

Tuffnell, Stephen, 'Anglo-American Inter-Imperialism: US Expansion and the British World, c. 1865–1914, *Britain and the World*, Vol. 7, Issue 2 (2014), pp. 174–95.

Waters, Chris, '"Beyond Americanization": Re-thinking Anglo-American Cultural Exchange Between the Wars', *Cultural and Social History*, Vol. 4, Issue 4 (2007), pp. 451–9.

Williams, Paul, 'A Commonwealth of Knowledge: Empire, Intellectuals and the Chatham House Project, 1919–1939', *International Relations*, Vol. 17 (2003), pp. 35–55.

Theses

Reid, Cecilie, 'American Internationalism: Peace Advocacy and International Relations, 1895–1916', unpublished PhD thesis (Boston College, 2005).

Websites

Alberta Heritage Digitization Project, <http://www.ourfutureourpast.ca/newspapr/brwsindx.asp?code=n1x≥ (last accessed 16 May 2014).

Baker, A. P., 'Brittain, Sir Henry Ernest [Harry] (1873–1974)', *Oxford Dictionary of National Biography* (Oxford University Press, 2004), <http://www.oxforddnb.com/view/article/30852> (last accessed 20 February 2012).

Boyce, D. George, 'Harmsworth, Alfred Charles William, Viscount Northcliffe (1865–1922)', *Oxford Dictionary of National Biography*

(Oxford University Press, 2004), <http://www.oxforddnb.com/view/article/33717> (last accessed 24 July 2014).

Boyce, Peter, 'Riley, Charles Owen Leaver (1854–1929)', *Australian Dictionary of Biography* (National Centre of Biography, Australian National University, 1988), <http://adb.anu.edu.au/biography/riley-charles-owen-leaver-8213/text14371> (last accessed 10 June 2014).

Ceadel, Martin, 'Cecil, (Edgar Algernon) Robert Gascoyne- [Lord Robert Cecil], Viscount Cecil of Chelwood (1864–1958)', *Oxford Dictionary of National Biography* (Oxford University Press, 2004), <http://www.oxforddnb.com/view/article/32335> (last accessed 3 March 2014).

Chatham House, The Royal Institute of International Affairs, <http://www.chathamhouse.org/about> (last accessed 24 August 2014).

Cull, Nicholas J., 'Public Diplomacy Before Gullion: The Evolution of a Phrase', *USC Center on Public Diplomacy*, <http://uscpublicdiplomacy.org/blog/060418_public_diplomacy_before_gullion_the_evolution_of_a_phrase> (last accessed 7 April 2014).

Foreign Relations of the United States, University of Wisconsin Digital Collections, <http://uwdc.library.wisc.edu/collections/FRUS> (last accessed various dates 2011–17).

Gaelic American, Chronicling America, Library of Congress, <http://chroniclingamerica.loc.gov/lccn/sn83045246/> (last accessed 14 May 2014).

Grieves, Keith, 'Geddes, Auckland Campbell, first Baron Geddes (1879–1954)', *Oxford Dictionary of National Biography* (Oxford University Press, 2004), <http://www.oxforddnb.com/view/article/33359> (last accessed 11 February 2014).

Haley, W., 'Stuart, Sir Campbell Arthur (1885–1972)', *Oxford Dictionary of National Biography* (Oxford University Press, 2004), <http://www.oxforddnb.com/view/article/31732> (last accessed 2 April 2012).

'House of Rothschild Controls Our Lives', <http://www.realjewnews.com/?p=14> (last accessed 14 May 2014).

Institute for the Study of Globalization and Covert Politics, 'The Pilgrims Society: A Study of the Anglo-American Establishment', <http://wiki-spooks.com/ISGP/organisations/Pilgrims_Society02.htm> (last accessed 14 May 2014).

Mackay, Ruddock and H. G. C. Matthew, 'Balfour, Arthur James, first earl of Balfour (1848–1930)', *Oxford Dictionary of National Biography* (Oxford University Press, 2004), <http://www.oxforddnb.com/view/article/30553> (last accessed 31 January 2014).

Native Plant Database, Lady Bird Johnson Wildflower Center, the University of Texas at Austin, <http://www.wildflower.org/plants/result.php?id_plant=EPRE2> (last accessed 20 August 2014).

'Portrait of Benjamin Franklin (Wilson-White House), 1759', <http://www.benfranklin300.org> (last accessed 19 July 2013).

Robson, Brian, 'Frederick Sleigh Roberts, first Earl Roberts (1832–1914)', *Oxford Dictionary of National Biography* (Oxford University Press, 2004), <http://www.oxforddnb.com/view/article/35768> (last accessed 18 November 2013).

Robson, Christopher, 'The Pilgrims' Society of Great Britain', <http://www.pilgrimsociety.org/history.pdf> (last accessed 3 October 2011).

Stearn, R. T., 'National Service League (*act.* 1902–1914)', *Oxford Dictionary of National Biography* (Oxford University Press, 2004), <http://www.oxforddnb.com/view/theme/95555> (last accessed 1 May 2012).

USC Center on Public Diplomacy, 'What Is PD?', <http://uscpublicdiplomacy.org/page/what-pd> (last accessed 13 September 2014).

The Waldorf-Astoria Archive, <http://www.waldorfarchive.org/> and <http://www.waldorfnewyork.com/about-the-waldorf/hotel-history.html> (last accessed 9 May 2014).

Williamson, Philip, 'Norman, Montagu Collet, Baron Norman (1871–1950)', *Oxford Dictionary of National Biography* (Oxford University Press, 2004), <http://www.oxforddnb.com/view/article/35252> (last accessed 3 February 2014).

Index

EU representative:
Easy Access System Europe
Mustamäe tee 50, 10621 Tallinn, Estonia
Gpsr.requests@easproject.com

www.ingramcontent.com/pod-product-compliance
Lightning Source LLC
Chambersburg PA
CBHW050348270326
41926CB00016B/3646